Applying the *Kaizen* in Africa

Keijiro Otsuka • Kimiaki Jin
Tetsushi Sonobe
Editors

Applying the *Kaizen* in Africa

A New Avenue for Industrial Development

Editors
Keijiro Otsuka
Graduate School of Economics
Kobe University, Kobe, Japan

Tetsushi Sonobe
National Graduate Institute for Policy
Studies (GRIPS)
Tokyo, Japan

Kimiaki Jin
Japan International Cooperation
Agency (JICA)
Tokyo, Japan

ISBN 978-3-030-08243-7   ISBN 978-3-319-91400-8   (eBook)
https://doi.org/10.1007/978-3-319-91400-8

© The Editor(s) (if applicable) and The Author(s) 2018. This book is an open access publication.
Softcover re-print of the Hardcover 1st edition 2018
Open Access This book is licensed under the terms of the Creative Commons Attribution 4.0 International License (http://creativecommons.org/licenses/by/4.0/), which permits use, sharing, adaptation, distribution and reproduction in any medium or format, as long as you give appropriate credit to the original author(s) and the source, provide a link to the Creative Commons license and indicate if changes were made.
The images or other third party material in this book are included in the book's Creative Commons license, unless indicated otherwise in a credit line to the material. If material is not included in the book's Creative Commons license and your intended use is not permitted by statutory regulation or exceeds the permitted use, you will need to obtain permission directly from the copyright holder.
The use of general descriptive names, registered names, trademarks, service marks, etc. in this publication does not imply, even in the absence of a specific statement, that such names are exempt from the relevant protective laws and regulations and therefore free for general use.
The publisher, the authors and the editors are safe to assume that the advice and information in this book are believed to be true and accurate at the date of publication. Neither the publisher nor the authors or the editors give a warranty, express or implied, with respect to the material contained herein or for any errors or omissions that may have been made. The publisher remains neutral with regard to jurisdictional claims in published maps and institutional affiliations.

Cover Illustration: Kheng Ho Toh / Alamy Stock Photo

This Palgrave Macmillan imprint is published by the registered company Springer Nature Switzerland AG
The registered company address is: Gewerbestrasse 11, 6330 Cham, Switzerland

Foreword

The Japanese word "*Kaizen*" originally means "improvement". It is a management philosophy and know-how that brings about continuous improvement of quality and productivity. *Kaizen* is a human-oriented approach which fosters teamwork, self-reliance, creativity and ingenuity. Although *Kaizen* is a long-term approach consisting of small steps and with little investment, it promotes the very core capabilities of firms such as production and management, which will be essential for the firms' growth. Recently, *Kaizen* is also starting to attract the world as a growing foundation of capabilities towards innovation.

JICA has been conducting *Kaizen* projects in 8 African countries and training programs for more than 25 countries in Africa, which have demonstrated thought-provoking results. However, it cannot be said that *Kaizen* is widely known in Africa. For this reason, this book explains what *Kaizen* is, how it was applied in developing countries and how concrete tools and methodologies are implemented while explaining the empirical knowledge obtained through practical achievements, as well as theoretical reasons, to support the belief that *Kaizen* is an effective entry point for industrial development in Africa.

The book targets policy makers, government officials and practitioners in charge of industrial development and economic transformation in African countries. It is also useful for researchers and students who are interested in economic transformation and capacity development. The book sends messages that are easy to understand and easy to start. I believe that this book will contribute to the wider dissemination of *Kaizen* management and promote further industrial development throughout Africa.

JICA Research Institute   Nobuko Kayashima
Tokyo, Japan

Preface

This book is the result of a collaboration between development economists (K. Otsuka and T. Sonobe), staff of the Japan International Cooperation Agency (JICA) (K. Jin and M. Suzuki), Japanese *Kaizen* consultants (S. Sugimoto and T. Kikuchi), and the first Director General of the Ethiopian *Kaizen* Institute known as the EKI (G.T. Mekonen). This project was a natural and logical project. Initially two economists (Otsuka and Sonobe) recommended the late Prime Minister of Ethiopia, H.E. Meles Zenawi, to introduce *Kaizen* into Ethiopia in 2007. The Prime Minister subsequently set up the EKI to train Ethiopian *Kaizen* experts for nationwide dissemination in 2011 and requested that JICA assist the EKI. JICA decided to implement a series of the *Kaizen* projects and to send Japanese *Kaizen* experts to the EKI. These experienced *Kaizen* experts have collaborated with enthusiastic and competent EKI staff working on the dissemination of *Kaizen* in Ethiopia ever since.

The two economists believe that the introduction of *Kaizen* is an effective entry point into the industrialization of Africa based on their vast amount of empirical research on the development of manufacturing industries in East and South Asia and sub-Saharan Africa. Their views are expressed in Chaps. 1 and 6. The two JICA staff are confident about the significant impact of *Kaizen* on the efficiency of enterprise management based on JICA's ample aid experience in Asia as well as careful review of incipient *Kaizen* projects in sub-Saharan Africa. Their views are shown in

Chap. 2 and in Sect. 4.4. The two *Kaizen* consultants have experienced success in disseminating *Kaizen* in several developing countries. In Chaps. 3 and 4, they discuss what *Kaizen* is, why it is useful for industrial development, and what types of *Kaizen* are useful in Africa. Finally, and possibly most importantly, a leader from within the *Kaizen* movement in Ethiopia is convinced from his own experience that, if the idea of *Kaizen* is properly understood and applied to enterprise management, it can be an effective tool for industrial development not only in Ethiopia but also in many other countries in sub-Saharan Africa. The Ethiopian experience is discussed in Chap. 5.

Although their reasons are substantially different, the authors all share the same view that *Kaizen* is an invaluable tool for successful industrial development. Therefore, when the idea of publishing the edited book on *Kaizen* was brought about by Seiji Sugimoto, author of Chap. 3, his fellow contributors agreed without hesitation. Since there has been an increasing interest in *Kaizen* in sub-Saharan Africa, we believe that it is timely and useful to jointly publish a book that explains the justifications for *Kaizen* from the viewpoints of development economists, foreign aid practitioners, *Kaizen* consultants, and a leader in the dissemination of *Kaizen*.

We are indebted to a number of people who were instrumental in implementing *Kaizen* projects and preparing this volume. In particular, we would like to thank the former Japanese Ambassador to Ethiopia, Mr. Kinichi Komano, who bridged the relationship between former Prime Minister Meles Zenawi, Japanese economists, and JICA in the early stages of launching the *Kaizen* dissemination activities in Ethiopia. We are also heavily indebted to Mr. Newai Gebre-ab, former Chief Economic Advisor to the Ethiopian Prime Minister, for his sincere support for the *Kaizen* projects in Ethiopia. Additionally, we are highly appreciative of the earnest support for the dissemination of *Kaizen* provided by the subsequent Japanese Ambassador, Mr. Kazuhiro Suzuki. We would like to acknowledge the contributions made by Professors Kenichi and Izumi Ohno, who also introduced former Prime Minister Meles to *Kaizen* activities in Tunisia and significantly promoted *Kaizen* through the Industrial Policy Dialogue between the Ethiopian government and the National Graduate Institute for Policy Studies (GRIPS) Development Forum/JICA. We would also like to thank Professor Akio Hosono for his helpful comments during the contributors' workshop in Tokyo on October 26, 2017.

We appreciate the generous support given by the JICA Research Institute in preparing this book. We would also like to thank Naotaka Yamaguchi and Akari Ichigi for their administrative assistance and Fumiyo Aburatani for her editorial work. Finally, we would like to express our sincere appreciation for the work of the *Kaizen* experts in Japan and in the developing countries, who have proven the effectiveness of *Kaizen* through their continuous efforts in their respective workplaces. Without their endeavors and successes, we would not have had any basis upon which to publish this book. Therefore, we would like to dedicate our book to those experts working on the ground and those people who believe in one's potential to improve the future economy of poor countries, or those who have a *Kaizen* mind.

Graduate School of Economics	Keijiro Otsuka
Kobe University	
Kobe, Japan	
Japan International Cooperation Agency (JICA)	Kimiaki Jin
Tokyo, Japan	
National Graduate Institute for Policy Studies (GRIPS)	Tetsushi Sonobe
Tokyo, Japan	

Contents

1 How *Kaizen* Brightens Africa's Future   1
   Tetsushi Sonobe

2 Role of *Kaizen* in Japan's Overseas Development
   Cooperation   31
   Kimiaki Jin

3 *Kaizen* in Practice   69
   Seiji Sugimoto

4 *Kaizen* and Standardization   111
   Tsuyoshi Kikuchi and Momoko Suzuki

5 *Kaizen* as Policy Instrument: The Case of Ethiopia   151
   Getahun Tadesse Mekonen

6 *Kaizen* as a Key Ingredient of Industrial Development
   Policy   199
   Keijiro Otsuka

**Appendix: Teaching Material for Classroom Training
and the Manual for In-Company Training** 225
Kimiaki Jin, Tsuyoshi Kikuchi and Seiji Sugimoto

Index 259

Notes on Contributors

Kimiaki Jin is a Senior Assistant Director, Private Sector Development Group, Industrial Development and Public Policy Department, JICA, Japan. He served as a Chief Representative of JICA in Ethiopia from 2013 to 2017 and in the UK from 2009 to 2013. He was a Director from 2007 to 2009 of the East Africa Division in JICA's Africa Department and a part-time lecturer from 2009 to 2015 at the Center for Sustainability Science (CENSUS), Hokkaido University. He served for two more periods with JICA in Ethiopia, from 1990 to 1993 and from 2003 to 2006.

Tsuyoshi Kikuchi is a Senior Advisor to Japan Development Services Co., Ltd., Tokyo, Japan. He holds a PhD in International Development and is an expert in *Kaizen* and industrial promotion for small and medium-sized enterprises (SMEs). He worked for JICA *Kaizen* project as a team leader to Tunisia (2006–2008), Ethiopia (2011–2014), Argentina (2009–2010) and Mexico (2014–2015). He served as a JICA Advisor to Kenya (1978–1980), Indonesia (1998–2000) and Ethiopia (2001–2003) and a United Nations Industrial Development Organization (UNIDO) Senior Industrial Development Field Advisor to Tanzania covering Malawi, Uganda and Seychelles (1986–1988). He has been working as a Staff and Deputy Managing Director of Engineering Consulting Firms Association (ECFA), Tokyo, for 33 years.

Getahuna Tadesse Mekonen is a certified Principal *Kaizen* Consultant. He served in senior government positions in different ministries and agencies. He played an active role from 2009 to 2016 as a counterpart to JICA projects and in establishing and leading the Ethiopia *Kaizen* Institute (EKI) as a Director General. He was the initiator of the Ethiopia *Kaizen* strategies, roadmap and TIISO model. He has published three *Kaizen* books in Ethiopian local language. He was also involved in JICA-sponsored research projects and several public policy and strategy studies.

Keijiro Otsuka is a Professor of Development Economics at the Graduate School of Economics, Kobe University. Prior to joining Kobe University, he was a Professor at the GRIPS from 2001 to 2016 and a core member of *World Development Report—Jobs* from 2011 to 2012. He has published 130 articles in internationally renowned journals and is a co-author or co-editor of 23 books. He received the Purple Ribbon Medal from the government of Japan in 2010.

Tetsushi Sonobe is a Vice President of the GRIPS and a Professor of Development Economics there. Before joining GRIPS, he was the Program Director of the Foundation for Advanced Studies on International Development and a Professor at Tokyo Metropolitan University. He has published several books and many journal articles on cluster-based industrial development and *Kaizen* based on more than 30 case studies and field experiments that he conducted in East Asia, South Asia, sub-Saharan Africa and Central America.

Seiji Sugimoto is a Chief Advisor to Japan Development Services Co., Ltd., Tokyo, Japan. He is a certified Small and Medium Enterprise Management Consultant and a certified Professional Engineer (technical disciplines of Industrial Engineering and Industrial Management). He worked for the JICA *Kaizen* project as a core team member in charge of training to Tunisia (2006–2008), Argentina (2009–2010) and Ethiopia (2011–2014) and has been a leader to Ethiopia (2015–). He has published one book and is a co-author of three others.

Momoko Suzuki is a Deputy Director, Team 2, Private Sector Development Group, Industrial Development and Public Policy Department, JICA, Japan. She holds a master's degree from Sussex University, Institute for Development Studies (IDS). She has been working for JICA since 2002 and has experience in Africa and private sector development. She has worked in the JICA Ethiopia Office from 2006 to 2010. She has been working on *Kaizen* projects in Africa since 2014. She is currently working with New Partnership for Africa's Development (NEPAD) on the Africa *Kaizen* Initiative and standardization of *Kaizen* in Africa.

List of Figures

Fig. 1.1 *Kaizen* tools, systems, methods, and principles. (Source: Created by the author) — 9

Fig. 1.2 Roots, trunk, and branches of *Kaizen*. (Source: Created by the author) — 14

Fig. 1.3 Tools and their designated storage spaces in an electric cable factory in Dar es Salaam, Tanzania, 2016. (Source: Created by the author) — 18

Fig. 1.4 Results of an RCT of *Kaizen* management training in Tanzania in terms of the adoption of improved management practices and value-added approaches. (Source: Calculated by the author based on the author's survey data) — 24

Fig. 2.1 Image of capacities. (Source: JICA Capacity Assessment Handbook (2008)) — 40

Fig. 2.2 Countries/organization and periods of JICA projects on quality and productivity improvement. (Source: Created by the author based on JICA reports) — 45

Fig. 2.3 A cyclical concept of the *Kaizen* mind-set. (Source: Created by the author) — 59

Fig. 3.1 Two types of *Kaizen* (problem-solving and task-achieving). (Source: Created by the author) — 70

Fig. 3.2 Inherent technologies and management technologies. (Source: Created by the author) — 75

Fig. 3.3	Example of layout change in the factory. (Source: Created by the author)	91
Fig. 3.4	Loosened bolt instantly made visible with simple *Kaizen*. (Source: Created by the author)	93
Fig. 3.5	Total optimization and partial optimization. (Source: Created by the author)	96
Fig. 3.6	Basic principles of QC circle activities. (Source: Created by the author based on "Fundamentals of QC Circle (1980)," JUSE Press, Ltd.)	99
Fig. 4.1	Basic concept of the Toyota Production System (TPS). (Source: Nakano (2017, 13)). *Elimination of "muri," "mura" and "*muda*": Toyota has identified as "*mudas*" seven types of non-value-adding waste in business or manufacturing process, that is, *overproduction, waiting (time on hand), unnecessary transport or conveyance, over-processing or incorrect processing, excess inventory, unnecessary movement* and *defects*. Liker (2004, 28–29) added an eighth waste to the abovementioned seven wastes, that is, *unused employee creativity*)	118
Fig. 4.2	The basic concept of a Lean Production System. (Source: Nakano (2017, 17). ** Elimination of "*muda*": Womack and Jones (1996) add one more "*muda*" to the seven that Toyota identified as non-value-adding wastes, that is, *service which does not meet the customer's requirement*)	119
Fig. 4.3	An image of future *Kaizen* for African enterprises (MSEs). (Source: Prepared by the author)	139
Fig. 5.1	Organizational structure of EKI. (Source: EKI 2016a, b, c)	169
Fig. 5.2	TIISO Model. (Source: Mekonen 2015b)	178
Fig. 5.3	TIISO Model—5 steps and 20 activities. (Source: Mekonen 2015b)	179
Fig. 6.1	A recommended logical sequence of industrial development policies. (Source: Prepared by the author)	202
Fig. A1	*Kaizen* house. (Total Quality Management (TQM), Toyota Production System (TPS), and Total Productive Maintenance (TPM) are three major pillars of *Kaizen* and 5S gives foundations for these three pillars. Teamwork of the staff sustains all of them.) (Source: Created by the authors)	240
Fig. A2	Pareto diagram. (Source: Created by the authors)	252
Fig. A3	Histogram. (Source: Created by the authors)	253

Fig. A4	Cause and effect diagram. (Source: Created by the authors)	253
Fig. A5	Stratification. (Source: Created by the authors)	254
Fig. A6	Scatter diagram. (Source: Created by the authors)	255
Fig. A7	Temperature check sheet. (Source: Created by the authors)	255
Fig. A8	Graph. (Source: Created by the authors)	256
Fig. A9	Control chart. (Source: Created by the authors)	256

List of Tables

Table 1.1	Real GDP growth rates by resource dependence type (% per year)	2
Table 2.1	Disaggregation of capacity development	41
Table 2.2	Transfer of *Kaizen* from Japan to developing countries	43
Table 2.3	Chronology of Singapore PDP	46
Table 3.1	Characteristics of two types of *Kaizen*	72
Table 3.2	List of technologies frequently used for *Kaizen*	77
Table 3.3	Forms of consulting organization	105
Table 4.1	Similarities and differences between Six Sigma and TQM	117
Table 4.2	Similarities and differences between BPR and *Kaizen*	123
Table 4.3	Six Sigma (SS)/L(Lean)/L&SS methods and key personnel	127
Table 4.4	Basic *Kaizen* technologies (methods, tools and procedures)	136
Table 5.1	Assessment criteria	158
Table 5.2	Assessment results of pilot companies	158
Table 5.3	Growth of consultants from 2014 to 2017 at EKI	168
Table 5.4	Enhanced job grade and remunerations	170
Table 5.5	Budget of EKI in million birr	170
Table 5.6	First-level *Kaizen*	176
Table 5.7	Second-level *Kaizen*	177
Table 5.8	Third-level *Kaizen*	178
Table 5.9	Different institutions reached by EKI	181
Table 5.10	Number of trainees and organized KPTs	182
Table 5.11	Number of KPTs organized in Metehara Sugar Industry	183

Table 5.12	Monetary value (nominal) of *Kaizen* achievement in Metehara Sugar Estate	184
Table 5.13	Monetary gains (nominal value) of *Kaizen* in Ethiopia	184
Table A1	5S total evaluation sheet	229
Table A2	Red-tag	230
Table A3	*Muda* checklist	242
Table A4	Standard operation sheet	243

1

How *Kaizen* Brightens Africa's Future

Tetsushi Sonobe

Sub-Saharan Africa, the large part of the African continent lying to the south of the Saharan desert, has long been a synonym for economic stagnancy. As shown in the first line of Table 1.1, however, the real gross domestic product (GDP) of this region has grown by more than 4 percent per year for the last two decades, a much higher growth rate than it had three to five decades ago. These data may however appear to suggest that the relatively high growth in the 2000s was driven mainly by internationally high prices of oil and other natural resources, because Nigeria, a large resource-dependent economy, grew rapidly, while South Africa, which is as large but less resource-dependent, had lower growth rates (see lines 2 and 4 of Table 1.1). Moreover, another ten highly resource-dependent countries recorded high growth (see line 3). But as line 5 shows, aside from South Africa the less resource-dependent economies have also managed to grow steadily over recent decades. Ethiopia, Tanzania, Ghana, Kenya, and Rwanda are included in this group.

T. Sonobe (✉)
National Graduate Institute for Policy Studies (GRIPS), Tokyo, Japan
e-mail: sonobete@grips.ac.jp

Table 1.1 Real GDP growth rates by resource dependence type (% per year)

Period	1986–1995	1996–2005	2006–2010	2011–2015
(1) 48 sub-Saharan countries	1.3	4.6	5.6	4.1
(2) Nigeria	1.0	7.2	7.2	4.7
(3) 10 other highly resource-dependent countries	−0.8	4.9	7.8	4.5
(4) South Africa	1.3	3.3	3.1	2.1
(5) 36 other less resource-dependent countries	2.8	4.2	5.7	4.9

Source: Created by the author using data from the World Bank

Notes: Those countries that earned on average more than 20 percent of their GDP from oil, natural gas, coal, and other mineral resources during the period 2001–2015 are called "highly resource-dependent countries" in this table; the remaining countries are referred to as "less resource-dependent countries." The average growth rates of each group of countries as well as that of the 48 sub-Saharan countries are the weighted averages of the GDP growth rates of individual countries with weights being their respective GDP levels

Africa has witnessed several favorable changes. First, the cost of transportation has been drastically reduced thanks to significant investment in infrastructure supported by several developed countries and China. Second, mobile phones have spread across the continent, reducing communication costs substantially. As a result, farmers and traders now know the latest prices for agricultural produce and other goods in remote markets. Moreover, mobile phones can be used to send and receive small amounts of money to cover transactions of goods and services, including those that could not previously be affected. Third, in many African states, the so-called structural adjustment programs (SAPs) have eliminated harmful government controls and regulations and privatized state-owned enterprises and parastatals. Although the SAPs created confusion initially, it seems that the favorable effects of the reforms are now being felt. Fourth, the regionally isolated markets have been integrated into the initiatives of the East African Community (consisting of 6 countries), the Southern African Development Community (15 countries), and the Economic Community of West African States (15 countries).

Lower costs of transportation and communication, freer economic activities in the private sector, and regional economic integration appear to have improved the functioning of markets, boosted market transactions, and contributed to the development of the division of labor and specialization between enterprises. Some economic historians refer to economic growth driven by increasing market transactions as *Smithian* growth (Mokyr 1990, 2017). There is a consensus among economists, however, that for economic growth to be sustainable in the long-run, it must be driven also by productivity gains. In a very narrow sense, productivity means output per unit of input. The term, however, can include the improvement of product quality and the introduction of new products, as well as an increase in the narrowly defined productivity relationship. The long-term economic growth driven by productivity gains in this broader sense is called *Schumpeterian* growth.[1] Smithian growth has always been important. Schumpeterian growth has assumed importance as the main engine of long-run economic growth since the Industrial Revolution in today's developed and emerging economies. In Africa, however, it has not yet reached this point.

To enhance productivity growth in Africa, there is a prerequisite. To see what the prerequisite is, it seems useful to review what productivity is. In general, productivity gain is likely to be missing where people equate it with the use of new machinery that embodies the latest technology and lament their unfavorable access to finance for such machinery. While it is true that productivity can be improved using new machinery, there are many cases in which new machinery and the embodied technology do not improve productivity at all. For example, the materials needed to be used by the machines may be delivered in too small a quantity or be too late, the machine operators may not be properly trained, and/or the machines may not have been well maintained. Conversely, if the initial situation is plagued by these problems, eliminating each of them will improve productivity even without having to introduce a new machine.

Clearly good management is a prerequisite for substantial improvements in productivity, even though the former may not necessarily deliver the latter. Without good management, productivity can only improve serendipitously.[2] That is, the prerequisite for making productivity gains

---

[1] Smithian growth was named for Adam Smith, who emphasized the importance of the division of labor; Schumpeterian growth was named for Joseph Schumpeter, who highlighted the role of innovation.

[2] Bruhn, Karlan, and Schoar (2010), among others, argue that managerial capital is missing in developing countries.

the major engine of economic growth is to cultivate management capabilities. The good news for Africa is that there is a human-friendly, inexpensive, common-sense approach to productivity gain that has proved effective in other regions of the world. Its name is *Kaizen*.

The rest of this chapter gives our definition of *Kaizen* (Section 1.1) and explains in Section 1.2 how this approach improves productivity, while it looks at the history of the concept in Section 1.3, and discusses the challenges and opportunities for adopting it in Section 1.4. Finally, Section 1.5 gives a brief introduction to the other chapters of this book.

1.1 What Is *Kaizen*?

Kaizen is now an international word appearing in the *Oxford English Dictionary*, which defines it as "a Japanese business philosophy of continuous improvement of working practices, personal efficiency, etc." Our definition is a little more detailed: *Kaizen* is the management philosophy and know-how that brings about continuous, participatory, incremental, and low-budget improvements in quality, productivity, cost, delivery, safety, morale, and environment (or QPCDSME).[3] Indeed, just like other philosophies, the concept includes both the humanities and the sciences. It is human-friendly and participatory. It is a collection of ideas and insights that many managers and workers from firms in the manufacturing and service sectors have created and refined through observations and experiments carried out over several decades in Japan and other parts of the world.

Kaizen improves productivity in a step-by-step, incremental, progressive manner. It has been used primarily in the manufacturing sector but has also been applied to health, education, public administration, and other services and can be applied to micro and small enterprises as well as medium and large firms. It can be applied to offices, retail shops, and service counters as well as machine shops, workshops, and garages, to

---

[3] A very similar definition appears on a webpage of the Japan International Cooperation Agency (JICA) and some other JICA documents. The only difference is that ours puts quality before productivity, because emphasis on productivity improvement in a narrow sense may lead to overproduction.

physical desktops as well as computer and smartphone desktops, and even to everyday life. Such versatility gives it a philosophical image.

Kaizen has spread throughout East Asia, Europe, and North America, boosting productivity in those regions. Industrial development has been successfully achieved in every developing country where the use of this approach has become widespread. *Kaizen* has improved productivity and product quality, hence the competitiveness of manufactured products in international markets. The growth of the manufacturing sector has transformed an agriculturally based economy into an industry-based one. In labor-abundant countries, *Kaizen* has helped the development of labor-intensive industries, thereby helping such countries achieve inclusive economic growth, and has reduced not only production costs but also the incidence of injury, machine breakdowns, and delayed delivery. It has improved morale and accountability. Thus, it may well be that the spread of *Kaizen* makes a society more proactive, transparent, and fair.

In Africa, Botswana began introducing *Kaizen* as early as in the 1990s and has been followed recently by Egypt, Tunisia, Ethiopia, Zambia, Tanzania, Ghana, Kenya, Cameroon, Senegal, Sudan, and the Republic of the Congo. However, the majority of business owners, managers, and workers in Africa remain unfamiliar with *Kaizen*. As the past experiences of *Kaizen* dissemination efforts suggest, an important task for the governments of African countries is to increase awareness through the provision of free training programs for business communities and the creation of model factories. It is also important to train the trainers who assist the managers and engineers of those firms that are willing to learn about *Kaizen*. Initially, the concept begins to spread from a single production line and a product to other lines and products within a firm. Those pioneering firms that earnestly put *Kaizen* into practice will see an increasingly substantial improvement in quality and productivity, and this will prompt their suppliers and customers to follow suit. *Kaizen* will thus spread from a few firms to many within an industry and from one industry to another.

During the early stage of dissemination, there will be an inequality of knowledge between the metropolitan area and less developed areas, and between large and small firms. For *Kaizen* to be disseminated more widely, governments and business associations can contribute by boosting awareness through contests, awards, and media campaigns. Such public support during the dissemination process is critically important, as is a commitment from political leaders. In the early stage of dissemination, however, neither political leaders nor government officials are familiar enough with the philosophy they should promote throughout the country. The best way to give politicians and bureaucrats an understanding and appreciation of the nature and values of *Kaizen* may be for them to start by introducing it to their own offices. However, once the public understands the value of this approach, the role of the government turns into one of institution building for quality control, to prevent substandard consulting or training services related to *Kaizen*.

Thus, with appropriate government policies, it is likely that Africa will succeed to disseminate *Kaizen* and to improve quality and productivity continuously. Moreover, Japan is willing to assist with its dissemination in Africa as it has successfully done in other developing countries. Before discussing this issue further, however, it seems useful to sketch the way in which *Kaizen* can improve quality and productivity.

1.2 How Does *Kaizen* Improve Quality and Productivity?

Consider a firm that has never tried to improve quality or productivity, and suppose that the firm's top-level management decided to try *Kaizen*. As its first *Kaizen* activity, it will encourage workers to classify operations and equipment in the firm into those that are really needed and those that are not. Having classified everything, the workers will then discuss the ways that they can dispose of those that they have identified as unnecessary. From this analysis, a broken machine that has occupied the center of a workshop for years will be removed for example. Since its removal will make workflows smoother, workers will feel better, and a small improvement is thus achieved.

The workers can also classify their own activities into those that add value to customers, those that do not add any value but are indispensable, and those that may be regarded as meaningless. By abandoning non-value-adding activities, productivity may improve. As workers will have achieved this improvement without new methods or new machinery being imposed upon them by upper management, they can feel a sense of ownership over the process. Top management is also happy because productivity has been improved without any significant monetary investment.

Once productivity is improved, a firm may consider expanding its level of production. To expand production, the firm may try to recruit young workers. As hiring highly educated workers is expensive, the firm may try to employ less qualified workers, but they may not be "employable" in the sense that they might damage the quality of products and services and lower productivity, and not be worth even their low wages. In general, the trade-off between labor quality and labor costs in Africa is steep. This is particularly so in those countries where secondary education is far from universal and the quality of education remains a big problem. This constraint poses a challenge to many African entrepreneurs.

The exceptions are rich entrepreneurs, who may not be bothered by this constraint. This is largely because rich entrepreneurs can hire college graduates fluent in English or French to provide business process outsourcing services, such as call center and data entry services for foreign customers. Additionally, they may hire more skilled professionals or "smart boys" to provide computer programming services. Such services may have large demands and high prices, but they allow rich entrepreneurs to earn positive profits despite the high labor cost.

In this regard, *Kaizen* offers a solution for many entrepreneurs who may be financially constrained and not able to afford to employ such a highly educated and skilled workforce. The problem associated with the employment of uneducated and unskilled workers is not just their lack of knowledge and skills, but also includes their lack of etiquette when working together with other people, and a lack of confidence in their own ability to acquire knowledge and skills. For example, after using a hammer and a screwdriver, workers may not return them to where they should be. As a result, other workers in the same workshop must waste a considerable amount of time looking for those tools. Without *Kaizen*, managers would simply attribute these actions to the workers' lack of discipline and education and would fail to take any countermeasures. A basic function of the methodology is therefore to serve as an effective job training tool for such workers and instill in them a positive mindset. Thus, *Kaizen* makes it possible to employ ordinary people, and even those who would be otherwise unemployable.

The more advanced part of *Kaizen* offers a variety of tools for spotting problems, for finding solutions, for motivating workers and managers to participate in its activities, or for managing cycles of planning, implementing, reviewing, and setting targets for further improvement. By adopting and assimilating a variety of tools to improve QPCDSME continuously, even initially small firms can reach or go beyond international standards, so that they can make inroads into export markets in developed countries or receive orders from world-class leading brands, or if they are tourism firms, attract the most quality-conscious tourists.

To summarize, *Kaizen* makes it possible to give initially unskilled, undisciplined workers the discipline to work efficiently and to continuously improve QPCDSME. With support from top-level management, it is possible for such workers to make the quality of their products reach international standards. Since *Kaizen* is also an inexpensive approach, it can help both small firms and large firms in any sector. That is to say, *Kaizen* can make ordinary people, who do not have particularly high levels of education or talent, productive.

These attributes of *Kaizen* help in those industries that intensively use the labor of ordinary people. The development of such industries will provide abundant job opportunities for ordinary people. Thus, if *Kaizen* is disseminated throughout a country, it will deliver not only rapid but also inclusive and sustainable economic growth, which is beneficial for a broad range of the population.

1.3 How Was *Kaizen* Born and How Has It Grown? Roots, Trunk, and Branches

Some *Kaizen* tools are used as a set or in a sequenced manner for the same purpose. Such a set of tools is called a method. A set of some methods that share similar purposes or some common threads is called a system. Thus, systems, methods, and tools have a containment relationship as illustrated in the upper part of Fig. 1.1. For example, the Toyota

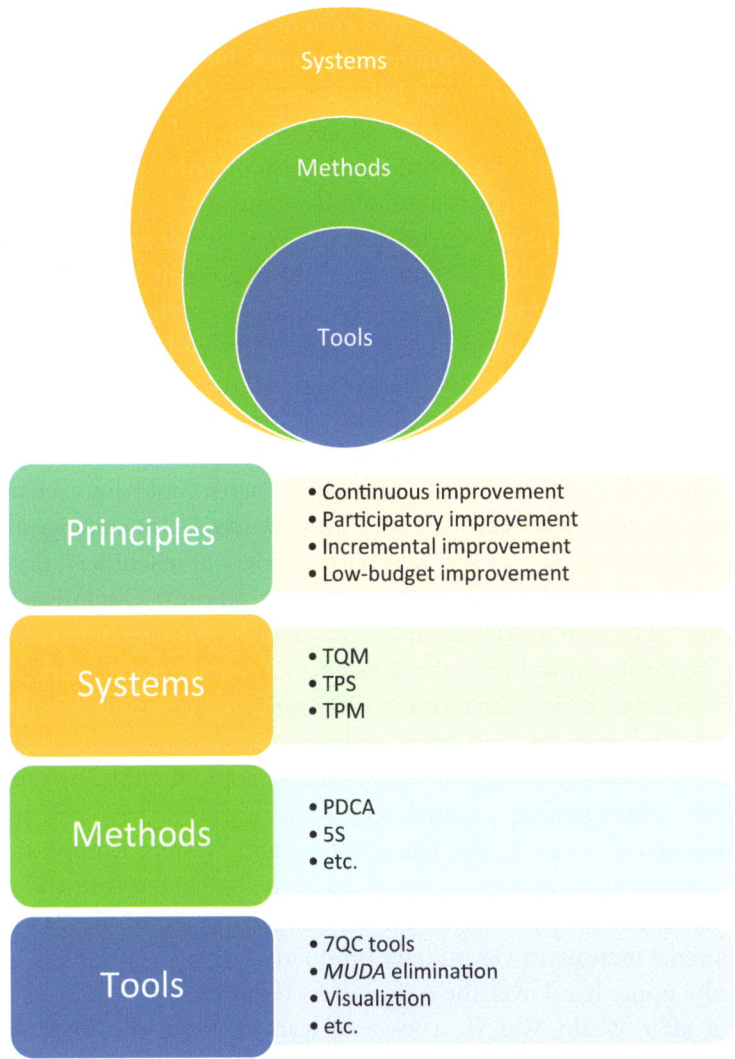

Fig. 1.1 *Kaizen* tools, systems, methods, and principles. (Source: Created by the author)

Production System (TPS) is a *Kaizen* system and contains several methods, each of which in turn contains some tools. Despite this illustration, it is not the case that every tool belongs to a specific method and that every method belongs to a specific system. Some tools and methods are included in more than one system or in all systems. Also, it is not the case that different systems are unrelated. On the contrary, they share the same principles that make people regard them as parts of *Kaizen* (see the lower part of Fig. 1.1). The next section gives a brief account of the historical processes in which *Kaizen* tools, methods, and systems have emerged and the continuity, participatory, incremental, and low-budget principles, which constitute the methodology, have been formed.

The history of modern management has been dated to at least 1801, when Ely Whitney, an American inventor, demonstrated the idea of interchangeable parts with ten guns whose parts could be exchanged without affecting the way that the guns worked. Interchangeability required workshops to be organized with a variety of machinery, jigs and other equipment, and the concept of tolerance. In turn, "Taylorism" and "Fordism" enhanced the development of Scientific Management substantially. Taylorism introduced the concepts of standardized work, time study, work standards, management dichotomy demarcating the roles of managers and workers, and process charts and motion study. Fordism introduced assembly lines, flow lines, and mass production. In general, Scientific Management exerted considerable influences on socioeconomic development in the United States and Western Europe and to a lesser degree in other parts of the world in the late nineteenth and early twentieth century. Its power was manifested during World War II by the phenomenal increase in US military productivity, which gave the United States the upper hand over the Axis powers (Hamilton 2014).

Soon after World War II, a wave of learning from the West swept through Japan. In the manufacturing sector, the demand for learning, especially from the United States, surged because the quality of Japanese products was too low to compete on the world market. Moreover, Japanese business people understood with increasing clarity how large the productivity gap between the United States and Japan had become. Naturally Japanese business people were eager to know what had boosted the quality and productivity of their US counterparts and how they could catch up. To meet this demand for knowledge, the Japan Management Association (JMA), the Union of Japanese Scientists and Engineers (JUSE), and the Japan Productivity Center (JPC), among other institutions, were busy inviting experts from the United States and sending missions over there to draw lessons from the US experiences.

These Japanese pioneers and their firms faced two major difficulties in transferring the American "way" to Japan. First, the scale of production was much smaller in Japan than in the United States, even though many of the pioneering firms were leading firms and relatively large by Japanese standards of the time. Scientific Management, especially the set of methods and tools for Ford-style mass production, was thus not very useful for them. Second, many of their employees were reluctant to accept Taylorism or Fordism, or their offshoots. In those days, labor unions were much more influential than today, and their leaders thought that unemployment would increase if productivity improved. In addition to the fear of unemployment, workers were possibly influenced by Charlie Chaplin's movie, *Modern Times* to think that Taylorism and Fordism would ignore human dignity and treat them like machine parts.

Various attempts were made to overcome these difficulties. After a process of trial and error, the pioneers began making Scientific Management in Japanese firms flexible and human-friendly. This was the beginning of their creation of *Kaizen*, that is, their great efforts to modify, adopt, and customize the American way to conform to small production sizes and to worker sentiment. One firm's small success in this line of effort was imitated by other firms, which then added new ideas. Even during this process, new ideas and practices were incessantly created by practitioners and academicians in the United States, Japan, and elsewhere. Japanese firms would aggressively and independently adopt and then customize those new ideas and practices to conform to their respective needs. From the results of these customization attempts, cream would be skimmed by other firms. As Imai (1986, 1997) points out, *Kaizen* is a compilation of those ideas and practices which have an established reputation of being effective, and it has continuously been growing. Our image of *Kaizen* is of a big tree that is already 70 years old but is still growing with newly emerging branches. The remainder of Section 1.3 is an attempt to characterize *Kaizen* using this metaphor and to trace the growth of the tree over time as far as we can.

1.3.1 Roots

Quality control was brought to Japan by two prominent quality gurus: Dr. E. Edwards Deming and Dr. Joseph M. Juran (Umeda 2001). In the summer of 1950, JUSE invited Dr. Deming to give seminars and to present a training program on Statistical Quality Control (SQC) for Japanese entrepreneurs, engineers, and scholars. The main emphasis was placed on improving the quality of products by applying statistical tools to production processes. In the same year, JUSE also extended an invitation to Dr. Juran; however, it was not until 1954 that he finally came to Japan to introduce the concept of quality control as a vital management tool for improving management performance. These two training programs were fascinating eye-openers. Many training participants immediately acted to introduce quality control in their firms, which tended to be the largest manufacturing firms in Japan.

However, while studying and applying SQC, many engineers and managers across the world found it unsatisfactory. While SQC helped them reduce defects in products, the extent of the reduction was not enough. In their view, a major reason for this was that quality control activities were conducted and coordinated only by quality control sections or departments. Against this background, a new framework of concepts and methods called Total Quality Control (TQC) was popularized in the United States by Dr. Armand Feigenbaum (1956, 1961). TQC emphasizes the importance of integrating the various quality improvement efforts made within different sections of a firm. SQC was soon replaced by TQC, which in turn was replaced by Total Quality Management (TQM).

The second and third roots transplanted from the United States to Japan were Training Within Industry (TWI) and Industrial Engineering (IE), both of which had boosted the productivity of the US military during the war. TWI refers to internal training programs provided by firms for their own workers. IE is a framework of concepts and methods for improving work efficiency and dates to the early 1900s when Frederick Taylor led the Efficiency Movement in the United States. It was during the 1920s that IE was first introduced to Japan and adopted by several Japanese firms. In the 1950s, the Toyota Motor Corporation began providing internal training programs known as "productivity courses" or "P-Courses" to its workers as a way of teaching them IE methods, such as process analysis, operation analysis, time study, and motion study. The architect of the P-Course, Dr. Shigeo Shingo, taught around 3000 workers over 25 years and his students went on to teach many others (Kato and Smalley 2011). The P-Course was copied by other firms and then customized to their needs. In this way, internal training programs proliferated in Japan.

The fourth root of *Kaizen* is preventive maintenance, a collection of methods for the detection and prevention of machinery malfunction and breakdown. This aspect of the approach was transferred from the United States to Japan in the 1950s (Suzuki 1994). It later grew into a larger framework of concepts and methods called Total Productive Maintenance (TPM).

1.3.2 Trunk and Branches

Figure 1.2 lists the systems, methods, and tools that are considered to be part of *Kaizen* and superimposes the list onto a picture of a large tree. The metaphor of a tree is useful for gaining an overview of how *Kaizen* has been developed and how it is used today. At the bottom of the list are Statistical Quality Control (SQC), Training Within Industry (TWI), and preventive maintenance. As mentioned earlier, SQC was replaced by Total Quality Control (TQC) and then Total Quality Management (TQM). Further, job training became so common that it was no longer called TWI, and preventive maintenance was replaced by Total Productive Maintenance (TPM). Thus, SQC, TWI, and preventive maintenance are roots of *Kaizen* not only because they are its origins, but also because they are no longer visible within firms and other organizations.

By contrast, Industrial Engineering (IE) remains visible, even though it has a long history and is a part of the origin of *Kaizen*. For this reason, it is included in the trunk part of Fig. 1.2. IE offers various methods and tools such as time analysis, work sampling, process analysis, and layout change. Roughly speaking, it emphasizes close observation, measurement, and analysis of processes, work, and so on. IE is useful for spotting work inefficiencies and finding their causes. Thus, it is often used to eliminate *MUDA* (a Japanese word meaning the wasteful use of time and materials).

Fig. 1.2 Roots, trunk, and branches of *Kaizen*. (Source: Created by the author)

Taiichi Ohno, the architect of the Toyota Production System (TPS), classified the typical waste found on workshops floors into seven different types: overproduction, waiting (due to miscoordination, delayed supply of parts, and machinery breakdowns), transport (that could be reduced by designing efficient production processes or layouts), processing (that is unnecessary or excessive), inventory (that is unnecessary or excessive), motion (that does not create any value for customers), and correction (inspection and rework). Note that while the correction of defects would add some value, the time needed to carry out corrections could be saved if the production process were better designed. Two concepts related to *MUDA* that also lead to inefficiency are MURI (overburden) and MURA (unevenness).

It is often said that the Toyota Production System (TPS) is one of the origins of today's *Kaizen*. TPS is still visible and its copies and variants are used extensively across the world. The underlying aim of TPS is to improve QPCDSME by reducing negative elements like *MUDA*, MURI, and MURA. Just-in-Time and Jidoka are the two integrated organs or major methods of TPS. Kanban is a tool for Just-in-Time. The idea of reducing negative elements is referred to as "lean."

To achieve higher quality, TQC emphasizes the concerted efforts of various groups within a firm. Seeing the way forward, Prof. Ishikawa of the University of Tokyo proposed two important additions to TQC.[4] The first was continuous improvement. It should be noted that "continuous improvement" is an expression included in the definition of *Kaizen* contained in the *Oxford English Dictionary*. For Japanese people, "*Kaizen*" as an everyday word means improvement in general and does not specifically mean continuous improvement.

The second addition to TQC made by Prof. Ishikawa is the involvement of everyone in the continuous improvement of quality, rather than just the involvement of the various groups directly related to quality control. Everyone means every manager and every worker; yet for workers to be involved meaningfully, they must have the skills and knowledge to operationalize the concepts and methods for quality improvement. One

---

[4] Prof. Kaoru Ishikawa is the father of the Japanese style of TQC, which differs from the TQC concepts of Dr. Armand Feigenbaum (1956, 1961). Prof. Ishikawa was an advocate of Company-Wide Quality Control (CWQC). In Japan, the quality management framework evolved from SQC to CWQC, TQC, and then to TQM.

way to make workers knowledgeable and skillful is to provide them with internal training programs. Toyota's P-Course is an example of such a program. Prof. Ishikawa proposed another way of achieving this, where workers voluntarily form small groups and share their knowledge and skills with other members of the group. Such small groups are called Quality Control Circles (QCCs). The purpose of QCCs is twofold: the first is the sharing and acquiring of knowledge and skills, and the second is the application of that knowledge and skill to finding and solving problems faced by workers within their workplace (Ishikawa 1985).

A focus on workers and their learning is also an important feature of Total Productive Maintenance (TPM). This concept views equipment breakdowns as the tip of the iceberg leading to a large set of potential troubles and offers methods and tools for eliminating the sources of trouble. TPM is a comprehensive approach to maximizing equipment efficiency and effectiveness by involving all managers and workers in the upkeep and maintenance of the equipment they are working with. This reduces the problem of relying on machine operators and maintenance staff as the sole groups responsible for maintenance. It also makes the factory environment safer and helps to avoid rust, and oil and gas leakages. In fact, TPM goes beyond maintenance in the sense that it enhances workers' skill levels by providing them with training, allows them use statistical tools to work on focused problems, and encourages them to interact with other circle members. The application of TPM is not limited to plant equipment but also includes office furniture, fixtures, and equipment.

The question arises as to what knowledge and skills the workers and managers should acquire through training courses, QCC, or any other devices. In the P-Course, IE was an important part of the curriculum. The set of knowledge and skills to be acquired should also include the 7QC tools, the new 7QC tools, the concepts of *Muda*, *Muri*, and *Mura*, and their various symptoms. The 7QC and new 7QC tools are used in quantitative and qualitative analyses, respectively, to identify a problem and its solution, or for checking that the problem has been solved. Since *Muda* elimination and QC tools can be used for other purposes than quality control, they are included in the category of general-purpose tools in Fig. 1.2.

A question may arise as to why workers agree to get involved in improvement efforts and to learn about various concepts and methods. How are they motivated? There are three kinds of incentives for workers to get involved. First, monetary incentives, such as bonuses and salary or wage increases, may be given to outstanding teams of workers or individual workers. Second, recognition and commendation may motivate workers. Third, people tend to be motivated by the feeling of being successful; therefore, a sense of success acts as another incentive. Because *Kaizen* is an inexpensive approach, the second and third incentives are important.

To make workers to feel successful quickly, it is often useful to begin with 5S, a set of five activities whose Japanese names start with the S sound (and their translations into other languages also start with the S sound if possible): *seiri* (sort), *seiton* (set in order), *seiso* (shine), *seiketsu* (standardize), and *shitsuke* (sustain). The first two S's, sorting and setting in order, are particularly important for this purpose because they can quickly produce a small level of success. Sorting refers to the classification of everything on the shop floor into two categories: necessary items and unnecessary items, or value-adding items and non-value-adding items. After this classification is made, those items that were identified as unnecessary or non-value-adding are eliminated from the shop floor, thus creating space and reducing the amount of time wasted looking for necessary or value-adding items. "Setting in order" is the act of assigning a storage space to each tool or instrument, such as a hammer and a wrench in the workshop or a document file in the office, and making sure that every tool or instrument is returned immediately after use, as illustrated by the photo in Fig. 1.3. This practice delivers high efficiency because the time wasted on searching is drastically reduced. There are easy steps to get started on the 2S and to break the ice among workers and managers so that they choose to take up new challenges toward productivity and quality improvement.

The above discussion makes plain why *Kaizen* has the following outcomes (see the lower part of Fig. 1.1):

1. Continuous improvement: *Kaizen* continuously improves productivity in a broad sense or QPCDSME specifically, through the making of incre-

Fig. 1.3 Tools and their designated storage spaces in an electric cable factory in Dar es Salaam, Tanzania, 2016. (Source: Created by the author)

mental changes. The continuity of improvement is maintained through the Plan-Do-Check-Act (PDCA) cycle. *Kaizen* offers different tools for performing each step of the cycle, as will be explained in Chap. 5.
2. Participatory improvement: *Kaizen* encourages everyone in a firm to participate in continuous improvement. It provides easy steps for getting started and participating. There are some ways, including QCC, to ensure full participation that are discussed below.
3. Incremental improvement: *Kaizen* achieves productivity gain through a series of small steps of improvement. This does not mean that *Kaizen* does not help innovation take place. On the contrary, it keeps firms agile in responding to and profiting from innovation.
4. Low-budget improvement: *Kaizen* does not require heavy expenditure. On the contrary, it begins by eliminating *MUDA* or waste. However, it is not about downsizing. As *Kaizen* taps into the insights and wisdom of workers, and the spirit of cooperation and self-esteem, and because it seeks full participation, the means of eliminating waste must be compatible with improving safety, the working environment,

and employee satisfaction. It should also be noted that if all inefficiencies are eliminated, further improvement may require large-scale investment; however, up until this point, the method is inexpensive.

It may be useful here to add some remarks on the full participation principle. In Japan, a common practice is to create small teams of workers because this is, or at least it was until recently, an effective way of ensuring the involvement of workers in activities aimed at bringing about improvement. Such teams would be called the 5S committee, the Standard Operation Committee, or the Total Productive Maintenance Committee, if they were not already classified as Quality Control Circles (QCCs). These small groups consisted of five to seven workers in the same place or process, who were well organized and guided by principles and procedures developed for them by JUSE (1985). From 1962, the popularity of QCC activities in Japan increased. In the mid-1980s, its popularity reached a peak with a majority of businesses in Japan, including 73 percent of all manufacturing businesses, having active QCCs (Ogawa 2011).

In the United States, however, TQC was not as popular at this time and QCCs were almost non-existent, most likely due to the US employment and pay systems, but also possibly because of cultural factors.[5] In any case, US manufacturers were outperformed by their Japanese counterparts from the 1970s through to the 1980s, in terms of quality and productivity. Responding in the 1980s, US manufacturers conducted a serious study of the Japanese-style TQC, and as a result of this research, Total Quality Management (TQM) was created.

The concept of TQM adopts the idea of continuous improvement and emphasizes policy deployment and cross-functional teams, which were already being used in Japanese firms. Policy deployment refers to concrete goals and targets that are deployed in divisions, departments, and sections to implement a company-wide medium- or long-term plan. At different levels, including the company-wide level, PDCA cycles are repeated to check the status of implementation and to revise the plan based on feedback from frontline employees or shop floor workers. A cross-

---

[5] In the Japanese system, unlike the US system, "employees need not fear for their jobs, expect to share in the fortunes of the firm, do not anticipate leaving for another employer, and have a say in the directions the firm will take" (Milgrom and Roberts 1992, 350–351).

functional team (CFT) of people from different departments and with different expertise is formed to study and propose solutions to a given issue so that top management can make a good decision. CFTs revive inter-departmental communication, coordination, and cooperation. TQM became popular in the United States in the late 1980s and early 1990s, contributing to an improvement in quality and to the recovery of the US manufacturing sector.

In Japan, the diffusion of TQM was initially very slow. Japanese firms, however, began to move from TQC to TQM in the mid-1990s after having looked at the successful recovery of the US manufacturing sector and having plunged into a recession themselves. Their shift to TQM was accompanied by an emphasis on management or a rebalancing of the roles played by top-down and bottom-up decision making. Interestingly, while US firms seldom have QCCs, many Japanese firms have modified TQM and maintained QCCs.

In Fig. 1.2, Lean Manufacturing and Six Sigma are included in the *Kaizen* tree. They were developed outside Japan after US manufacturers began re-importing the concept. We admit that these methods are in a gray zone in the sense that they do not really meet all the *Kaizen* principles; however, they have emerged from its systems and methods as new branches. We may refer to those management systems, methods, and tools that share a few such principles but not all of them as "*Kaizen* derivatives," or "Western-style *Kaizen*." It is also noteworthy that the quality management system principles commonly known as the International Standards Organization (ISO) family was developed in Europe from the 1950s, and has been periodically updated to meet changing environments and new developments, thereby providing an alternative perspective of management (Hoyle 2000). We will discuss this issue further in Chap. 4.

1.3.3 Dissemination of *Kaizen* to the SME Sectors in Japan

The roots of *Kaizen* were transferred from the United States to Japan, especially to its large corporate sector. Aside from the activities of JPC, JUSE, and academics, the leading role in developing this concept was played by the spontaneous and independent (or non-coordinated) efforts made by large firms. The dissemination of *Kaizen* to small and medium enterprises (SMEs) began later and was carried out at varying speeds. In some sectors, where SMEs supplied important parts and components to large companies, dissemination proceeded smoothly as SEMs could obtain information on *Kaizen* from their transacting partners. In other sectors, the access of SMEs to information on *Kaizen* remained unfavorable until the government reinforced its efforts to boost awareness by various measures, including the upgrading of the *Shindanshi* (Small and Medium Enterprise Management Consultant) system toward the end of the 1960s.

Kaizen was welcomed by SMEs probably because it is effective whether production or operation is small or large. Unlike the Fordism approach, *Kaizen* offers to SMEs a variety of methods and tools that helped them reduce the costs of the small-quantity production of high-quality products that satisfy consumer preferences. Examples include Just-in-Time, Kanban, single-minute-die-exchange, waste elimination, and visual management.

In the 1960s, Japanese people, including leading economists, viewed SMEs as a kind of burden on economic growth (Shinohara 1961). Subsequently, however, SMEs became widely recognized as a major driver of the growing competitiveness of the Japanese manufacturing industries (Asanuma 1997). In terms of timing, such a drastic change in the view of SMEs coincided with the diffusion *Kaizen* across the SME sector.

1.4 Opportunities and Challenges for Africa as a Late Adopter

Japan caught up with higher income economies by taking advantage of technology transfer. *Kaizen* made the attempts of Japanese firms to transfer technology successful because it gave Japanese workers (including middle managers) discipline; as a result, they were able to acquire new knowledge and skills. As we observed in the previous section, *Kaizen* itself was a product of the copying and modifying of Western ideas; thus Japan is known for exploiting the second-mover advantage. Some East

Asian countries have taken the third-mover advantage by subsequently applying *Kaizen* as a way of substantially improving quality and productivity, in their march to join the ranks of the middle-income or even high-income countries.

Africa is becoming a continent of hope with a bright future. While it is true that Africa will have to rise to some challenges to assure bright future, there are some opportunities that it can enjoy. The next sections consider both the major challenges and the opportunities for Africa.

1.4.1 Challenges

Challenge 1: In other continents, *Kaizen* has proven to be one of the best approaches, if not the very best, for creating discipline in workers and making them capable of upgrading their knowledge and skill sets. Still, the question remains as to whether it will work effectively in Africa. In short, is the concept transferable to Africa? Can workers in Africa accept *Kaizen* and feel comfortable enough to implement it? American firms, Chinese firms, European firms, and East Asian firms have modified *Kaizen*; thus, a challenge for African workers and firms is to absorb, assimilate, and customize it for their own purposes.

Challenge 2: The commitment of the top-level management to support and encourage workers to undertake activities that include *Kaizen* is indispensable. When, through hard work and perseverance, workers succeed in bringing about some improvement, top management should appreciate the achievement. When workers request permission to try work-space layout changes for example, top management should positively consider it. Without knowing the value of *Kaizen*, however, it is difficult for top management to commit itself, and without having achieved success, it is difficult to convince top management of the value of *Kaizen*. Thus, securing a commitment from top-level management will be a challenge.

Challenge 3: Although *Kaizen* is human-friendly and approachable, it requires very basic skills such as literacy and numeracy. In those countries where universal lower-secondary education is far from the reality, it may take longer time to widely diffuse *Kaizen*.

Challenge 4: According to a certain survey, less than 30 percent of firms that received *Kaizen* training in the past continue to practice *Kaizen*. Is it possible to make *Kaizen* more sustainable?

1.4.2 Encouraging Findings and Opportunities

Entrepreneurs are those who see opportunities where others see challenges. Challenges 1 and 2 above have been overcome in several countries. Challenge 3 was not encountered in East Asia and Latin America, but it would be absurd to postpone efforts to disseminate *Kaizen* in Africa until education levels rise sufficiently. Challenge 4 is a common problem associated with management or business skill training programs. Consider record keeping, one of the most basic business practices. Those small business owners who participate in business skill training programs are reminded by trainers of the importance of keeping records of sales, purchases, inventories, and so on, but many fail to continue to keep records. Whether to keep records is not a matter of knowledge but eventually a matter of habit. Thus, it is not surprising that many of the recent attempts at impact evaluations found statistically insignificant impacts of business training programs for micro and small enterprises on profitability and growth (McKenzie and Woodruff 2014).

Those business persons who do not keep records would not continue to practice *Kaizen* if they participated in a *Kaizen* training program. If a training participant keeps records, he or she may not necessarily continue to practice *Kaizen*. Nonetheless there are some encouraging findings from recent studies. Figure 1.4 shows the results of a randomized controlled trial (RCT) conducted in the garment industry in Tanzania by Higuchi et al. (2017), where firms were randomly assigned to treatment and control groups.[6] One of the three treatment groups was invited to a classroom lecture course, another was offered an on-site training course by instructors, and the third treatment group was offered both classroom lecture and on-site training courses. Both courses cover basic *Kaizen*

---

[6] Among related studies are Karlan and Valdivia (2011), Mano et al. (2012), and Higuchi et al. (2015).

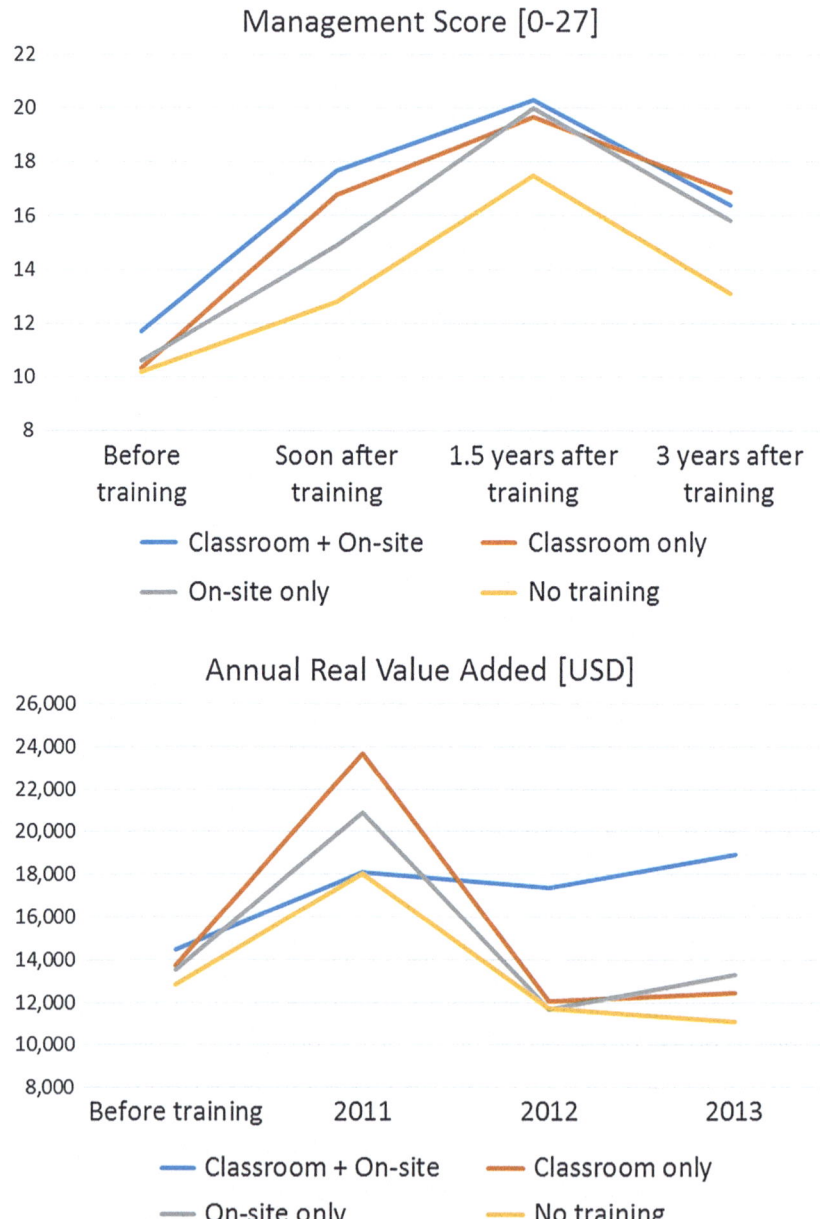

Fig. 1.4 Results of an RCT of *Kaizen* management training in Tanzania in terms of the adoption of improved management practices and value-added approaches. (Source: Calculated by the author based on the author's survey data)

practices and basic business training.[7] The control group received neither of these training courses.

The results show that improved management practices, measured by a management score,[8] were adopted more or less equally, for a while, after training by the groups receiving classroom and on-site training, only classroom training, and only on-site training. The control group receiving no training also adopted some improved management practices due to imitation. The management score, however, began declining 1.5 years after this training, presumably because the trainees sorted out irrelevant practices. A major finding is that only the group receiving both classroom and on-site training continued to increase value added, which indicates that the combination of conceptual training in the classroom and practical training on site leads to the sustainable growth of enterprises.

The finding of the RCT study that *Kaizen* management training improves enterprise performance by improving management practices, even without improving infrastructure and providing subsidized credits, strongly indicates that this form of management training is an effective first step for industrial development. Thus, it seems clear that it is desirable to train several specialists in the principles of *Kaizen* management and to offer several management training courses, thereby increasing the number of competent entrepreneurs. This is what has been happening in Ethiopia, where the government established the Ethiopian *Kaizen* Institute, and where Japanese *Kaizen* experts have been sent to train selected Ethiopians about this form of management, who will later be dispatched to factories and training centers (see Chap. 5).

If competent entrepreneurs are nurtured by management training, many enterprises will develop, and this will lead to congestion in the existing industrial clusters as well as in other original locations. Then the demand for industrial parks in the suburbs of cities will increase. Investment in industrial parks will have high pay-offs if the government allocates space to promising entrepreneurs. If the government also provides financial support only to those promising entrepreneurs, the risk of

---

[7] The latter covered elements of business strategy, marketing, and book keeping and used the Start/Improve Your Business training materials developed by the International Labor Organization (ILO).

[8] This is measured by the number of improved management practices out of 27 recommended ones.

failure in the allocation of investment funds will be reduced. In this way, the TIF approach is likely to enhance the likelihood of the success of industrial development significantly.[9]

Finally, it should be stressed that the policy of increasing the number of competent entrepreneurs by means of *Kaizen* management training will contribute to the establishment of competitive markets, which, in turn, is expected to reduce corruption and preferential treatment of specific industries and enterprises (Otsuka and Sonobe 2011).

Given these encouraging findings, it seems that African firms and workers will enjoy the following opportunities:

Opportunity 1: *Kaizen* has been adapted and customized in North America, East Asia, Europe, and Latin America and has become accepted by different cultures and employment systems. The availability of its latest version is advantageous to Africa.

Opportunity 2: The Japan International Cooperation Agency (JICA) and other organizations in Japan and elsewhere have made considerable efforts to disseminate *Kaizen* worldwide. They are now bringing all their know-how to Africa.

Opportunity 3: Botswana, Ethiopia, and some African countries have been promoting national *Kaizen* movements. Other countries can learn lessons from their efforts and experiences.

Opportunity 4: In many African countries, local consultants are being developed, and local institutions that have a commitment to promoting *Kaizen* movements are being established. It is hoped that other countries will soon follow suit.

Opportunity 5: The New Partnership for Africa's Development (NEPAD) and JICA have begun to coordinate the promotion of a Pan-African *Kaizen* movement aimed at the resilient and sustainable development of the continent. At the Tokyo International Conference for African Development (TICAD), due attention was also given to the promotion of *Kaizen* as a key support element. These initiatives will help

---

[9] Although we did not discuss it explicitly, the general education of labor force particularly through schooling is extremely important. We did not take up this issue, as it is a part of overall economic and social policy, rather than of specifically industrial development policy.

political leaders commit themselves to supporting, motivating, and financing *Kaizen* movements.

Opportunity 6: *Kaizen* in the public sector will make public administration efficient and transparent. There are already projects promoting such activities in the public sector in other continents. The lessons learned from such projects will be available to African nations.

Opportunity 7: Development partners are providing different capacity enhancement programs. Among them is the African Business Education (ABE) initiative, proposed by the Japanese government in 2013. One thousand African youths are now receiving higher education in Japan. The trainees, as future leaders of private and public sectors, will take away some practical lessons from Japan and employ them in their home countries.

1.5 The Structure of the Book

Kaizen has grown into a spreading tree with new ideas budding out of its trunk and branches. Some of the new ideas may have stifled obsolete ideas with the shade they cast, but many old tools and methods remain useful for multiple purposes. This chapter has given a brief account of how this tree has grown. It has also discussed what challenges and opportunities the dissemination of *Kaizen* in Africa will face. It is hoped that Africa will in the not-too-distant future have a role model, a successful person whose business thrives because of its efficient work force practicing *Kaizen*, and who will inspire African youth beyond national borders. Clearly, it is desirable to integrate separate national *Kaizen* movements into a Pan-African *Kaizen* movement.

The rest of this book is organized as follows. Chapter 2 reviews the Asian experience of *Kaizen* dissemination. It shows that the transfer of knowledge of this model from Japan to other countries has not always been easy. But the chapter finds also that *Kaizen* knowledge can be customized to the economic, social, and cultural contexts of the host country so that the knowledge works out nicely there. It argues that the process of customization and localization is innovative and can create new knowledge. Chapter 3 describes how *Kaizen* is practiced in small, medium, or large enterprises, and improves their operation in developing countries. Chapter 4 compares "Japanese-style *Kaizen*" or simply *Kaizen*, on the one hand, and "Western-style *Kaizen*," including the Six Sigma and Lean Production models whose standards have recently been developed by the International Organization for Standardization (ISO), on the other. The chapter discusses the expected impacts of ISO's involvement and the direction of *Kaizen* dissemination desirable for Africa's future. Chapter 5 addresses the issue of the transferability of *Kaizen* to developing countries on the African continent by reporting in detail the Ethiopian experience of this process. Because Ethiopian society is much more diversified in terms of ethnicity, religion, and culture than Japanese society, these characteristics might have had some influence, but they did not hamper the transfer and dissemination of *Kaizen*. Chapter 6 concludes the book with discussion of implications for industrial development policy.

References

Asanuma, B. (1997). *Nihon no Kigyo Soshiki – Kakushinteki Taio no Mekanizumu [The Innovative Adjustment Mechanism of Organizations of Japanese Firms].* Tokyo: Toyo Keizai Shinpo-sha.

Bruhn, M., Karlan, D., & Schoar, A. (2010). What Capital Is Missing in Developing Countries? *American Economic Review, 100*(2), 629–633.

Feigenbaum, A. V. (1956). Total Quality Control. *Harvard Business Review, 34*(6), 93–101.

Feigenbaum, A. V. (1961). *Total Quality Control.* New York: McGraw-Hill.

Hamilton, N. (2014). *The Mantle of Command: FDR at War 1941–1942.* Boston: Houghton Mifflin Harcourt.

Higuchi, Y., Nam, V. H., & Sonobe, T. (2015). Sustained Impacts of *Kaizen* Training. *Journal of Economic Behavior and Organization, 120*, 189–206.

Higuchi, Y., Mhede, E. P., & Sonobe, T. (2017). *Short-and Medium-Run Impacts of Management Training: An Experiment in Tanzania.* GRIPS Discussion Paper. Tokyo: National Graduate Institute for Policy Studies.

Hoyle, D. (2000). *ISO 9000 Quality Systems Handbook* (4th ed.). Oxford, UK: Butterworth-Heinemann.

Imai, M. (1986). *Kaizen: The Key to Japan's Competitive Success.* New York: McGraw-Hill.

Imai, M. (1997). *Gemba Kaizen: A Commonsense, Low-Cost Approach to Management*. New York: McGraw-Hill.

Ishikawa, K. (1985). *What Is Total Quality Control? The Japanese Way* (trans: Lu, D. J.). Englewood Cliffs, NJ: Prentice Hall. Originally published in Japanese as *Nihonteki Hinshitsu Kanri* in 1981. Tokyo: JUSE Press.

JUSE, QC Circle Headquarters. (1985). *How to Operate QC Circle Activities*. Tokyo: JUSE Press.

Karlan, D., & Valdivia, M. (2011). Teaching Entrepreneurship: Impact of Business Training of Microfinance Clients and Institutions. *Review of Economics and Statistics, 93*(2), 510–527.

Kato, I., & Smalley, A. (2011). *Toyota Kaizen Methods, Six Steps to Improvement*. New York: Productivity Press.

Mano, Y., Iddrisu, A., Yoshino, Y., & Sonobe, T. (2012). How Can Micro and Small Enterprises in Sub-Saharan Africa Become More Productive? The Impacts of Experimental Basic Management Training. *World Development, 40*(3), 458–468.

McKenzie, D., & Woodruff, C. (2014). What Are We Learning from Business Training and Entrepreneurship Evaluations Around the Developing World? *World Bank Research Observer, 29*(1), 48–82.

Milgrom, P., & Roberts, J. (1992). *Economics, Organization and Management*. Englewood Cliffs: Prentice Hall.

Mokyr, J. (1990). *The Lever of Riches: Technological Creativity and Economic Progress*. New York: Oxford University Press.

Mokyr, J. (2017). *A Culture of Growth: The Origins of the Modern Economy*. Princeton: Princeton University Press.

Ogawa, S. (2011). "1990 neniko ni okeru Nihon no Shoshudan Katsudo" [Small Group Activities in Japan Since the 1990s]. Yokohama Keiei Kenkyu. *Yokohama Business Association Society, 32*(1), 183–198.

Otsuka, K., & Sonobe, T. (2011). *A Cluster-Based Industrial Development Policy for Low-Income Countries*. World Bank Policy Research Working Paper 5703. Washington, DC: The World Bank.

Shinohara, M. (1961). *Nihon Keizai no Seicho to Junkan [Growth and Business Cycles of the Japanese Economy]*. Tokyo: Sobun-sha.

Suzuki, T. (1994). *TPM in Process Industries*. New York: Productivity Press Originally published in Japanese as *Sochi Kogyo no TPM* in 1992. Tokyo: Japan Institute of Plant Maintenance.

Umeda, M. (2001). *Seven Key Factors for Success on TQM*. Tokyo: Japanese Standards Association.

Open Access This chapter is licensed under the terms of the Creative Commons Attribution 4.0 International License (http://creativecommons.org/licenses/by/4.0/), which permits use, sharing, adaptation, distribution and reproduction in any medium or format, as long as you give appropriate credit to the original author(s) and the source, provide a link to the Creative Commons license and indicate if changes were made.

The images or other third party material in this chapter are included in the chapter's Creative Commons license, unless indicated otherwise in a credit line to the material. If material is not included in the chapter's Creative Commons license and your intended use is not permitted by statutory regulation or exceeds the permitted use, you will need to obtain permission directly from the copyright holder.

2

Role of *Kaizen* in Japan's Overseas Development Cooperation

Kimiaki Jin

Japan International Cooperation Agency (JICA) has been working on the promotion of productivity improvement in different countries in the developing world as its Technical Cooperation (TC) project. One of the core systems of knowledge utilized in these activities is *Kaizen* as described in this book. It has a wide range of methodologies and tools with a very rich insight backed up by a long history of experiences. They are very scientific and analytical as well as human-centered. This chapter discusses factors affecting successful *Kaizen* promotion projects through reviewing the past projects in Southeast Asia, Latin America and some countries in Africa. It attempts to promote further understanding of *Kaizen* through disaggregation of several concepts based on theories of knowledge, learning and development cooperation. The chapter does not touch on details of technical tools which will be explained in other chapters (particularly in Chap. 3), but tries to connect its own arguments with the chapter on

---

K. Jin (✉)
Japan International Cooperation Agency (JICA), Tokyo, Japan
e-mail: Jin.Kimiaki@jica.go.jp

© The Author(s) 2018
K. Otsuka et al. (eds.), *Applying the Kaizen in Africa*,
https://doi.org/10.1007/978-3-319-91400-8_2

standardization (Chap. 4), the case in Ethiopia (Chap. 5) and the broader argument on industrialization in Africa (Chap. 6).

This chapter describes the history of *Kaizen* transfer based on the framework of TC. Section 2.2 explains the theoretical framework of TC in order to understand the characteristics of knowledge transfer. Section 2.3 reviews the history of *Kaizen* projects under the framework provided by Section 2.2. Section 2.4 sorts out key lessons and challenges of *Kaizen* knowledge transfer and elucidates the challenges of TC as well.

2.1 Technical Cooperation (TC) in Japan's Official Development Assistance (ODA)

Technical Cooperation (TC) of the Japanese government with overseas countries started in 1955 in combination with reparations for World War II, after Japan had joined the Colombo Plan in 1954. TC consists of programs of education and training at the home country or abroad, or services of consultants, advisors, teachers and administrators in recipient countries, according to the Organisation for Economic Co-operation and Development (OECD) glossary.[1] In other words, TC is the provision of know-how to recipient countries in the form of personnel, training and research. In the case of a JICA TC project, a group of Japanese experts/consultants are dispatched to a recipient country and work together with the members of a counterpart organization. Although some parts of TC are provided to facilitate the implementation of loan and capital grant aid projects, Japan has been implementing TC as one of stand-alone activities to support capacity development of recipient countries under the category of bilateral grants.

The Japanese government established the Overseas Technical Cooperation Agency (OTCA) as an implementing body of TC in 1962 and reorganized it to the Japan International Cooperation Agency (JICA) by merging with the Japan Emigration Service (JEMIS) in 1974. Reflecting Japan's rapid economic growth created and sustained by its strong human resource base, and closer diplomatic ties with the

---

[1] http://www.oecd.org/dac/dac-glossary.htm#TC

Association of Southeast Asian Nations (ASEAN) countries, in 1981, Japanese Prime Minister Zenko Suzuki announced the launch of a comprehensive package of human resources development projects in ASEAN countries[2] as a part of its Official Development Assistance (ODA). One of the projects in five ASEAN countries was the Productivity Development Project (PDP) in Singapore that started in 1983 and which lasted for a period of seven years, which attempted to transfer various *Kaizen* knowledge and tools. This is because then Prime Minister Lee Kuan Yew of Singapore specifically requested the Japan Productivity Center (JPC) to transfer Japan's productivity development movement to the country (NPB and JICA 1990; JICA 2014b). In Thailand, JICA started the Productivity Development Project in 1994 which lasted for five years. *Kaizen* has become a symbolic know-how that Japan has transferred to Singapore and other developing countries as one of the secrets of Japan's economic achievement in the postwar period. And the transfer of *Kaizen* is one of the significant successes that Japan has contributed to the industrial development in Singapore[3] and Thailand through human resource development. In this way, TC of Japanese ODA has become one of the major instruments to transfer know-how of productivity improvement to developing countries, whose details are explained in Section 2.3 of this chapter.

Japanese ODA including TC has been enjoying good reputation among recipient countries in East Asia. However, among Western donors, technical assistance which mainly associates with implementation of capital investment projects was not so appreciated especially in the context of sub-Saharan Africa's development. The concepts of TC and technical assistance (TA) have been (and continue to be) used interchangeably in many arguments in the development discourse. Both TC and TA have the same goal of capacity building in many cases. However, there are attempts to distinguish between the two terms, as pointed out by McMahon, a World Bank consultant. His analysis suggests that TC is broader in focus, trying to increase the level of knowledge, skills, technical

---

[2] http://www.mofa.go.jp/mofaj/gaiko/bluebook/1982/s57-shiryou-401.htm
[3] The government of Singapore organized the national productivity movement from 1981 that JICA has supported through its TC, which accelerated economic growth of the country.

comprehension or productive aptitudes of residents of a developing country. In contrast, TA refers to activities whose main contribution is to design or implement a given project or program (McMahon 1997).

In 1996, the Operations Evaluation Department of the World Bank evaluated TA provided by the Bank between 1971 and 1991. Its report points out that to design institutional development (ID), TA requires an intimate knowledge of local practices and how decisions are really made, since ID efforts are very sensitive to cultural, social and political factors beyond the control of project management (WB 1996). The report states that out of 1689 approved projects during 1971–1991, only 29% of them have sufficient impact on ID. The report concludes that although the outcomes of TA have varied widely, the efficacy and cost-effectiveness of TA overall has been disappointing, especially in sub-Saharan Africa. Another point is that TA is often donor- (or supplier-) driven with little commitment of recipient countries (McMahon 1997). Although there are several arguments on the effectiveness of TA, the overall conclusion of the World Bank is that it has been a microcosm, donor-driven, with little evidence that it has done much to improve local institutions (Morrison 2005). Other donors concerned with aid effectiveness such as the Department for International Development (DFID) now share a similar understanding that technical assistance is not very effective, partly because of the high transaction costs that are involved (Killick 2008).

Based on the above arguments, TC was often criticized by some of the Western donors as failing to meet actual recipient countries' needs. Therefore, Japan's TC project was also viewed as "old-fashioned" and "inefficient" assistance among Western donors (Arase 2005). Even recently, Kodera (2016) points out that JICA's TC and training programs have not received due attention from the bankers of multilateral financing institutes because of TC's micro-nature and also JICA's inability to articulate its own know-how accumulated on the ground in an international context. Therefore, there is a pressing need for JICA to scale up impact of TC as well as to convert JICA's plenty of tacit knowledge on technology transfer into an explicit one and share it with the international society.

The other part of arguments on TC is much more positive, symbolized in the concept of capacity development, which the next section explains. In the framework of ODA in Japan, TC has been a vital tool to accelerate economic growth in the context of development in East Asia. One of the arguments is about Japan's ODA Model that was presented by the working group of economic cooperation in the national council of industrial structure of Japan as a very successful model of development cooperation (METI 2005). The concept of the Japan's ODA Model is a combination of hard infrastructure development through capital aid, soft infrastructure and industrial human resource development through TC, which stimulate production, trade and investment by the private sector. In fact, Japanese ODA has been a major tool that contributes to economic growth in Southeast Asia.

The TC has been particularly focusing on development of human skills and know-how, technical guidelines, vocational training and higher education, institutional setup, regulatory frameworks, quality control and standardization system for the country as well as for the region. These focuses on industrial development show clear contrast with the ODA by the Western donors which shifted away from industrial development and concentrated on the social sector particularly since the 1990s.

Kato (2016) lists human resources development and field orientation as key characteristics of Japan's ODA. He points out two focuses of human resource development to cooperation; one is formal education, particularly basic education, and another is cooperation that nurtures people's *practical problem solving capacity*. The latter includes promotion of the *Kaizen*-type problem solving activities as a typical Japanese model. He added that many development practitioners involved in JICA projects believe that this type of capacity can be acquired through experience in the workplace (*gemba*). Human resource development is an absolute priority unanimously upheld by Japanese development workers almost like an obsession, according to Kato. The following sections elaborate this concept of human resource development through illustrating the experience of transfer of *Kaizen*.

2.2 Theoretical Framework of Technical Cooperation

Kaizen is a set of knowledge, methodologies and tools for quality and productivity improvement as broadly described in Chap. 1. It has been transferred to developing countries as a part of Japan's TC projects aiming at knowledge transfer and institutional setup. However, as the World Bank report correctly stated, TC for institutional development is very sensitive to cultural, social and political factors of the recipient countries. Therefore, in order to understand the challenges of *Kaizen* transfer to developing countries, how the JICA's TC has managed to deal with such influential factors needs to be explained. The key concepts to manage them are (1) "customization of knowledge" through collective work of local and foreign experts, (2) practical approach through "learning by doing" in addition to classroom or seminar-type trainings and (3) leading and supplementary roles of the public sector. By the way, in the author's terminology, the word "localization" and "customization" are interchangeable. Localization is a concept of modification explained from the viewpoint of the supply side who works on "standard" approaches. The word "customization" is one from the recipient side who works on its own reality on the ground. Technical application of *Kaizen* methodologies and tools is described in Chap. 3 by Sugimoto, and this chapter focuses on the soft part of *Kaizen* knowledge transfer to developing countries.

2.2.1 Customization of Knowledge

A typical process of development begins with an introduction of a scientific and rational way of doing things into traditional systems of the society. In many cases, scientific and rational approaches are of Western origin. Japan has experienced a dramatic introduction of such modern Western ways of doing things into traditional Japanese systems, first through the Meiji Restoration starting in 1867 and second after defeat in World War II in 1945. In both experiences, Japanese society was necessitated to accept and digest Western ways of new technologies and incorporate them into its own systems in order to secure its diplomatic survival and promote reconstruction of the country. Development of the *Kaizen* approach that is started from introducing the concept of productivity management from the US is one of symbolic efforts of the country.

Through the modernization process of Japan during the Meiji Restoration, there was a key concept shared among Japanese people, which is the *Wakon Yosai* [Japanese spirit, Western knowledge] approach. This is because people know that the society prefers to maintain its own cultural and traditional system as core values through development while accepting external knowledge and technologies. Knowledge is always linked with the culture and environment from which it comes. And knowledge is deliberately interpreted to be applicable to the social values and environment of which it goes in. This balanced process is one of the key factors for successful introduction of new knowledge, even under the recent and rapid globalization. Development of *Kaizen* based on the US technology is a process of customizing foreign knowledge and improving along the context of its own. Sawamura (2002) argues that this *Wakon Yosai* approach based on Japan's own experience of modernization as a non-Western developed country provides foundations for Japanese development cooperation.

Kaizen systems and methodologies consist of two major dimensions. One is a rational and scientific dimension based on measurement, calculation and standardization, or engineering dimension in other words. Another is a human-focused participatory dimension that is often called as "*Kaizen* philosophy" or "*Kaizen* mind-set." These two dimensions, engineering and human-focused, are contrasting and often analyzed and discussed in different development discourses. Engineering parts are common knowledge applied globally while human-focused parts are always social context-specific. Chambers (1997) points out that an engineering issue can be managed by a top-down, blueprint approach that is essential for physical construction. On the other hand, the issues related to people have uncontrollable and unpredictable features. He argues that many of the errors of development effort have followed from trying to apply the blueprint approach, which works with controllable and predictable things, to processes with uncontrollable and unpredictable people. Even in the manufacturing industry, the human features are not negligible as far as production process depends on human labor and management. Therefore, the double rational/scientific and human-focused dimensions in *Kaizen* are a result of the efforts of how to apply the engineering approach to Japanese society. Because *Kaizen* has such human-focused participatory dimension, it is applicable in different societies if it is properly managed and adjusted in the local context. That is already proved through the process of successful dissemination of *Kaizen* in the US, Europe, Asian countries and other parts of the world.

The participatory approach is essential to customize or at least adjust *Kaizen* activities to each workplace environment, since many people often resist changes brought externally. However, Nonaka's knowledge creation theory in which the Japanese approach has its foundation provides further advantage of the participatory approach. Nonaka (1991) points out the importance of tacit knowledge by quoting the words of a philosopher, "we can know more than we can tell." His theory is constructed through analyzing the processes of innovation in Japanese major manufacturing companies. During application of *Kaizen* tools to a company, managers and workers who participate in the process can propose useful ideas even without knowing logical justification explicitly. Nonaka and Toyama (2003) further argue that knowledge is a reality viewed from a certain angle. The same reality can be viewed differently depending on from which angle or context one sees it. They argue that people have their own cultural and historical contexts which give the basis for one to interpret information to create meanings. These arguments imply that effort of knowledge transfer from outside of the society, such as TC, needs to be built on intensive interaction between those who see the reality from different angles. One of the key features of *Kaizen* promotion in the countries JICA has been working with is customization of original *Kaizen* in the context of the working culture and environment in the recipient country through participatory process of management and frontline workers in companies.

As a result, JICA's *Kaizen* concept applied to its TC projects covers a much broader concept of productivity improvement activities than the narrow sense of the *Kaizen* definition shared within Japanese manufacturing industries. In developing countries, the capacity of people at the beginning of the project is quite different from the one in Japan, so the emphasis on how to utilize the variety of *Kaizen* tools should also be different. 5S (sort, set in order, shine, standardize and sustain), a basic tool of housekeeping, plays quite an important role in the initial stage of *Kaizen* introduction as stated in the latter part of this section, which is one of customization through TC. On the other hand, in the US, *Kaizen* was further developed to Business Process Reengineering (BPR), Lean Manufacturing and Six Sigma, as described in Chap. 4, based on its technical level of industry as well as characteristics of the national labor market and the employment systems in the US. The author assumes that the approach of productivity improvement can be more engineering-oriented, such as BPR, under the condition of a dynamic labor market, in which workers are easily replaceable. In contrast, in the customary society with a static labor market and long-term employment system, the approach may be more human factor-oriented.

Furthermore, the International Organization for Standardization (ISO) based in Switzerland is promoting standardization of productivity improvement in which Six Sigma is a core system promoted as global knowledge (see Chap. 4). In contrast, the Japanese *Kaizen* approach has a characteristic to adjust itself to the local context and incorporate local knowledge, if properly handled by people who know such local contexts. Quality Control (QC) Circle is a tool to utilize such local knowledge in the company level into *Kaizen* activities while stimulating ownership and satisfaction of workers, although further customization is required for effective operation as explained in Section 2.4 of this chapter.

2.2.2 Learning by Doing

Another point to understand *Kaizen* knowledge transfer by TC is "learning by doing," which is also related to a characteristic of knowledge. In the context of knowledge transfer for development, King and McGrath (2004) refer to two broad tendencies in theory and practice. One tendency is that knowledge is universally applicable and can be captured in a set of synthesized notes on best practice and hence be transferable. This is termed the technological approach. Another broad tendency is termed the social approach, which emphasizes that much of what is really useful knowledge is embedded in the experience of individuals and could not be easily captured and codified, such as tacit knowledge. This thought emphasizes the importance of learning together, which may be designated as experiential approach. King argues that the Japanese approach focuses more on learning-by-doing, experience-based approach and context-specific knowledge than the Western type of approach that focuses on codified knowledge such as the UK's. This argument explains that the effective transfer of knowledge such as *Kaizen* from Japanese experts to counterparts needs experience-sharing through collective work at *gemba* in addition to provision of manuals and classroom training. For implementation of JICA's TC projects, Japanese *Kaizen* experts always work together with their counterparts through on-the-job training (OJT) in the recipient organization and target companies.

With regard to the concept of capacity development, JICA's Capacity Assessment Handbook (2008) disaggregates capacity to technical capacities, core capacities and enabling environment. Technical capacities refer to specialized knowledge and skills of particular sectors and technologies. The core capacities are the central force in capabilities in handling issues such as discipline, will, attitude, leadership and management capabilities which are needed for producing desirable results through the use of technical capacities. The core capacities are complex and have a nature whereby they can only be improved by following a complicated course that contains such steps as learning through trial and error, inner reflection and self-development. Figure 2.1 shows the image of capacities particularly emphasizing the importance of the core capacities by using an iceberg as a metaphor. A major part of the core capacities is invisible because it is underwater but sustains visible parts of capacities. *Kaizen* activities in their basic stage can address the formation of these core capacities through learning by doing 5S (sort, set in order, shine, standardize and sustain).

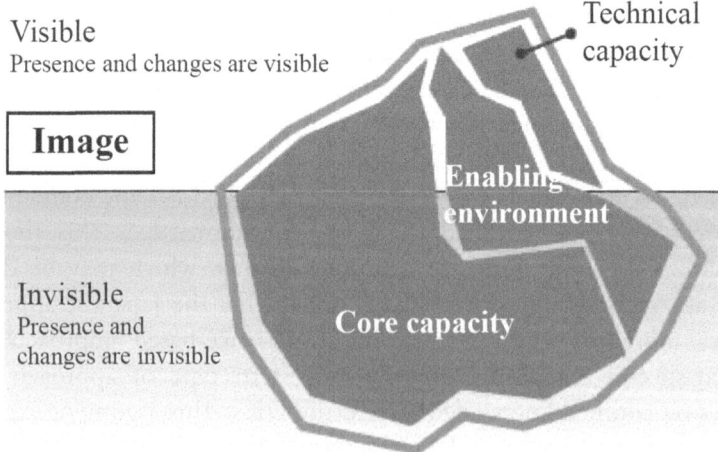

Fig. 2.1 Image of capacities. (Source: JICA Capacity Assessment Handbook (2008))

These core capacities are related to people's mind-set on punctuality and obedience to the rules, which have far-reaching impact on operation and maintenance of machineries, infrastructure and performance of service delivery. In many developing countries especially in sub-Saharan Africa, development of core capacities for a mass of people is crucial for further development of technical capacities.

Moreover, for the localization/customization process, in many cases, the right focuses and points of adjustment that should be made are not known before actual application on the ground. There is always a risk of failure as well as potential of improvement to be better. Therefore, trial and error is an effective process, which is also shared by Western academics such as Easterly (2006), who highly values the "searchers" position. He points out that "searchers" admit that they do not know the answers in advance and try to disentangle complicated political, social, institutional and technological factors. These features require the "learning-by-doing" approach.

Table 2.1 shows the classification of capacity development activities divided into institutional development and human resource development of individuals, and further break down to technical aspects and human aspects. Human aspects of both institution and human resources can be developed through the participatory approach and core capacity can be developed through learning by doing. Each part is mutually influential and regulative, and so the learning-by-doing approach is one of essential building blocks for comprehensive capacity development.

Table 2.1 Disaggregation of capacity development

	Technical aspects	Human aspects
Institutional development	Institutional structures, infrastructure, equipment, IT, resource allocation	Decision-making system, labor management system (and corporate culture)
Human capacity development	Technical capacity (sector-specific technologies, skills and knowledge management)	Core capacity (discipline, will, attitude, motivation, leadership of individuals)

Source: Created by the author

2.2.3 Role of the Public Sector

Since *Kaizen* is a set of know-hows applied in industry, foreign direct investments (FDIs) can be a vehicle of transferring to developing countries. In fact, many Japanese private companies which invest in Asian countries disseminate *Kaizen* in the region. However, the history shows that the public sector can accelerate its transfer by a series of supportive arrangements. Moreover, there are critical arguments of leaving technology transfer to market mechanisms (see Chap. 6).

Prime Minister Meles Zenawi who decided to bring *Kaizen* to Ethiopia explained his intention on technology transfer in his article on the Developmental State (Zenawi 2012). He pointed out that technology cannot be efficiently supplied to developing countries by the market mechanism because of the virtuous cycle of knowledge creation established through joint actions of the public and private sectors in developed countries and the vicious cycle of the low-technological development trap unbreakable by market forces in developing countries. Hence, he argued that non-market intervention is needed for developing countries to accelerate their catch-up process. Stiglitz and Greenwald (2014) also assert that investment in learning and innovation may not be optimal in unfettered markets because they are characterized as being public goods with spillover effects and sunk costs.

Even without knowing such academic arguments, the Japanese government has been proactive to introduce foreign knowledge from abroad and provided technical support to the private sector during Japan's catch-up process and economic growth. The Japanese government has also been providing TC to developing countries especially in Southeast Asia, particularly focusing on small and medium-sized enterprises (SMEs) in the field of industrial development. This is because SMEs are not in an advantageous position in technology transfer or the acquisition process, but the presence of them who can enter into the supply chain of FDIs as a supporting industry is essential for sustainable economic growth. And because FDIs limit their technical support to current subcontractors, there is room for the public sector to provide technical support to wider but selected SMEs who are conscious about productivity improvement and willing to enhance their supply capacity. Chapter 6 of this book analyzes the role of the public sector in provision of *Kaizen* training, which supports capacity

Table 2.2 Transfer of *Kaizen* from Japan to developing countries

	Japan		Developing countries	
Public domain	JICA and the expert team ⟶		The organization providing business development services	
	↑	TC	↓	Training/ Consultancy
	↑		↓	Services
Private domain	Companies	⟹ FDIs	Companies	

Source: Created by the author

development of entrepreneurs as well as identifies promising ones for further support. To accelerate industrialization, the public sector can play more roles in infrastructure development and finance.

Table 2.2 shows a concept of complementarity of FDIs and TC in *Kaizen* promotion in Southeast Asia that is explained in the next section. Though the main channel of *Kaizen* transfer is from companies in Japan to companies in developing countries through FDIs, JICA mobilizes Japanese experts and transfers *Kaizen* to the organization who promotes productivity improvement in the developing country, such as the National Productivity Board in the case of Singapore. The organization further transfers *Kaizen* to private companies in the country.

Through Japanese TC projects, *Kaizen* is also applied to hospital management in Sri Lanka and 15 other countries in Africa. The main approach of these projects is to introduce 5S and Total Quality Management (TQM), which improve working environment of hospital staff and subsequently improve quality of services, occupational safety and motivation of the staff. In this case, the role of the public sector is unarguably important.

2.3 *Kaizen* Dissemination in the ODA Framework

In Southeast Asia, JICA implemented productivity development projects in Singapore and Thailand. The one in Singapore started in 1983 and has a monumentally high profile. It was on a large scale in terms of the number of Japanese experts involved in TC because of commitments of high-level political leaders in both countries. In the case of Thailand, the project was affected by the Asian financial crisis in 1997 and extended for two years. Apart from these two countries, Malaysia also introduced *Kaizen* by its own efforts without JICA. Since the 1990s, JICA has been expanding its *Kaizen* promotion to Latin America, and to Africa which started during the boom since the latter part of the 2000s. Figure 2.2 shows a list of the past and ongoing JICA projects on productivity improvement[4] in various parts of the world and their periods of cooperation.

2.3.1 Cases in Southeast Asia

Singapore is the first country that JICA has provided TC on quality and productivity development. Based on the request from Prime Minister Lee Kuan Yew, JICA started its Singapore Productivity Development Project (PDP) as a TC in 1983 and continued until 1990. The counterpart in the Singaporean side was the National Productivity Board (NPB) that was established in 1972 under the Ministry of Labor. Prior to the request of the project to the Japanese government, the Singaporean government launched the national productivity movement and NPB published a report of the Committee on Productivity in 1981 that analyzed the "Japanese System" of productivity improvement with around 30 recommendations to its own government regarding management and labor systems to be introduced in Singapore (JICA 1986). In 1981, Prime Minister Lee also discussed with the Chairman of JPC[5] who is one of the main promoters of the *Kaizen* movement in Japan. Although the initial concept of the human resource development project had focused on vocational training, the Singaporean government changed its subject to productivity improvement based on such preparation. Table 2.3 shows the chronology of the PDP formulation and implementation.

---

[4] The table shows only the projects focusing mainly on productivity improvement. There are many other projects supporting SME development, which are not indicated in the list.
[5] The Chairman of JPC was Mr. Kohei Goshi who also visited Singapore to discuss with PM Lee, according to an interview with JPC staff.

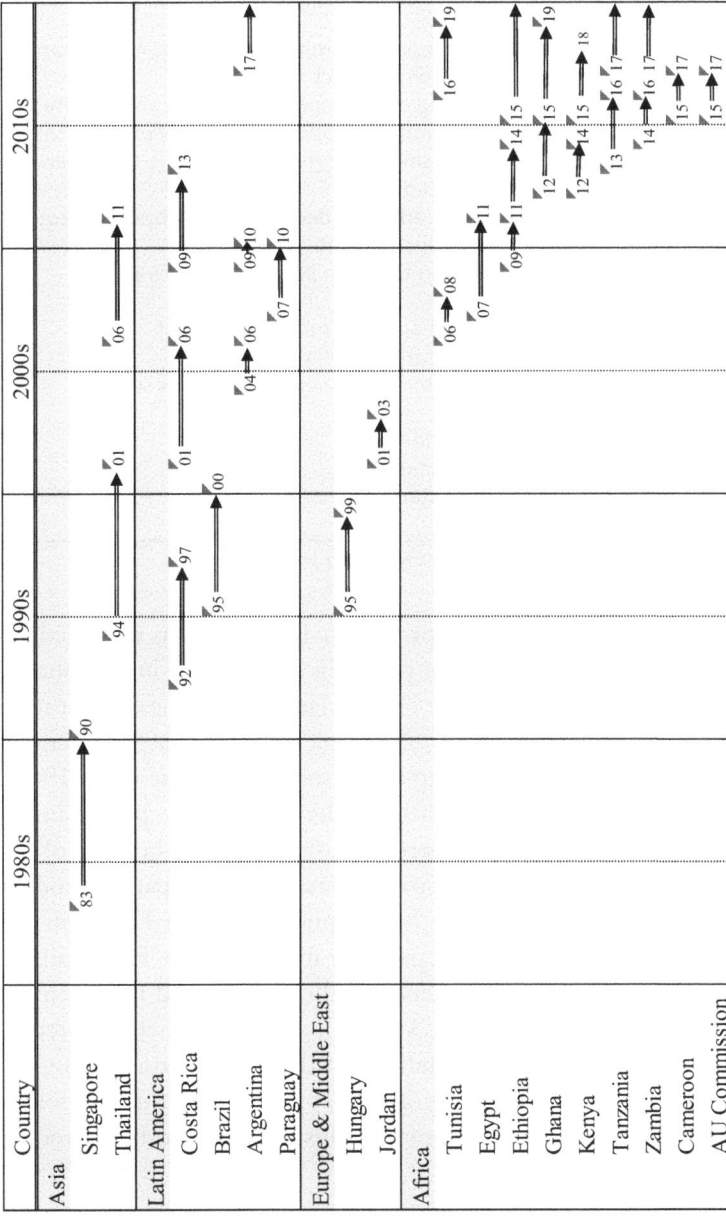

Fig. 2.2 Countries/organization and periods of JICA projects on quality and productivity improvement. (Source: Created by the author based on JICA reports)

Table 2.3 Chronology of Singapore PDP

1972		NPB was established
1981	Jan	PM Zenko Suzuki of Japan committed to the ASEAN Human Resources Development Project
	Apr	The Singaporean delegation proposed to set up an Institute for Continuing Occupation Development at the meeting in Tokyo
	Jun	PM Lee Kuan Yew of Singapore met Kohei Goshi, Chairman of Japan Productivity Center
1982	Mar–Jun	The Ministry of Labor and NPB decided to re-propose a project focused on the productivity movement
	Jun	A Singaporean mission to Japan presented a new project proposal on PDP
1983	Jun	Signing of the project agreement (the Record of Discussion) and preparatory phase started
	Oct	A first group of long-term Japanese experts was sent to Singapore
1985	Apr	Restructuring phase started
1986	Nov	Implementing phase started
1988	Jun	Consolidation phase started
1990	Jun	The project ended

Source: Created by the author based on NPB and JICA (1990)

The PDP started as a five-year project in 1983 and was extended for two years until 1990. Progress of the project is summarized in four phases, namely, the preparatory phase (June 1983–March 1985), the restructuring phase (April 1985–October 1986), the implementing phase (November 1986–June 1988) and the follow-up or consolidation phase (June 1988–June 1990) (NPB and JICA 1990). In the preparatory phase, initial efforts were made by Japanese experts to promote understanding of the Singaporean side on the basic theory and concept of the Japanese productivity movement based on *Kaizen* before practicing actual tools in the field. This is because the JICA's preparatory mission of the PDP pointed out that the Singaporean side understood the complicated management system of Japan superficially (JICA 1986). However, such theoretical approach could not satisfy NPB staff so, in the restructuring phase, the approach was changed[6] to a more practical application of *Kaizen* tools in order to show tangible improvement in industries first and then proceed

---

[6] The Japanese side discarded tens of thousands of pages of textbooks prepared for the PDP before its start, in order to show a clear change of approach to the Singaporean side, according to the interview with JPC staff.

to understanding the concept (JPC 1990). On-the-job training for the NPB staff was introduced to equip them with relevant skills, which was a typical "learning-by-doing" approach adopted in the reconstructing phase. In the implementation phase, the role of Japanese experts shifted from leaders of activities to advisors to NPB staffs who became actual consultants to provide training and consultation services to the companies. In the consolidation phase, fundamental productivity practices such as 5S were firmly entrenched in the industry.

Throughout the project, the following fields and methodologies of *Kaizen* were covered:

- Management and Supervisory Development (MSD)
- Labor-Management Relations (LMR)
- Quality Control Circles (QCC)
- Industrial Engineering (IE)
- Total Quality Control (TQC)
- Audio-Visual (AV) Technology
- Productivity Measurement
- Occupational Safety and Health
- Consultancy for Small and Medium Enterprises

Concrete indicators of outputs of the project were:

1. 196 Singaporeans were trained in Japan,
2. over 200 Japanese experts were dispatched and exposed to Singaporean industries,
3. 4000 participants were trained using materials developed by PDP,
4. more than 200 SMEs have benefited from assistance given by the NPB consultants and Japanese experts,
5. SMEs can seek assistance from a pool of the 191 referral consultants and 30 associate consultants set up by the NPB,
6. 5.4% of the whole workforce in the country became members of the QCC, and
7. over 100 companies introduced 5S (NPB and JICA 1990).

These outputs further contributed to the annual growth rate of productivity in Singapore, which was 4.5% between 1980 and 1995, as the then Deputy Prime Minister Tony Tan Keng Yam acknowledged[7] at the inauguration of the 1996/1997 productivity campaign in Singapore. At the end of the project, JPC (1990) which is the main player of the project in the Japanese side published a retrospective report on lessons learned from the project. It says that the project had focused on TQC, QCC and IE as priority target methodologies of TC in the restructuring phase. However, through the activities on the ground, the project members realized that neither workers of most factories were well organized nor factories were clean. Although the NPB side requested to learn Total Productive Maintenance (TPM), real problems in the factories were far basic than the level of TPM, and the capacity of the NPB staff was not as high as expected. Therefore, Japanese experts re-proposed to introduce 5S as an initial step and gradually proceed to higher technologies. The JPC report also points out that the management technology is a comprehensive technology consisting of both science/engineering and sociology/human science, so that its essence would be understood only after applying to the actual workplace of production and services. The report further states that the Singaporean side should develop their own guiding principles of productivity improvement instead of applying the three guiding principles of productivity movement in Japan (expansion of employment; cooperation between labor and management; and fair distribution of the fruits of productivity improvement among labor, management and consumers).

Ohno and Kitaw (2011) draw several lessons from the PDP in Singapore. First, productivity improvement needs strong commitment from higher-level officials, organizations and individuals. Second, it needs a strong organization structure for policy coordination. Third, a cadre of private management consultants needs to be nurtured. These institutional frameworks can be the essence of creating productivity movement in any country.

In Singapore, much more advanced methodologies/tools of productivity improvement are now widely applied to various fields. Cirera and Maloney (2017) reported the cooperation between JPC and NPB (now known as SPRING) as a good case of a productivity program. Considering

---

[7] Press release saved at the National Archive of Singapore at http://www.nas.gov.sg/archivesonline/data/pdfdoc/1996103101/tkyt19961031s.pdf

current high economic competitiveness and technological advancement of the country, although productivity improvement is a result of a variety of influential factors, the author assumes that the productivity movement supported by PDP has created a foundation for the current economic success of the country. It is also worth mentioning that *Kaizen* has complementarity to other industrial development support measures that government can provide such as business development services and finance (JICA 1997; Lemma 2016). In fact, the NPB has further evolved into the Productivity and Standard Board (PSB) in 1996 and then the Standards, Productivity and Innovation Board (SPRING) in 2002 and now is providing support to enterprises in financing, capability and management development, technology and innovation, and access to markets.[8] This process of institutional development implies that *Kaizen* provides foundation for further creation of innovation.

In Thailand, the government established the Thailand Management Development and Productivity Center (TMDPC) in 1962 with the support of the International Labor Organization (ILO). In order to increase productivities of the country, the government planned to promote national-level productivity movement and requested TC to the Japanese government in 1991, which aimed to train the TMDPC for effective implementation of the movement. The Thailand Productivity Development Project started in 1994 and continued until 2001 (JICA 2000a). In 1995, the Thai government established a new institute, the Thailand Productivity Institute (FTPI), from here on the project was handled by FTPI. The project trained 46 counterparts, organized "Productivity Week," introduced 5S to the Prime Minister's Office and provided on-the-job training on On-site-Management Guidance to around 100 companies. Approximately 200 companies have visited the institute for consultation. In 1997, Thailand was hit by the Asian Financial Crisis, and the government launched the Industrial Reconstructing Plan in 1998, in which improvement of productivity was one of the issues to strengthen competitiveness of the country. The project was extended for two years to concretize its outputs. There was a negative phenomenon in the project; during the process of changing the

---

[8] https://www.spring.gov.sg/About-Us/Pages/spring-singapore.aspx

counterpart organization from TMDPC to FTPI in 1995, many TMDPC staff refused to move to the new institute because FTPI was planned to be privatized after five years. They were afraid of losing the status of public servants (JICA 1999).

The economy in Thailand has been dynamic and successfully fostering the development of the automotive industry. In 2005, total production of cars in the country was more than 1 million per year. In 2006, in collaboration with the Japan External Trade Organization (JETRO) and the Association for Overseas Technical Scholarship (AOTS)[9] in Japan, JICA launched the Automotive Human Resources Development Project for Supporting Industries for a period of 5 years in order to develop the dynamic supporting industry in Thailand. One of four major fields covered by the project was the Toyota Production System (TPS) that included Working Control, Continuous Flow, Standardized Work, and the Pull System. *Kaizen* is already incorporated into major production systems of manufacturers in Thailand as FDIs especially from Japan disseminated it in the 1990s and after. Therefore, demand for *Kaizen* was already high among SMEs in Thailand at the time when the project started (JICA 2004).

In the case of Malaysia, the National Productivity Center was established in 1962, which was reorganized as the National Productivity Corporation (NPC) in 1991 and again renamed as the Malaysia Productivity Corporation (MPC) in 2008. The NPC has been collaborating with JPC under the membership of the Asian Productivity Organization (APO) since 1983 as well as with the Union of Japanese Scientists and Engineers (JUSE) to promote QCC without involvement of JICA. The MPC has been enthusiastically promoting 5S by creating the 5S certificate and 5S audit.

In other Southeast Asian countries, FDIs by Japanese firms are major vehicles for *Kaizen* transfer. In these countries, although JICA hasn't implemented TC exclusively focusing on quality and productivity improvement, many TCs in industrial development have included training modules on *Kaizen*. The Association for Overseas Technical

---

[9] The Association for Overseas Technical Scholarship (AOTS) was established in 1959, reorganized to the Overseas Human Resources and Industry Development Association (HIDA) in 2012 and again changed to the Association for Overseas Technical Cooperation and Sustainable Partnerships (AOTS) in 2017.

Cooperation and Sustainable Partnerships (AOTS) in Japan is another implementing arm of Japanese ODA, who also provides *Kaizen* training to Asian countries. From 1980 until 2016, the AOTS received 16,560 training participants who joined the courses with *Kaizen* as a part of subjects and dispatched 2482 experts[10] to Asian countries. Moreover, JPC and JUSE have been independently expanding networks on quality and productivity improvement to Asian countries such as through the International Convention on Quality Control Circles.

These efforts on industrial human resources development focusing on quality and productivity improvement are essential parts of contributing factors of East Asian economic growth in conjunction with economic infrastructure development and promotion of investment climate (see Chap. 6).

2.3.2 Cases in Latin America

In Costa Rica, JICA had supported the Technical Instructor and Personnel Training Center for Industrial Development in Central America (Centro de Formacion de Formadores y Personal Tecnico para el Desarrollo Industrial de Centroamerica—CEFOF) in three phases—from 1992 to 1997, from 2001 to 2006 and from 2009 to 2013. CEFOF was established in 1992 as a community college for the purpose of training technical personnel in the industry of Central America. Through JICA's support, CEFOF had been providing training courses on 5S, Problem Solving Techniques, QC Seven Tools, TPM, Supervisory Training, Computer Applications as well as consultancy services on introduction of 5S to the companies. CEFOF also provided a training program mainly focusing on 5S to the companies in the Central America region (JICA 2005). At the end of the third phase, CEFOF had developed a network of consultants/facilitators/institutions working on productivity improvement to share information and provide support. CEFOF had organized seminars covering eight countries[11] in which 1797 participants were involved during the third phase period. A total of 56 consultants became certified facilitators on Japanese quality and productivity improvement (JICA 2014a).

---

[10] Data obtained from AOTS in August 2017.
[11] Belize, Costa Rica, Dominican Republic, El Salvador, Guatemala, Honduras, Nicaragua, Panama.

CEFOF became an organization under the Costa Rica Technical University (UTN) and was renamed as Centro de Calidad y Productividad—CECAPRO during the third phase of the project.

In Brazil, *Instituto Brasileiro Qualidade e Produtividade in Parana* (IBQP-PR) was a counterpart organization of the productivity and quality improvement project supported by JICA. Because IBQP-PR was a newly established institute when the project was started, the evaluation report of JICA (2000b) points out the importance of gradual approach with a flexible project design. The report also emphasizes the importance of on-the-job training as well as presentation of tangible results in addition to theoretical knowledge transfer.

In Argentina, JICA supported *Instituto Nacional de Tecnologia Industrial* (INTI) in two phases, from 2004 to 2006 and from 2009 to 2010, which focused on a supporting program for SME development. INTI and JICA launched the third phase in 2017 in which *Kaizen* would play an essential role in training programs supported by the projects. INTI retains around 100 consultants as its own staff who are working as a *Kaizen* trainer or a *Kaizen* instructor. This continuous and extended relationship between INTI and JICA proves the effectiveness of *Kaizen* application in Argentina (JICA, UNICO and JPC 2018).

In Paraguay, JICA supported *Centro Paraguayo de Productividad y Calidad* (CEPPROCAL) from 2007 to 2010 in order to strengthen its capacity for business consultation to SMEs and as a training provider. Through the cooperation with JICA, CEPPROCAL has developed a system to provide its services to SMEs by utilizing external personnel of the organization as pooled consultants (JICA 2009).

2.3.3 Cases in Africa

In the African continent, JICA has been supporting quality and productivity improvement in eight countries consisting of Cameroon, Egypt, Ethiopia, Ghana, Kenya, Tanzania, Tunisia and Zambia as shown in Fig. 2.2. All of the JICA projects in the African continent started after 2005 under the environment in which many African countries were achieving high economic growth. These countries particularly in sub-

Saharan Africa intend to achieve economic transformation through improving the productivity of their industries and service sectors and upgrading their competitiveness in the international market without relying on the price hike of oil and minerals produced in this continent. In addition, the African Union Commission (AUC) introduced *Kaizen* in 2009 by obtaining the support of the Spanish government for their own reform of the internal administrative system. Imai (2012) reports the case of the AUC as a model of removing *Muda* from the public sector organization in his second edition of *Gemba Kaizen*. He presents the 4P model (Physical workplace improvement, Process improvement, Policy review, and People involvement) for the AUC as a result of customization of *Kaizen*. From 2015, JICA has followed this effort and supported AUC *Kaizen* promotion that is based on the formulation of *Kaizen* taskforce and improvement of the AUC's standard operational procedures. Furthermore, the New Partnership for Africa's Development (NEPAD) Agency, in collaboration with JICA, has also started promoting *Kaizen* efforts among the AU member countries from 2016.

In sub-Saharan Africa, Ethiopia is a top runner which has introduced nationwide *Kaizen* activities, whose details are described by Mekonen in Chap. 5 of this book. One of the key factors that leads to successful *Kaizen* promotion in Ethiopia is a strong commitment of the government. In 2008, then Prime Minister Meles Zenawi directly requested transfer of *Kaizen* knowledge from the Japanese government. Meles clearly pointed out to the mission members sent by the JICA headquarters that he wanted the *Kaizen* approach among other tools of industrial development and business development services. The reason why he had chosen *Kaizen* can be read in his article (Zenawi 2012), in which he argues about two distinct national innovation systems for economic development. One is the mission-oriented system which is characterized by investments in large public and private research infrastructure for the continuous generation of new ideas and technologies. This system that is found in the UK, US and France is also sustained with relatively high mobility of labor force and capital from mature to new technologies. Another is called the diffusion system that invests more efforts in human resources development which is found in Germany, Japan and Korea. This system is related to higher education and training of engineers/

craftsmen to create continuous upgrading of standards. He concludes that while the mission-oriented system is good for the front runner, the diffusion system is effective in mastering existing technologies during the catch-up process in developing countries. Therefore, Meles had deliberately chosen the Japanese *Kaizen* which is a typical model of innovation under the diffusion system. Because of his clear orientation to *Kaizen* based on his distinctive policy research, the government of Ethiopia has been enthusiastically scaling-up *Kaizen* application to both private and public sectors. The government established the Ethiopia *Kaizen* Institute (EKI) after a year and a half of verification of the applicability of *Kaizen* to the country. EKI has been very proactive in promoting *Kaizen* even without involving Japanese experts after mastering basic tools and methodologies. Eye-opening details are described in Chap. 5.

In Ethiopia, there is significant FDI influx into the garment and leather industries in the past decade. Many of them come from Asia, particularly from China, and are practicing some *Kaizen* tools such as 5S in their factories built in Ethiopia. Managers of the factories who came from China or Taiwan are already familiar with these tools even without knowing the origin of *Kaizen*. They spend huge efforts to train newly recruited young local workers on basic disciplines starting from how to use the toilet and proceeding to the importance of keeping rules and regulations and then technical skills of cutting and sewing. 5S is an effective tool for them to teach discipline to these workers. Therefore, the government-led *Kaizen* promotion in Ethiopia may have good complementarity with its enthusiastic policy of FDI attraction.

Prior to JICA's cooperation with Africa, there are two countries, Burkina Faso and Botswana, that have attempted to transplant *Kaizen*-type productivity improvement activities in Africa. In Burkina Faso, the World Bank supported *Kaizen* dissemination from 1989 until 2000 and the United Nations Industrial Development Organization (UNIDO) supported it from 1999 to 2003. Uesu (2011) discussed by citing the report of UNIDO in 2005 that despite some important achievements and the important role of the organization that promoted QCC, the results of application varied between companies and were judged as "mixed." Based on the review of the case in Burkina Faso, Uesu concludes by making four[12] recommendations on *Kaizen* promotion in developing countries that includes: (1) the government should play a proactive role to encourage the private sector in improving quality and productivity and (2) the imported system should be tailored in accordance with the circumstances and the capacity of the country. Regarding the latter, she explains that the companies that were successful in promoting QCC had made small adjustments in accordance with the difference in employment systems between Japan and Burkina Faso, while others who failed had not.

In Botswana, the NPB in Singapore supported productivity improvement from 1991 to 2000, which is reported by Kitaw (2011). He concludes that the impact of the productivity improvement program in Botswana has not been as high as expected, by referring to the downward trend of the country's rating in the Global Competitive Index, ranked 66th in 2009/2010, 76th in 2010/2011 and 80th in 2011/2012. However, the support by Singapore's NPB had terminated ten years before this downward trend began, so further research is needed. And the conditions of African economies between the stagnating 1990s and the growing 2010s are quite different, so the absorptive capacity of companies and the environment surrounding them in the continent might be different too.

2.4 Key Lessons and Challenges

The author picks up three lumps of the lessons learned from the cases of *Kaizen* promotion in many developing countries in different parts of the world through TC. First, the importance of a set of institutional arrangements must be discussed so as to concretize the foundation of *Kaizen* promotion. Second, development of core capacities of human resources is important for the entry point of productivity improvement in many developing countries. And core capacity is related to the concept of the *Kaizen* mind-set, which is always a black box of *Kaizen*. Needless to say, it is important to understand the inside of the black box. Third, customization of the methodologies and tools is essential in order to create workable systems based on each local context of the country.

---

[12] The other two recommendations are (1) involving and motivating the top management is key and (2) long-term capacity building and institutional building are required.

2.4.1 Institutional Arrangements

In Singapore, the NPB was established in 1972 and the Committee of Productivity was established in 1981 as critical steps of the productivity movement before starting the JICA project. In Ethiopia, EKI was established in 2011, after two years since the country was exposed to *Kaizen* for the first time. For the substantive dissemination of *Kaizen*, it is crucial for a developing country to establish a specialized organization in charge of promotion, most probably in the public domain if dynamism of the private sector is not strong enough. The role of the government is decisive of triggering and sustaining productivity improvement because required knowledge has the nature of a public good with large spillover effects; thus, transfer of knowledge cannot be optimal in unfettered markets. The organization should be able to receive a sufficient amount of allocated resources for its activities, not only to cover recurrent costs but also capital budget.

Ohno (2011) selects six criteria for successful *Kaizen* promotion as a national movement: they are (1) strong personal commitment of the top leader, (2) establishment of core organizations responsible for implementation, (3) presence of supporting institutions and mechanisms, (4) implementation of a massive campaign, (5) provision of standardized training programs and (6) enhancement of capability of the private sector. It might be fortunate if all the six criteria are fulfilled at once in many African countries. The establishment of the core organizations and a strong commitment by the government that make a massive campaign possible by using basic tools such as 5S are priority issues to create momentum. The commitment of a top visionary political leader is unquestionably important as we saw in Singapore and Ethiopia, though it can be a challenge too. In both countries, the prime ministers took distinctive initiatives of transplanting quality and productivity improvement activities into their own countries.

For effective transfer of technology, ownership of the government in the recipient side is indispensable, which can provide momentum of scaling-up the outputs of the TC project. As the World Bank points out, the output of TC tends to be microcosm and limited in impact. This is the nature of TC that aims to create a good replicable model under the environment of the recipient country, which does not necessarily include a scale-up mechanism until the successful model is established. And impacts of the model in the macro-level may not be easily visible in the short term, while the micro-level outcomes are tangible. Therefore, without strong commitment of the recipient government, TC cannot successfully proceed to the scaling-up stage, and be called "supply-driven" by the donor. Therefore, effective institutional setting by the recipient government for the smooth scale-up of *Kaizen* practices to wider targets than the initial project is a requirement of a successful case.

Furthermore, for the successful *Kaizen* activities on the floor of factories, firm commitment of the management of a company is an imperative duty. It is very naive to talk about workers' participation only without commitment and leadership of the management of a company. Workers never perform well under poor management in the factory even when applying *Kaizen* tools and methodologies. Therefore, the organization should be equipped with the capability of sensitizing the managements of companies or to select companies that have motivated managements.

Two challenges must be listed at this point. One is high turnover of the trained staff in the core organization. It is a common challenge of JICA's human resource development projects especially in a country with high mobility of labor in the market. There are two observed countermeasures; one is the case in Ethiopia that creates a monetary and in-kind incentive for the staff to remain in the organization, and another is observed in the cases of Singapore and Paraguay that create a sizable pool of consultants outside of the organization to be mobilized on a contract basis.

Another challenge is the commitment of high-level political leaders. The two successful leaders mentioned repeatedly are highly prominent, well-informed and visionaries in the history of development. In order to draw commitment of political leaders, it is important to create opportunities for them to be exposed to tangible evidence and successful cases in addition to written information, which should not be a chicken and egg argument. Hence, leaders of *Kaizen*-implementing organizations need to be strategic to draw and maintain commitment of top political leaderships.

2.4.2 Core Capacities and the *Kaizen* Mind-Set

Although the abovementioned institutional arrangements can promote the process of human capacity development, there is a substantial issue that often receives less attention in technology transfer, which is development of core capacities. Requirement of sector-specific technologies to produce quality products is evident, so the managements may proactively introduce new techniques/skills and machineries. However, development of core capacities, such as discipline, will and attitude, is a prerequisite to sustain acquisition of technical capacities. For the labor-intensive production lines in a factory, if one person does not properly handle the assigned work, it will affect the quality of final products. Even when automation and mechanization are in progress, safe and accurate operation requires such discipline. In African countries, one of the reasons for low labor productivity seems to be caused by the low level of core capacities, which severely affects organizational capacities and performance of collective work. Lack of punctual time management wastes available time of all the participants in the work process, like a 15-minute delay of the meeting for 8 people wastes 2 hours of person-time. Time is a precious resource that is often neglected in a low-productive work process.

5S is a suitable method for improving core capacities because it focuses on very basic housekeeping issues. It trains people to keep simple rules; for example, every worker has to return a tool, which the worker uses, to the original place after use. The worker has to sort every material in the right order and make them findable for other workers. These simple arrangements of 5S are relatively easy to achieve with tangible outputs of productivity improvement in many workplaces, including factories and offices even in Japan now.

We may call core capacities as the mind-set of people. However, the word "mind-set" gives us an image of something difficult to change because of its ambiguous outline. The word mind-set can be disaggregated into more concrete words including motivation and self-confidence. For motivation, JICA is developing an approach to stimulate it in rural development projects named Smallholder Horticulture Empowerment and Promotion (SHEP) based on the Motivation and Self-Determination theory in psychology

(JICA 2016). For accuracy, daily training with incentive and punishment may work. For self-confidence, accumulation of small successes can be influential. In Ethiopia, the author observed mind-set change as one of the major outcomes of *Kaizen* promotion because of the weak core capacity of the majority of workers including discipline and punctuality. The author believes that the mind-set of someone is a phenotype of her/his own capability under a certain environment.

Figure 2.3 illustrates a cyclical concept of the *Kaizen* mind-set. People who have little motivation can create little but tangible improvement by using relatively basic *Kaizen* tools without any additional resource allocation. The improvement can create little satisfaction and self-confidence, which guide him/her to further target setting and motivation. The outside of cyclical arrows in the figure shows *Kaizen* tools and promotion measures as extrinsic factors, and the inside shows a concept of *Kaizen*-type mind-set as intrinsic elements that have a strong link with core capacity. Such mind-set is not a precondition of *Kaizen* activities but results of the progresses. This cyclical stimulation of mental and occupational improvement can be fueled with small steps of successes and encouragements from outside. Then people may feel like "we can create many improvements" without a fear of change. In

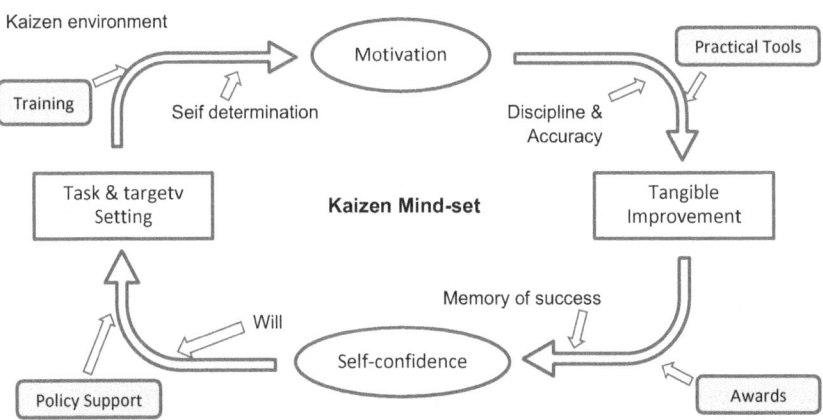

Fig. 2.3 A cyclical concept of the *Kaizen* mind-set. (Source: Created by the author)

order to trigger this cycle, a Japanese *Kaizen* expert asks the factory workers during consultation if they have any production process they feel unsafe or burdensome. Then the expert tries to solve the problem with basic *Kaizen* tools as to show a tangible result, which convinces the workers that *Kaizen* is beneficial to them.

A fundamental challenge may be the "cultural aspects" of *Kaizen*. One of the long-lasting questions on the effectiveness of *Kaizen* is that it may not be transferable to the society with a different culture because *Kaizen* is adapted to Japanese culture founded on homogeneity of society and unique religions. The question needs to be answered by demonstrating actual successful cases of transfer, such as Singapore and Ethiopia. In terms of literature, Recht and Wilderom (1998) have studied the effectiveness of the *Kaizen*-oriented suggestion system in Slovenia and argue that organization culture consists of the employment system, management-worker relation and internal information flow of the company that can be changeable by application of *Kaizen* even under different national cultures. Perry (1997) analyzes applicability of TQM in Africa and concludes that it might be as easy to introduce into African countries as into other countries because of the high level of collectivism in Africa. However, he adds that it cannot be a simple transplant but it needs be modified to fit in the African context.

2.4.3 Customization

The concept of *Kaizen* that JICA has been transferring to developing countries includes a variety of methodologies and tools. Typical processes of customization are (1) selection of methods and tools based on prevailing problems in the target companies, (2) modification of operational rules of methodologies/tools based on management-labor relations and social problems the company faces and (3) reformulation of methodologies/tools in response to social systems such as education, employment and economic trend. These processes need to be initiated by people who have knowledge and ideas on details of systems and problems.

One of customization observed is a broad application of 5S coupled with 5S auditing and 5S certification developed in many developing countries. 5S is a popular and easy method for the initial stage of *Kaizen* introduction, which is also very effective as repeatedly said. Another customization is observed in the project in Singapore in the restructuring stage. Methodology of the technology transfer in Singapore was changed from "a sequence of deepening theoretical understanding first" to "a combination of theoretical classroom training (CRT) and practical in-company training (ICT)" in the short cycle, followed by further on-the-job training, which is a typical approach of learning by doing.

Further customization may be the adjustment of application of methodologies/tools to the common employment systems such as lifetime employment or short-term contract and the wage system. Uesu (2011) points out that the QC circle in Japan is undertaken most often as unpaid voluntary work after working hours, which is difficult to do in the same manner in developing countries. If collectivism among workers is high in the society, group work may be effective like the *Kaizen* Promotion Team (KPT) in Ethiopia described in Chap. 5. Social coherence and the mutual support system symbolized by the extended family system in Africa seem similar to the one in Asia than in the US. Customization of *Kaizen* in Africa might be in a different direction from the case in the US and the UK since dynamism of labor mobility in the labor market, style of collectivism shared in society and level of core capacities of people are different between Africa and the US or the UK.

Regarding the guiding principles of the productivity movement, in 1955, the Japanese government and JPC announced three principles: (1) expansion of employment; (2) cooperation between labor and management; and (3) fair distribution of the fruits of productivity improvement among labor, management and consumers, as mentioned before (JPC 2005). African countries may need to have similar but different guiding principles of their own for sustainable *Kaizen* practices with broad participation of workers. Although increase in wage without productivity increase may negatively affect competitiveness of the company, the managers and workers can agree that wage increase be linked to productivity improvement in order to maintain competitiveness. If this is agreeable, both parties will have incentive to improve productivity.

How to further evolve the *Kaizen* system under the recent rapid development of information technology is a challenge to be mentioned. Volume of data and information accessible to policymakers, consultants, managers, engineers and workers in companies is rapidly increasing through the development of the Internet. Efficiency of communication among stakeholders is increasing drastically by using different information software such as e-mail, text message, social media as well as the Internet of Things. And operation systems and role of workers may change in accordance with the development of information technology (IT) and artificial intelligence (AI). Based on these circumstances, the methodologies and tools of *Kaizen* can be and should be further developed.

Another, and perhaps a more fundamental, challenge on customization of *Kaizen* as a device of TC is embedded in its decision-making system of ODA. In many ODA projects, fundamental decision-making on designing and implementation is made at the head office in the home country, even though beneficiaries of the project are in the recipient country. In contrast with domestic development projects of the government, ODA projects tend to have an information gap to conduct smooth monitoring and evaluation. And the donor government is obliged to be accountable to their own taxpayers in the home country. Therefore, the donor organization tends to set a rigid Monitoring and Evaluation (M&E) framework with a short timeframe of assessment to judge the performance. However, as the author explains, by its nature successful TC needs learning by doing. That means concrete answer on how to solve problems is not exactly known by stakeholders at the early stage of projects. The decision-making process in the head office of donors needs to be sensitive about these aspects and be flexible in operation. Otherwise, the head office may tend to decide its withdrawal from essential but difficult issues and allocate resources to only easy issues with already established methodologies.

2.5 Conclusions and Implications

Because knowledge and technologies are essential to our development, their transfer from one society to another is an imperative task to accelerate the process. However, knowledge transfer is not a simple task. Global knowledge needs be localized for effective utilization, and local knowledge can be shared widely and can become a global standard. History shows that the process of customization of quality control methods from the US has created *Kaizen* in Japan, which has become global knowledge. Localization of *Kaizen* in the African context may create further useful knowledge to accelerate the catch-up process of many people in developing countries. *Kaizen*, with the fundamental characteristics of a low-cost, gradual and inclusive approach, has huge potential. And *Kaizen* consists of a wide range of tools from basic to advanced, which also ensures applicability to many people with different capabilities in a variety of countries.

Through reviewing the academic literatures, the reports of past projects and empirical knowledge accumulated in JICA obtained from experiences in Japan, Africa, Asia and Europe, it can be said that quality and productivity improvement through *Kaizen* methodologies are very effective for Africa. The following are some conclusions on how to introduce *Kaizen* in African environments.

- For effective transfer of *Kaizen*, the government and its top leaders can play significant roles through a set of institutional arrangements including creation of and support to the core implementing organization of productivity improvement, allocation of adequate resources to create impacts and promotion of a national movement guided by strong commitment of the top leaders as observed in Singapore and Ethiopia.
- For sustainable improvement of quality and productivity of work, the core capacities need to receive due attention since they provide the bases for further technical capacity development including operation and maintenance skills of machineries and infrastructure. The required efforts to develop core capacity include not only obtaining theoretical knowledge but more essentially learning through actual experiences of trial and error.
- The *Kaizen* mind-set of people is a result of a continuous and cyclical *Kaizen* exercise of small successful experiences, self-confidence, further target setting and motivation. This mind-set can be the base of creating change and making proactive contribution to improvement.
- Since knowledge transfer is influenced by both technical and human aspects, the process of customizing *Kaizen* tools and methodologies in the local context while maintaining the core value of *Kaizen* is indispensable for long-lasting quality and productivity improvement activities.

Apart from these human aspects, details of the technical feature of the *Kaizen* system, methodologies and tools are described in Chap. 3. Some of the technical tools are much more scientific, objective and universally applicable than the above features. And how to justify *Kaizen* and maximize its effects in a broader context of industrial development are further points discussed in Chap. 6 as it has been playing in economic growth in Southeast Asian countries.

When we cannot do things smoothly, we may ask two questions to ourselves, namely "are we doing right things?" and "are we doing things right?" It is already proven that *Kaizen* is applicable in many workplaces in a different environment in its entirety or in part. The right question is how to apply *Kaizen* in the African context. JICA's effort on standardization of *Kaizen* along the African context focuses precisely on this question through sorting out know-how obtained from customization in each country and sharing with others (see Chap. 4). Needless to say, success needs active contribution of people in Africa.

References

Arase, D. (2005). Introduction. In D. Arase (Ed.), *Japan's Foreign Aid, Old Continuities and New Directions* (pp. 1–19). Oxon: Routledge.

Chambers, R. (1997). *Who's Reality Counts? Putting the First Last.* Rugby: Practical Action Publishing.

Cirera, X., & Maloney, W. (2017). *The Innovation Paradox, Developing-Country Capabilities and the Unrealized Promise of Technological Catch-Up.* Washington, DC: World Bank Group.

Easterly, W. (2006). *The White Man's Burden.* New York: Oxford University Press.

Imai, M. (2012). *Gemba Kaizen Second Edition: A Commonsense Approach to a Continuous Improvement Strategy.* New York: McGraw-Hill.

Japan International Cooperation Agency. (1986). *Singapore Kyowakoku Seisansei Kojo Project (Asean Hitozukuri Project) Sogo Chosa Hokokusho* (Comprehensive Study Report on Productivity Development Project in Singapore), ASEAN Human Resources Development Project, JICA Kokaigi JR-86-54.

Japan International Cooperation Agency. (1997). *Kokogyo Project Follow-Up Chosa (Kaizen) Hokokusho, Dai Ichi Bunsatsu, Dai Ichi-bu, Kaizen Donyu wo Chushintoshita Seisansei Kojo Gijutsu Iten* (Report of the Follow-Up Study on Projects in Mining and Industry Sector *(Kaizen)*, Part 1 of Volume 1 – Technology Transfer of Productivity Improvement focusing on introduction of *Kaizen*), JICA Kochokei JR-07-114.

Japan International Cooperation Agency. (1999). *Thai Okoku Seisansei Kojo Project Shuryoji Hyoka Hokokusho* (Terminal Evaluation Report on Productivity Development Project in the Kingdom of Thailand), JICA Kokai-1 JR-99-19.

Japan International Cooperation Agency. (2000a). *Thai Okoku Seisansei Kojo Project (Follow up) Shuryoji Hyoka Hokokusho* (Terminal Evaluation Report on Productivity Development Project Follow up in the Kingdom of Thailand), JICA Kokai-1 JR-00-38.

Japan International Cooperation Agency. (2000b). *Brasil Renpokyowakoku Seisansei/hinshitu Kojo Shuryoji Hyoka Hokokusho* (Terminal Evaluation Report on Improvement of Productivity and Quality Control in Federative Republic of Brazil), JICA Kokai-1 JR-00-09.

Japan International Cooperation Agency. (2004). *Asean Chiikini Okeru Susonosangyo Ikusei Kyoryoku Jigyo no Arikatani Kansuru Kisochosa Hokokusho* (Basic Study Report on Cooperation Projects Focusing on Development of Supporting Industry in ASEAN Region), JICA Keizai-JR-04-040.

Japan International Cooperation Agency. (2005). *Costa Rica Seisansei Kojo Project Shuryoji Hyoka Chosadan Hokokusho* (Report of the Terminal Evaluation Mission for Productivity Improvement Project in Costa Rica), JICA Keizai JR-05-121.

Japan International Cooperation Agency. (2008). *Capacity Assessment Handbook: Project Management for Realizing Capacity Development*. Tokyo: JICA Research Institute.

Japan International Cooperation Agency. (2009). *Paraguay Kyowakoku Hinshitsu Seisansei Center Kyoka Keikaku Project Shuryoji Hyoka Hokokusho* (Terminal Evaluation Report of the Project for Strengthening Quality and Productivity Center in Paraguay Republic), JICA Sangyo JR-09-109.

Japan International Cooperation Agency. (2014a). *Costa Rica Chushokigyo no Hinshitsu Seisansei Kojo ni Kakaru Facilitator Noryoku Kojo Project, Chubei Karibu Koiki: Shuryoji Hyoka Hokokusho (Terminal Evaluation Report of the Regional Project, Central America and Caribbean Countries: On Capacity*

Development of Facilitators for Quality and Productivity Improvement in SMEs Hosted by Costa Rica). Tokyo: Japan International Cooperation Agency.

Japan International Cooperation Agency. (2014b). Feature, 60 Years of Japanese ODA: History, The *Kaizen* Project, Laying the Groundwork for Singapore's Growth. *JICA's World January, 4–5.*

Japan International Cooperation Agency. (2016). *Introduction to the Psychology of International Cooperation, Seventeen Motivation Case Studies Collected from the Field*. Tokyo: Japan International Cooperation Agency.

Japan International Cooperation Agency, UNICO International, and Japan Productivity Center. (2018). *Project Kenkyu Africa Kaizen Shien-ni-kakaru, Hyojun Approach Sakutei Chosa (Study on Standardizing Kaizen Approaches for Further Dissemination and Deployment in Africa)*. Tokyo: Japan International Cooperation Agency.

Japan Productivity Center. (1990). *Singapore Seisansei Kojo Project, ASEAN Hitozukuri Project Gijutsu Iten-no Rinen to Jissen ni Kansuru Hokokusho*. Tokyo: Japan Productivity Center.

Japan Productivity Center. (2005). *Seisansei Undo 50nenshi*. Tokyo: Japan Productivity Center.

Kato, H. (2016). Japan's ODA 1954–2014: Changes and Continuities in a Central Instrument in Japan's Foreign Policy. In H. Kato, J. Page, & Y. Shimomura (Eds.), *Japan's Development Assistance, Foreign Aid and the Post-2015 Agenda*. Hampshire: Palgrave Macmillan.

Killick, T. (2008). Understanding British Aid to Africa: A Historical Perception. In *GRIPS Development Forum Report; Diversity and Complementarity in Development Aid*, http://www.grips.ac.jp/forum-e/D&CinDA.htm

King, K., & McGrath, S. (2004). *Knowledge for Development? Comparing British, Japanese, Swedish and World Bank Aid*. London: Zed Books.

Kitaw, D. (2011). Chapter 5 Botswana's Productivity Movement. In *Kaizen National Movement, a Study of Quality and Productivity Improvement in Asia and Africa*. Tokyo: JICA-GRIPS.

Kodera, K. (2016). Japan's Engagement with Multilateral Development Banks: Do Their Professional Paths Really Cross? In H. Kato, J. Page, & Y. Shimomura (Eds.), *Japan's Development Assistance, Foreign Aid and the Post-2015 Agenda* (pp. 19–35). Hampshire: Palgrave Macmillan.

Lemma, A. (2016). *The Role of Kaizen in Economic Transformation*. London: Overseas Development Institute. https://www.odi.org/publications/11067-role-kaizen-economic-transformation

McMahon, G. (1997). *Applying Economic Analysis to Technical Assistance Projects*. Washington, DC: World Bank.

Ministry of Economy, Trade and Industry (METI). (2005). *Wagakuni no Keizai Kyoryoku no Seikokeiken wo Fumaeta Japan ODA Model no Suishin (Promotion of Japan ODA Model Based on the Success of Economic Cooperation)*, Interim Report of the Working Group of Economic Cooperation, the National Council of Industrial Structure. Tokyo: Ministry of Economy, Trade and Industry.

Morrison, K. (2005). The World Bank, Japan and Aid Effectiveness. In D. Arase (Ed.), *Japan's Foreign Aid, Old Continuities and New Directions* (pp. 23–40). Oxon: Routledge.

National Productivity Board (NPB) and Japan International Cooperation Agency (JICA). (1990). *Further Fields to Conquer... A PDP Commemorative Publication*. Singapore/Tokyo: National Productivity Board/JICA.

Nonaka, I. (1991, November–December). The Knowledge-Creating Company. *Harvard Business Review*, 96–104.

Nonaka, I., & Toyama, R. (2003). The Knowledge-Creating Theory Revisited: Knowledge Creation as a Synthesizing Process. *Knowledge Management Research and Practice, 1*(1), 2–10.

Ohno, I. (2011). Chapter 1 Overview: National Movements and the Synthesis of Selected Country Experiences. In *Kaizen National Movement, a Study of Quality and Productivity Improvement in Asia and Africa*. Tokyo: JICA-GRIPS.

Ohno, I., & Kitaw, D. (2011). Chapter 3 Productivity Movement in Singapore. In *Kaizen National Movement, a Study of Quality and Productivity Improvement in Asia and Africa*. Tokyo: JICA-GRIPS.

Perry, C. (1997). Total Quality Management and Reconceptualizing Management in Africa. *International Business Review, 6*(3), 233–243.

Recht, R., & Wilderom, C. (1998). Kaizen and Culture: On the Transferability of Japanese Suggestion System. *International Business Review, 7*(1), 7–22.

Sawamura, N. (2002). Local Spirit, Global Knowledge: A Japanese Approach to Knowledge Development in International Cooperation. *Compare: A Journal of Comparative and International Education, 32*(3), 339–348.

Stiglitz, J., & Greenwald, B. (2014). *Creating Learning Society*. New York: Colombia University Press.

Uesu, S. (2011). Chapter 4 Quality Control Circles in Burkina Faso: Lessons Learned and Implications for Other Developing Countries. In *Kaizen National Movement, a Study of Quality and Productivity Improvement in Asia and Africa*. Tokyo: JICA-GRIPS.

World Bank (WB). (1996). *Lessons & Practices: Technical Assistance*. Washington, DC: Operations Evaluation Department, World Bank.

Zenawi, M. (2012). States and Markets: Neoliberal Limitations and the Case for a Developmental State. In A. Noman et al. (Eds.), *Good Growth and Governance in Africa, Rethinking Development Strategies*. New York: Oxford University Press.

Open Access This chapter is licensed under the terms of the Creative Commons Attribution 4.0 International License (http://creativecommons.org/licenses/by/4.0/), which permits use, sharing, adaptation, distribution and reproduction in any medium or format, as long as you give appropriate credit to the original author(s) and the source, provide a link to the Creative Commons license and indicate if changes were made.

The images or other third party material in this chapter are included in the chapter's Creative Commons license, unless indicated otherwise in a credit line to the material. If material is not included in the chapter's Creative Commons license and your intended use is not permitted by statutory regulation or exceeds the permitted use, you will need to obtain permission directly from the copyright holder.

3

Kaizen in Practice

Seiji Sugimoto

As was discussed in Chap. 2, *Kaizen* is already popular and widespread throughout the world. This chapter describes, from a technical standpoint, how *Kaizen* impacts actual work in the workplace. Section 3.1 of this chapter explains the objectives, stakeholders involved in practices, and types of technology, methodology, and tools of *Kaizen*. Section 3.2 describes detailed features of *Kaizen* with a focus on technological aspects and implementing structure. Section 3.3 identifies eight guidelines of *Kaizen* implementation for the consultants and workers who want to introduce *Kaizen* in the workplace and the management who want to accelerate *Kaizen* activities. Finally, Section 3.4 discusses the advantages and challenges for introducing and promoting *Kaizen*, followed by the conclusion. The chapter includes many concrete examples of practice and cases on the ground based on the experiences of the author, which give a clear picture of *Kaizen* implementation.

S. Sugimoto (✉)
Consulting Division, Japan Development Service Co., Ltd., Tokyo, Japan
e-mail: sugimoto@cba.att.ne.jp

3.1 *Kaizen* as an Integral Part of Technology

This section illustrates the very broad and comprehensive knowledge and technologies covered under the concept of *Kaizen* by focusing on its objectives, promoting institutions, and types of technologies and tools in order to draw a complete picture of *Kaizen*.

3.1.1 Two Types of *Kaizen* Based on Objectives

In factories in the early stage of starting *Kaizen* activities, good entry points are production processes that workers feel are difficult or unsafe or that create an unstable quality of products. Ideally through *Kaizen* a factory would develop processes that are easy to operate without safety risks and produce consistently quality products as compared to the state before implementing *Kaizen*. Gaps between the ideal state and the current state are recognized as problems to be solved through *Kaizen* (JIS Q 9024 2003). Figure 3.1 shows this comparison between the ideal state and the current state. The complete gray circle on the left side indicates the ideal state and the incomplete circle with a dotted line indicates the current state. The missing part shown by the dotted line in the circle indicates the gap between the ideal state and the current state, which represents problems to be solved by *Kaizen*.

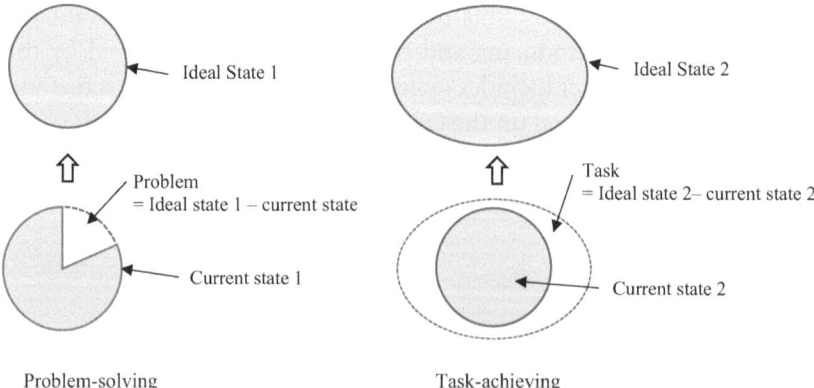

Fig. 3.1 Two types of *Kaizen* (problem-solving and task-achieving). (Source: Created by the author)

A concrete example of a gap between the ideal state and the current state can be illustrated by a case in a T-shirt producing factory. A garment company produces T-shirts following the steps of purchasing the textile, cutting and sewing it to be a T-shirt, and then printing a pattern on it. A finished T-shirt is packed as a complete product. In this factory, the quantity of T-shirts to be produced per person per hour is the performance indicator of the operation. Its target number is 3 T-shirts per person per hour based on the initial design of the factory; this target is the ideal state. However, if the actual production is 2.6 T-shirts per person per hour, the gap between 3 and 2.6—0.4 T-shirt—is the shortfall and the problem to be solved by *Kaizen*. The left side of Fig. 3.1 shows this ideal state of 3 T-shirts per person per hour as "Ideal state 1," 2.6 T-shirts as "Current state 1," and 0.4 T-shirts as a problem.

There is another type of ideal state that is indicated as "Ideal state 2" in the right side of Fig. 3.1. Even if the current state is the same as the ideal state 1, the company may face new competition in their target T-shirt market within a three-year period from imported products made in China or Bangladesh where labor cost is lower and productivity is rapidly improving. If the company recognizes such potential competition in the target market and decides to increase its own productivity by three times within three years, such a target is not a problem, but a task set to realize a managerial strategy. This is shown as "Ideal state 2." This situation is indicated as a gap between the gray circle shown as "Current state 2" and an oval labeled "Ideal state 2." Such a state is a target of a different dimension, which cannot be achieved through the same procedure of problem-solving (Nitta 1999).

For both ideal states—one from the view of the workplace and the other from management—*Kaizen* can be defined as activities that fill the gap between the current state and the ideal state by solving problems or achieving tasks on an operational level. In fact, proactive companies that introduce *Kaizen* while receiving training and consultancy services always keep in mind the ideal state of the company, understand the current state of the company correctly, recognize gaps between the ideal state and the current state, and are willing to fill these gaps. On the other hand, companies without an interest in *Kaizen* do not possess at least one of the following: "image of the ideal state," "understanding of the current state," "recognition of a gap," or "willingness to fill the gap."

Table 3.1 Characteristics of two types of *Kaizen*

	Problem-solving type of *Kaizen*	Task-achieving type of *Kaizen*
Ideal state	Objective and target already set	Objective or benchmark to be achieved in future
Approach	Bottom-up approach is major	Top-down approach is major
Magnitude of gap	Relatively small gap	Relatively large gap
Focus of *Kaizen* activities	Identification of root cause that creates gap is important	Idea and planning to fulfill large gap is important
Resources to be input (labor, facilities, time, etc.)	Relatively small amount of input/resource	Relatively large amount of input/resource
Implementer of *Kaizen*	Workers in factory, QC circles, cross-functional team	Management, engineer, and technician

Source: Created by the author

Table 3.1 shows key characteristics of the above two types of *Kaizen*. The prevailing features of the problem-solving type of *Kaizen* are a bottom-up approach with relatively small inputs, while the task-achieving type of *Kaizen* is often initiated by a top-down approach with larger inputs of resources.

3.1.2 Background Information on *Kaizen*

This sub-section provides background information related to three issues on *Kaizen*. The first concerns the relationship between *Kaizen* and *mottainai*. *Kaizen*, which refers to the basic concept of "filling the gap between the ideal state and the current state," can also be understood as a mind-set that wants to remove the feeling of *mottainai*.[1] *Mottainai* is used to refer to situations where things that are still useful are disposed and where inherent capacity or functions are not fully utilized. For example, the feeling of regret at the disposal of offcuts of wood made after cutting parts for the products in a carpenter shop is a sense of *mottainai*. When you have made only 2.6 T-shirts under the production capacity of 3 T-shirts though

---

[1] *Mottainai* spread throughout the world thanks to the efforts of Ms. Wangari Maathai (Kenya), who was the first African woman to win the Nobel Peace Prize.

using the same material, labor, and machines, you may feel that the capacity is not fully utilized, a situation that can be called *mottainai*. *Kaizen* emerged from the wish to dissolve such a condition of *mottainai*. Japan, a resource-poor country by nature, was put in a condition of severe scarcity during the period from the defeat in the Second World War in 1945 until recovery of GDP per capita to the level of the pre-war economy in 1955. This is also a period when both the private sector and the government of Japan had enthusiastically introduced technologies from the United States related to quality and productivity improvement. Therefore, it can be said that *Kaizen* is an effort to realize maximum utilization of available labor, material, and money under conditions that cannot easily be changed.

The second point concerns the relationship between *Kaizen* and innovation. Because of the modest approach of *Kaizen*, it is often mistakenly thought that *Kaizen* does not create innovation, and especially radical innovation. However, *Kaizen* has been contributing to many incremental innovations in production lines in private companies, through sustaining basic capacity of production as well as promoting continuous improvement. Furthermore, capacities and know-hows developed through *Kaizen* activities in the workplace often contribute to realization of radical innovation particularly during the stage of trial production of a new product based on an innovative idea.

The third point is about the players working on *Kaizen* activities. There are two types of stakeholders in the promotion of *Kaizen*. One are the practitioners of *Kaizen* including private companies and public institutions who deliver public services such as hospitals, schools, and operators of transport service. The second are promoters of *Kaizen* such as consultants, trainers, and organizations who support the improvement of the quality and productivity of practitioners. The government and ministries concerned can be promoters of *Kaizen* based on their policy of and strategy for their own development.

The role of the government as a *Kaizen* promoter within an industrial development strategy is to strengthen international competitiveness of domestic companies and to promote the development of small and medium-sized enterprises (SMEs) for the sake of job creation (see Chap. 6). The government can also improve service delivery within public sectors. Although private businesses can promote *Kaizen* in developed countries where the private sector is strong enough, the organizations focused on improving productivity operate within the public domain in developing countries. In the case of Ethiopia, the government established Ethiopian *Kaizen* Institute (EKI), the details of which are described in Chap. 5.

Capacity and the number of capable consultants who can promote *Kaizen* to practitioners are essential factors for successful *Kaizen* dissemination. Therefore, the role and form of organization of consultants are explained in the Sections 3.3 and 3.4 of this chapter. On the other hand, there are many experienced large companies who already have built-in capacity for *Kaizen* activities within their corporate structure, such as Toyota. They can sustain *Kaizen* activities without external consultants.

3.1.3 Management Technologies and Inherent Technologies

The technologies involved in the production of goods can be classified into two types, namely, inherent technologies and management technologies. Inherent technologies mean the knowledge and technologies required to produce goods or services, which can create a physical change in the form or condition of materials, or a chemical change in the character of materials. In contrast, management technologies[2] mean those required to operate various inherent technologies in combination as a system, to smoothen the interface between humans and machines, and knowledge on motivation, behavior, thought processes, and so on of individuals and groups. Inherent technologies can produce goods, but management technologies including Total Quality Management (TQM), Industrial Engineering (IE), and Total Productive Maintenance (TPM) are essential to produce quality products in a stable manner with high productivity and low cost within a set delivery period.

While inherent technologies are specific to a particular industry, management technologies include many that are applicable to various industries. Quality control is an example (see Fig. 3.2). Thus, there is *Kaizen* performed by management technologies and *Kaizen* performed by inherent technologies. One example of the former is the improvement in productivity that results when one worker becomes capable of simultaneously operating two

---

[2] As the term "management technologies" is commonly used by many types of businesses, it should be mastered by *Kaizen* consultants at both the basic and intermediate levels.

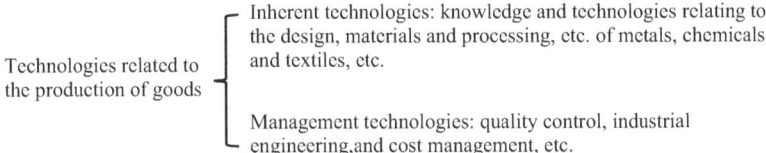

Fig. 3.2 Inherent technologies and management technologies. (Source: Created by the author)

lathes instead of one due to multiple activity analysis, which is a kind of IE tool. In contrast, when the productivity of lathe operation is improved due to an increase in the revolving speed following a change in the material of the bites, this is a type of *Kaizen* performed by the inherent technology of changing the material of the bites.

While broadly defined *Kaizen* can involve inherent technologies, *Kaizen* in the present context is narrowly defined hereafter in this chapter as *Kaizen* using management technologies for the following reasons:

(A) Management technologies including quality management, quality assurance, and reliability analysis play a major role in the ability to produce a certain quality of products in a constant manner, though inherent technologies play some role.
(B) The application of management systems such as IE (Industrial Engineering) and TPS (Toyota Production System) are indispensable to realize and maintain high productivity.
(C) The utilization of management tools such as VE (Value Engineering), cost planning, and standard cost are essential to create products with cost competitiveness.
(D) Management tools including scheduling, production control, and process management are required to manage and shorten delivery times.

For consultants who provide *Kaizen* services to various companies, becoming an expert on management technologies tends to have advantages because they are applicable to a wider range of industries than inherent technologies that focus on one specific industry. The combination between management technologies provided by *Kaizen* consultants and inherent technologies accumulated in the companies often broaden the options for *Kaizen* activities and enhance their effectiveness, especially for quality improvement and TPM.

3.1.4 *Kaizen* Systems, Methodologies, and Tools

Table 3.2 lists examples of *Kaizen* technologies which are used in the narrowly defined *Kaizen*. The vertical axis indicates the versatility of technologies and the difficulty of applied use, while the horizontal axis indicates different targets for technology application. Meta-*Kaizen* technology shown on the bottom includes terms that indicate the overarching procedures of *Kaizen* implementation through different *Kaizen* methodologies and tools in different levels.

Of the technologies listed in Table 3.2, those which are important core technologies for *Kaizen* are briefly explained below. Many of these technologies were developed in the US from the 1910s to the 1930s. They were introduced to Japan around 1950 with the instruction of the US. In the following, names underscored with a wave line are technologies introduced from the US and modified in Japan; names underscored with a straight line are technologies developed in Japan; and the names without an underscore are the technologies of US origin.

1. TQM (Total Quality Management)
   TQM is a system which combines ideas, tools, mechanisms, and so on designed to maintain and improve quality in general at companies. In the late 1950s, total quality control (TQC) was introduced to Japan with the emphasis that all employees from top management to front-line workers must participate in all departments, ranging from product planning and development, material procurement, marketing, sales, and after-services to personnel affairs and finance, in addition to the manufacturing department in order to produce high-quality products. Based on this idea, TQC combined with broader participation became widely used in Japan in the 1970s. In the US, this Japanized TQC was transformed into a top-down system to make it easier for the intentions of the top management to be thoroughly understood at the production floor. This revised approach was described as TQM. Japan imported this term, and TQC was renamed TQM in 1996.

Kaizen in Practice   77

Table 3.2 List of technologies frequently used for *Kaizen*

Levels		Target* of technology				
		Quality	Productivity	Cost	Delivery	Others
Advanced Kaizen		Taguchi method Experimental design Quality function deployment Reliability		Economic engineering NPV Target costing Activity-based costing	Decoupling point APS	
Intermediate Kaizen		⌐ ─ TQM ─ ─ ┐ │ Policy management │ │ Daily management │ └ ─ ─ ─ ─ ─ ─ ─ ┘ Statistical quality control Verification	⌐ ─ ─ TPS ─ ─ ┐ ⌐ ─ TPM ─ ┐ │ JIT │ │ Planed │ │ Jidoka │ │ maintenance │ │ Leveling │ │ │ │ SMED │ │ │ │ Kanban │ │ Autonomous │ │ Poka-yoke │ │ maintenance │ │ Cell production │ │ OEE │ │ TOC (Theory of constraint) │ └ ─ ─ ─ ─ ─ ┘ ⌐ ─ ─ ─ IE ─ ─ ─ ─ ┐ │ Multiple activity analysis │	Value engineering Value analysis Standard costing	Cell production MRP Pull production	Value stream mapping SWOT analysis Five forces analysis Value chain analysis Ergonomics
Basic Kaizen	Fundamental technology	Control chart Process capability index OC process chart	Process analysis Motion study, Time study Work analysis Work sampling Line balancing, Layout	Direct costing Cost accounting		
	Common** Kaizen tech.	●5S, ●7 QC tools, ●New 7 QC tools, ●Why–why analysis, ●Brain storming, ●TWI ●Visualization, ●Muda elimination, ●QC circle, ●Cross functional team, ●Suggestion system				
Meta Kaizen technology***		●PDCA, ●SDCA, ●QC Story, ●Problem solving procedure, ●Task achieving procedure ◎Project management				

* Target means purpose of each Kaizen technology.

** Common Kaizen technology is one that has several targets.

*** Meta Kaizen technology means ones that apply every other Kaizen technologies according to situation.

● shows essential technologies to be learnt in the basic level.   ◎ shows necessary technology to be learnt in the intermediate level.

Source: Created by the author

2. TPS (Toyota Production System)
   TPS is a production system developed by Toyota through a series of *Kaizen* efforts based on the philosophy of thoroughly eliminating *Muda* (waste; see (10) of this sub-section) and pursuing rational manufacturing. TPS is built on two main pillars. One is the idea of "stopping the machine at the moment any abnormality is detected, preventing the production of defective items" (called "jidoka"). The other is the idea of continuing production without stoppage by supplying only the kinds and quantities of items when they are needed for each production process (called "just-in-time") (Ohno 1978). There are not many companies even in Japan which are capable of adopting all pillars of TPS. However, TPS has made a significant impact on many enterprises in Japan as well as in the rest of the world in relation to the concept of *Kaizen* and how to proceed with *Kaizen*. The lean production system (or simply Lean) is a generalized production system which is modelled after TPS but renamed for better understanding by Americans (see Chap. 4).
3. Industrial Engineering (IE)
   The concept of industrial engineering, introduced by F.W. Taylor and F.B. Gilbreth, was developed as a technology to design, improve, and install a management system whereby people, materials, and equipment act together to perform their functions for the primary purpose of improving productivity (Fujita 1978).
4. TPM (Total Productive Maintenance)
   TPM increases productivity through the integrated maintenance of production facilities while aiming at achieving zero work accidents, zero defective products, and zero breakdowns. TPM is characterized by self-maintenance by operators and small group activities with full participation. The idea of the preventive maintenance of machinery arrived at Japan from the US around 1950. The original American idea of maintenance by staff who are exclusively responsible for the maintenance of machinery was Japanized to TPM with the full participation of everyone from the top executive to front-line workers based on the idea that front-line operators are also responsible for the maintenance of machinery by means of conducting preventive maintenance (Suzuki 1992).

The manual work in production is steadily being replaced by machines and the role played by machinery in production is growing not only in terms of productivity enhancement but also quality, cost, and delivery improvement. This trend is not limited to industrialized countries. In developing countries, there are many cases of the installation of second-hand machines that require careful maintenance. The importance of machinery maintenance in production in developing countries is often greater than in industrialized countries because second-hand machines often operate less reliably, have spare parts that take longer to obtain, and require a long and costly process to call a machine manufacturer's engineer from the country of manufacture for repair when a local agent is unable to repair a broken machine (which occurs fairly often). This is the reason why TPM is such an important *Kaizen* technology. The following box illustrates how a company in a developing country struggles to maintain machineries of production.

Box 3.1   Defunct Machines Cannibalized for Operating Machines

A visitor to a factory in a developing country often encounters the scene of a number of obsolete machines being simply stored instead of disposed of. This is a likely situation for the recommendation of the first S (sort) of 5S, that is, removal and disposal of unnecessary and non-urgent items from the production floor. However, it is essential to investigate the actual circumstances before making such a recommendation.

As mentioned earlier, many companies in developing countries use second-hand machines, many of which are no longer produced by the original manufacturers with no stock of the relevant spare parts. In this situation, defunct machines kept at a factory are often cannibalized for parts for operating machines. While there is a question of whether or not the storage of such machines resembling scraps to act as a source for spare parts is appropriate, the potential use of defunct machines in this manner should be considered before recommending "sort."

---

5. 5S (Five S)

The 5S stands for sort, set in order, shine, standardize, and sustain. For the purpose of improving the work environment to make it easier to work, unnecessary items in the workplace must be removed (sort), places to store necessary items determined with consideration for the ease of returning the items to the designated places after use (set in order), and cleaning regularly conducted (shine). These activities and states of things are normalized (standardize) and are made habitual practices in the workplace (sustain). As the 5S primarily reduces wasteful actions of "looking for things" and "transporting something" which do not produce any added value, both productivity and quality improve. Because the involvement of employees in the 5S provides the opportunity for them to recognize the value of *Kaizen*, *Kaizen* commonly starts with the introduction of the 5S. Many people tend to consider the 5S to be merely cleaning of the workplaces as they do not understand the unique definition of each S. The reality is that the proper execution of the 5S can produce much better effects than commonly anticipated.

6. 7 QC Tools (Seven Quality Control Tools)

    The 7 QC tools are a control chart, Pareto chart, cause and effect diagram, check sheet, histogram, stratification, and scatter diagram (Ishihara 1980). These represent the tools used for the present data analysis designed to discover the root causes of a problem using primarily numerical data. They are all old tools except for the cause and effect diagram (fishbone diagram or Ishikawa diagram) invented by Dr. Kaoru Ishikawa of Japan. It is said that the full application of the 7 QC tools can improve (solve) 95% of problems encountered at the production floor (Ishikawa 1989). New 7 QC tools (relations diagram (association diagram), affinity diagram, tree diagram, matrix diagram, matrix data-analysis diagram, PDPC (process decision program chart), and arrow diagram) that are suitable for analyzing qualitative data have also been developed, while the 7 QC tools are designed to analyze quantitative data.

7. Why-Why Analysis

    Why-Why analysis is a tool to logically investigate the cause(s) of a problem by tracing it back to its roots. At Toyota, employees are taught to repeat "why" five times to find or determine the true cause of a problem. The following box shows an application of the analysis.

Box 3.2 Root Causes Found in Sales Site

As a concrete case of identifying a root cause by using Why-Why analysis, let me cite my own experience in Argentina. In 2009, five shoemaking factories in Buenos Aires were selected as model factories for the transfer of *Kaizen* technologies through OJT to counterparts of the government. At that time, Argentina's GDP recorded negative annual growth of 5% due to the sharp recession that started in the previous year, even though the country had enjoyed nominal economic growth of nearly 10% a year over the previous four years. The first question I asked on visiting these factories was about the trend in turnover in the previous several years. All five factories were experiencing a downturn with a year-on-year decline of 20–30% except for one factory which had experienced a 50% decline in turnover. I found such a decline to be extraordinary and thought that both the factory and those hoping to assist *Kaizen* would be enthusiastic regarding efforts to improve quality and productivity, which is the standard practice of *Kaizen*, only after finding the true cause of this massive decline of the turnover, that is, why it occurred. The reason for any abnormality in the market needed to be investigated by regarding the market as a production floor, even though the subject matter falls outside the category of "*Kaizen* at the workplace." The first step I took was to invite front-line personnel from marketing and sales to get their opinions on quality, design, complaints, range, price, delivery time to shops, sales promotion, and after-sales service, including repair of the shoes made at their factory compared to other shoemakers. The findings of these interviews were that (1) the design and quality which crucially affect the turnover of their shoes were reputedly better than others, (2) the prices tended to be slightly higher than their competitors although they were unlikely to be the cause of twice the large decline in turnover compared to competitors, and (3) the shortcomings were a slightly longer delivery time and insufficient after-sales service.

To identify the cause of the rapid fall in the turnover, an interview survey was arranged with managers and so on of more than 30 leading retail outlets on matters related to shoes manufactured by this factory. Through these interviews, it became clear that the delivery time—almost twice as long as other manufacturer—was incompatible with the expectations of retailers facing the adverse impact of the recession, which necessitated prompt delivery to avoid the loss of sales opportunities due to being out of stock. This long delivery time was the true cause of the business slump at this factory.

Once this discovery had been made, it was time for "*Kaizen* at the production floor" to show its value. The target of "shortening the delivery

(*continued*)

> **Box 3.2 (continued)**
>
> time" was introduced and efforts were made to switch from large lot production to small lot production. It took some time to persuade the factory manager to switch the production system as he feared a decline in productivity in the near term due to an increased number of set-up changes associated with small lot production. However, switching to small lot production had a positive impact as the sales growth exceeded that of competitors after three months.
>
> Although this is a somewhat special case of Why-Why analysis, logical investigation of the cause of a problem coupled with verification of the solution through practical application narrowed the scope of the remedial measures to be implemented, resulting in the quick achievement of *Kaizen*.

8. TWI (Training Within Industry)

   TWI means the training of subordinates by a team leader or supervisor at a shop where the work is mostly routine. (In other words, it means "job instruction" along with such training themes as "job methods" on how to improve the job, "job relations" on how to handle human relations, and "job safety" on how to conduct work safely.) TWI is a training method which was originally developed in the US and disseminated during the Second World War. In Japan, TWI was disseminated during the post-war period.

9. Visualization

   Visualization means the sharing of information on work within an organization, which aims at contributing to the early discovery of problems and the promotion of *Kaizen* using charts, tables, and graphs. In some cases, sounds or lights are used for the same purpose.

10. *Muda* Elimination

    Any activity which does not produce added value is considered to be *Muda* (waste). *Muda* elimination literally means the elimination of over-production *Muda*, waiting *Muda*, transport *Muda*, over-processing *Muda*, inventory *Muda*, motion *Muda*, and defects *Muda* (together, they are called the seven *Muda*) (JMA 1980). For *Kaizen*, it is important to immediately deal with that *Muda* which can be easily reduced or eliminated in an early stage of *Kaizen* implementation. In this chapter, *Muda* elimination is frequently mentioned as a building block of TPS, in the detailed features of *Kaizen*, and to explain actual cases in the production sites, because it is one of the key entry points to various *Kaizen* activities.

11. QCC (Quality Control Circle)
    QCC is a small group formed at the workplace to improve work at the production floor. Even though the name contains QC, the actual themes for *Kaizen* are not restricted to quality (JUSE 1980). QCC emerged in 1962 based on the idea of Ishikawa (1989) mentioned in (6), taking its cue from the organizational activities of labor unions. It soon became widespread throughout the world. The participation of a small group(s) consisting of front-line workers in QCC as well as TQM and TPM is a distinctive feature of *Kaizen*.

12. Cross-Functional Team
    A cross-functional team is a team composed of required personnel who are enlisted from a variety of departments or positions to solve a general business challenge faced by the company. By definition, the team deals with problems or tasks that cannot be solved by a single department (JUSE 1980). This team is an important operational unit for TQM.

13. Suggestion System
    The suggestion system gives ordinary employees the opportunity to make suggestions regarding desirable improvements relating to their work to the middle or top management. This is an important tool for *Kaizen*. This system promotes *Kaizen* while creating a sense of participation in company management among ordinary employees.

14. QC Story (Quality Control Story)
    A QC story tells a standardized procedure for problem-solving or task-achieving plus matters related to the presentation of *Kaizen* results (Nitta 1999). Even though the term QC is used, the actual themes are not restricted to quality.

Although the above section explains management technologies, it must be noted that *Kaizen* management technologies must be combined with industrial technologies when improvements in the quality of products or the efficiency of equipment is intended. Even for other purposes of *Kaizen*, knowledge and experience of industrial technologies as well as cost and delivery times of products are useful to promote *Kaizen* activities.

3.2 Fundamental Features of *Kaizen*

3.2.1 TPS as a Symbol of *Kaizen*

This section examines the historical impacts of TPS (Toyota Production System) on Japanese-style *Kaizen* technologies.

The impact of TPS cannot be ignored when discussing *Kaizen* technologies for productivity enhancement. TPS is a unique production system based on unique ideas and its impact is felt not only in Japan but also in the rest of the world. TPS also offers useful hints for *Kaizen* for the distribution and service sectors in addition to the manufacturing sector. The uniqueness and originality of TPS are vividly reflected in the following five aspects:

1. To improve profitability, emphasis is placed on cost reduction through the elimination of *Muda* rather than through a higher product price and/or increased sales volume (Ohno 1978). Toyota currently leads the global automobile market in terms of annual vehicle production along with General Motors (GM) and Volkswagen, but once faced bankruptcy in 1950.[3] Learning lessons from this crisis, Toyota decided that the rigorous elimination of *Muda* should be the highest priority to ensure the survival and further development of the company and developed a number of *Kaizen* tools. This policy resulted in TPS which would later become the foundation for the lean production system.

   Throughout the company Toyota lists seven types of *Muda*, of which over-production *Muda* is considered to be the most vicious. The availability of required products at the required quantity and time is sufficient, as Toyota decisively considers any hasty production or production above the required quantity to constitute over-production *Muda*. Toyota's idea is that it is better to produce the necessary quan-

---

[3] After the Second World War, Japan experienced massive inflation. In 1947, J. M. Dodge, a banker dispatched to Japan by the US military to control inflation and the fiscal deficit, introduced drastic fiscal austerity measures. In the case of the automobile industry, while the sales prices of cars were officially controlled, raw materials and components, such as tires, were excluded from the price control regime. Consequently, automobile manufacturers faced a crisis of survival as their financial deficit increased with the larger output of vehicles. Toyota was no exception (Asahi Shinbun 2013).

tity even if it means a fall of the short-term productivity, negating the common sense associated with the scale merit of mass production. This idea is sustained by the scientific approach of measurement, analysis, and rationalization of the production system. TPS is quite different from Ford's famous production system, which is the sequential mass production of a single product leading to low-cost production and mass sales at a low price, assumed to result in increased profit (Wada 2009).

2. Many companies seek scale merit through the mass production of a single product. However, TPS rejects this idea as it creates *Muda* associated with over-production. Instead, even if it results in an increase in the number of set-up changes,[4] TPS aims to reduce the inventory level as well as lead time[5] through small lot production as much as possible. In the case of the press process, for example, as the work to change a die typically requires two to three hours to complete, there is a tendency to produce many products with the same die, reducing the number of set-up changes. However, this creates intra-lot waiting (lot processing delay)[6] and intra-process waiting,[7] extending the time necessary to complete the production (creating a longer delivery time). Because this operation produces more products than immediately required, it creates an in-process inventory, necessitating the allocation of space for its storage and transportation to this space. In the case of TPS, a new method was invented to shorten the die changeover time, as reducing the number of processed products using the same die does not decrease productivity. This method is called the single-minute exchange of die (SMED). SMED has shortened most of the die changeover times to less than ten minutes from the conventional two to three hours (Shingo 1980).

---

[4] A set-up change means the setting up of a new operation which is necessary to produce a different product. It includes the replacement of a die, jig, assembly parts and members, and other adjustments until quality is stabilized and pre-manufacturing confirmation of the work contents and cleaning is completed.

[5] Lead time means time required to process raw materials and assembly to produce a product.

[6] Intra-lot waiting means the idle time before and after a process, waiting for full build-up of the unit production volume.

[7] This is the state where an entire lot is waiting for processing work as the processing work involving the lot in question does not proceed.

3. Most companies employ a push production system whereby the amounts of the raw materials to be fed in the first process are determined by the estimated sales volume. In contrast, TPS is a pull production system whereby a production instruction (using a *Kanban*) is issued from the final process to the upstream processes to ensure that the required volume of products is produced when necessary in correspondence with the actual demand. In reality, a production instruction is also issued in a push production system not only to the first process but also to all other processes. Once a problem occurs at an intermediate process, the actual state of production begins to differ from the issued production instruction. In the case of the pull production system, the production instruction issued from a downstream process to its previous process can absorb a small fluctuation in the production volume, minimizing any adjustment between the plan and actual performance (Monden 1985). In other words, the production system of making to stock tries to "sell what is produced," while TPS tries to "make what is sold."
4. Most factories hold some stock (of raw materials, work in process, completed products, etc.) to avoid adverse impacts on immediate production and sales of an unanticipated situation, such as equipment breakdown, non-supply of raw materials, sudden time off by workers, occurrence of defective products above an assumed level, and so on. In TPS, the stock level is reduced to the lowest possible level to make any problem on the production floor visible, so that problems can be quickly rectified as measures designed to prevent the re-occurrence of the same problems are introduced. In other words, the former absorbs problems with stock, which may conceal the seriousness of such problems, while TPS tries to quickly find the occurrence of problems in order to take suitable steps to solve them quickly and prevent any further occurrence (JMA 1980).
5. In the case of continuous production involving a conveyor belt, the entire operation is divided into a series of simple tasks, each of which can be conducted by a single skilled worker. Such simple tasks, however, promote a feeling of boredom, often resulting in a decline of morale. With TPS, workers are encouraged to develop multiple skills. Moreover, the provision of opportunities to present thoughts and ideas

through participation in production floor small group activities and the proposal system leads to the capacity building of ordinary employees.

Companies positioned opposite to TPS described above are typically those that employ Ford's production system,[8] a mass production system relying on the interchangeability of parts and an assembly line using a conveyor belt. The system was developed over a period of five years from its initial conception to realization in the US, was established around 1910, and is still used by many factories around the world. In contrast, TPS is a production system resulting from thorough thinking by Toyota to obtain cost competitiveness in a high-mix low-volume production system. TPS was designed to enable the company's survival in the small post-war automobile market in Japan. The system was established as the result of *Kaizen* efforts over a period of some 20 years and its introduction to all Toyota plants was completed in 1962 (Wada 2009).

Although TPS has had a great impact on the philosophy and methods of *Kaizen*, it has become somewhat tacit knowledge because of the few systematic guidelines applicable to various types of companies unlike International Organization for Standardization (ISO) standards and also because of the use of many unique terms. The lean production system can be described as a system which has restructured the tacit knowledge associated with TPS and converted it to explicit knowledge so that it can be easily understood by non-Japanese companies. As such, it is an example of the globalization of TPS (see Chap. 4 for comparison between TPS and Lean).

3.2.2 Detailed Features of *Kaizen*

The following four matters describe general features of *Kaizen*:

(i) Pursues cost reduction through the rigorous elimination of *Muda*;
(ii) Aims to enhance the sense of participation in *Kaizen*, morale, and capabilities of front-line workers;

---

[8] Toyota production system and Ford production system can be compared with production based on order vs make-to-stock, pull production vs push production, pursuit of profit by small lot production vs pursuit of profit by large lot production, and so on.

(iii) Proceeds gradually from basic *Kaizen* to advanced *Kaizen* in correspondence with the capacity of the company or organization;
(iv) Gives priority to *Kaizen* relying on analytic thinking rather than large investment.

3.2.2.1 Cost Reduction Through the Rigorous Elimination of *Muda*

As described in the previous sub-section, *Kaizen* is strongly influenced by the philosophy of Toyota which is one of the most representative giant companies of Japan. The idea is to remove any negative aspects (*Muda*) to increase the profit. Though a company undertakes the sales promotion of its products against the products of its competitors, the product price and sales volume are largely determined by the market and cannot be totally controlled simply by internal efforts. In contrast, the elimination of *Muda* can be achieved solely by internal efforts and, therefore, can easily be a target for *Kaizen*.

3.2.2.2 Sense of Participation and Capacity Building Among Front-Line Workers

Kaizen aims at not only improving quality and productivity but also at enhancing the morale of workers along with their capacity. *Kaizen* is driven not by investment in *Kaizen* technologies or mechanical equipment but by investment in front-line workers, supervisors, and managers. The capacity building of these people through *Kaizen* activities makes it possible for them to tackle advanced *Kaizen* themes, progressing from simpler *Kaizen* in the beginning. When viewed from this angle, the production floor of Toyota can be described as "a learning organization." As will be mentioned later, one of the leading features of *Kaizen* is its emphasis on workers' logical thinking and empirical knowledge rather than money. *Kaizen* cannot simply be achieved with the application of *Kaizen* technologies. In addition to such technologies, interest in *Kaizen* among all stakeholders and a sense of participation and the capacity building of workers are essential. The positive effects of *Kaizen* only emerge and continue when the technological and human aspects are engaged with each other like a pair of wheels.

3.2.2.3 Gradual Application of *Kaizen* at Different Levels

As listed in Section 3.1.4, *Kaizen* includes a variety of systems, methodologies, and tools. They can be classified according to their level of applicability as basic, intermediate, or advanced *Kaizen* as indicated in Table 3.2. In the basic *Kaizen*, 5S is a typical first method to be introduced. That is because 5S (or at least 2S, sort and set in order) is an empirical prerequisite for balance improvements of production lines and reductions in the rejection rate. In addition, 5S can create tangible changes in the workplace, through which workers can recognize the benefits of *Kaizen* and be more supportive to it. After achieving a better work environment and stimulating the *Kaizen* mind of the workers, *Muda* elimination is the next step. Although *Muda* elimination includes practices at different levels from easy to difficult, the easiest one in terms of designing and implementation can be selected as the first step, which can foster further self-confidence in workers toward higher levels of *Kaizen*. When a small and medium-sized enterprise (SME) tries to introduce a comprehensive *Kaizen* technology system under Western ways of application such as Lean, Six Sigma, or ISO, it is often recommended to introduce the entire system at once. Since with *Kaizen* there is a way to start with an easy step, such as the 5S, *Kaizen* is easier to adopt by SMEs with a lower ability to apply *Kaizen* technologies. Metaphorically speaking, Six Sigma and ISO can be described as restaurants offering a full-course menu, while *Kaizen* is a restaurant offering an a la carte menu as well. It goes without saying which restaurant is easier to visit for a customer with limited digestive capacity as well as funds.

3.2.2.4 Relying on Analytic Thinking Rather Than Large Investment

Here is a useful example in Argentina. An old factory building which became cramped was replaced by a new larger factory, which the owner asked me to diagnose. The new factory was found to be more modern in appearance, but the job flow set by the shop-based machine layout where machines of the same type are positioned together remained the same.

One clear difference was that the distance between the machines in the new factory was much farther than before with an increased number of products in process being piled up around each machine. This view made the author instantly suspect that investment increased *Muda*. A relaxed machine layout lengthens the moving distance of goods, while an increased number of products in process not only lengthens the lead time but also increases the handling workload relating to work in process. Any investment not accompanied by the viewpoint of *Kaizen* can actually damage the quality and/or productivity in many cases. The example shown in the following box, which argues that relocation to a larger factory is made unnecessary due to *Kaizen* of the layout, comes from Ethiopia.

Box 3.3 Capacity Expansion Through a Change of the Layout

The owner of a feed factory which has a long rectangular shape of 6 m wide and 20 m deep wanted to relocate to a new larger factory in several months' time as the existing factory had become cramped due to increased production. The main machines, that is, crusher and mixer, are positioned at the far end of the factory building with an operating rate of 50%. The factory has one aisle almost at the center of the floor which runs from the entrance to the far end. Maize and other raw materials for mixed feed are placed on both sides of this aisle. With this kind of layout, raw materials are temporarily placed in designated areas and ultimately transported to the area of the machinery. Processed and mixed products are moved to the product yard near the entrance for subsequent loading onto trucks. Some 20 workers work at the factory, 70% of whom are engaged in the in-factory transportation, loading and unloading the raw materials and products from trucks (see Fig. 3.3).

All of the raw materials ultimately require transportation to the far end and completed products must be transported from the far end to the entrance. This is a layout whereby the lines of flow of goods and people have been made the longest. Under the instructions of the author, the machines are relocated near the entrance, while raw materials with a heavy weight in the final product (maize, etc.) are now stocked near the entrance. Those with a lighter weight in the final product (various minerals, vitamins, etc.) are stocked toward the far end. The work to change the layout was conducted over a weekend (Saturday and Sunday). On Monday, the productivity increased by 37% without any special instructions on how to conduct the work and the day's work was completed three hours before the factory's closing time. The workers responsible for transportation are

(continued)

Box 3.3 (continued)

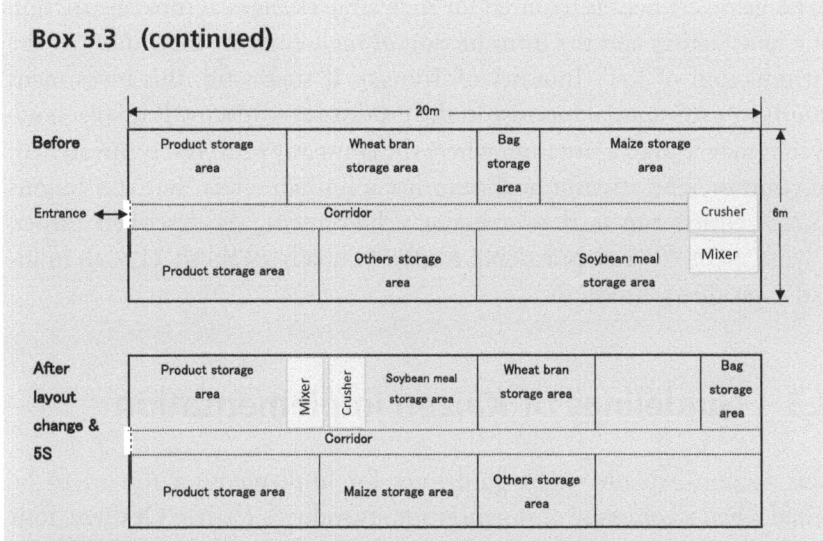

Fig. 3.3 Example of layout change in the factory. (Source: Created by the author)

said to be jubilant as their work is now less physically demanding. Trial calculation shows that no additional workers are required even if the production volume increases by 60%, meaning that the existing factory can cope with such level of production.

The example described in the box is a real case where the relocation of a factory and the recruitment of new workers, both of which can be considered strategic issues for business management, became unnecessary for several years due to the basic *Kaizen* which improved the factory layout. In this case, it is also possible to introduce a conveyor belt for in-factory transportation to replace manual labor by a mechanical means. However, the introduction of a conveyor belt without changing the layout constitutes the "mechanization of *Muda*,"[9] causing double *Muda*.

---

[9] If the current flow line (travelling route of people and goods) of 40 m can be shortened to 10 m by a change of the layout, a flow line of 30 m constitutes *Muda*. Investment in a conveyor belt for the transportation of goods while leaving a long line of flow means investment in the mechanization of a 30 m long wasteful line of flow. The author calls this the "mechanization of *Muda*" or "investment in *Muda*."

Large investment is required for such large changes as the construction of a new factory and the introduction of high-capacity machinery or the introduction of IoT (Internet of Things). If successful, this investment results in a substantial increase in the production capacity. If it fails, however, it may lead to a situation where the company's survival is threatened. In contrast, one attempt at *Kaizen* has a limited effect, but continuous *Kaizen* efforts can lead to a major achievement. As described earlier, Toyota spent 20 years practicing *Kaizen* to finally establish TPS, an innovative production system.

3.3 Guidelines of *Kaizen* Implementation

This section explains eight guidelines for implementing *Kaizen* to be noted when a company or organization introduces *Kaizen*. Of these, four are for consultants and workers, while the remaining four are for *Kaizen* management.

3.3.1 Four Guidelines for Consultants and Workers

1. Immediate action is the first priority, followed by continuous *Kaizen*.

Unlike administrative reform, *Kaizen* assumes the accumulation of small changes. Because of this, the cost is small, and any unsuccessful outcome does not cause much damage to the company. *Kaizen* can be implemented even when a new system for its implementation is not fully in place. It is sufficient to start wherever it can be started.

Let us consider work in which a machine operator checks any loosening of the bolts as part of self-maintenance for the purpose of retightening if loosened bolts are found. When the machine to be inspected uses the type of bolt shown in Fig. 3.4, daily checking using a spanner in many places is time-consuming. The drawing of a narrow line which runs continually from the bolt, nut, and base as shown here makes it easier to detect any loosening as a misaligned line means a loosening of

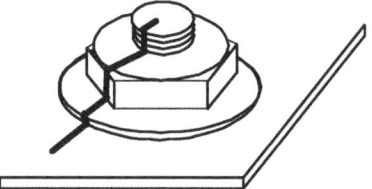

Fig. 3.4 Loosened bolt instantly made visible with simple *Kaizen*. (Source: Created by the author)

the bolt. The simple act of drawing a line constitutes an act of *Kaizen* when implemented.

An immediate action is very important for *Kaizen*, and it is not necessary to be afraid of failure when attempting *Kaizen*. Failure should be treated as an experience to be referred to for new attempts that take a different approach. In Japan, there is a company which awards prizes to the QC circles experiencing a major *Kaizen* failure for the purpose of encouraging the implementation of *Kaize*n in the first place.

2. On-the-spot observation is more important than deskbound discussions.

In some countries, highly educated engineers with professional knowledge may not like the idea of visiting the field as they dislike getting dirty with machine oil. They discuss the causes of problems in the conference room based on advanced professional knowledge learned at university or graduate school. For example, they list as many possible causes of a problem that they can think of during a brainstorming session and compile these causes in the form of a cause and effect diagram. The causes indicated on such a diagram, however, are simply possible causes. In general, the number of real root causes of a problem is one or slightly more. Cases are observed where efforts are made to come up with measures for all possible causes without narrowing down the likely root causes. The implementation of all measures requires massive human resources as well as funding in addition to the length of time needed to find the real root cause(s). As such, this approach is unproductive. Failure to narrow down the root causes can be attributed to insufficient on-the-spot observation in most cases.

While the logical pursuit of the root cause using Why-Why analysis is helpful, the validity of the finally identified cause must be verified in the field. In the case of *Kaizen* at the production floor, the root cause of a problem is assumed to lie at the production floor and clues for a solution are often expected to be found at the same production floor, as the example in the following box portrays.

> **Box 3.4 The Cause of Defective Product and Tips of *Kaizen* Detected on the Sites**
>
> This is a case of a factory that produces canvas shoes in Argentina. In response to a request from the factory management who wanted to reduce the rate of defective products, the author and trainees who would be *Kaizen* consultants in the counterpart organization of Japan International Cooperation Agency (JICA) project started consulting on quality improvements in collaboration with the Quality Control (QC) staff of the factory. First, based on the theory of QC, we counted defect rates in accordance with type of shoes, side (left or right) of pairs, and six parts of each shoe and then drew a Pareto chart. The result showed that the most common defect, about half of all defects, was mal-adhesion between a particular part of shoe soles and the canvas. The next step as a common method was to prepare a fishbone diagram that indicated possible causes of defects identified through a brainstorming session. However, such practices may not bring productive results if the site observation is not conducted carefully enough. Therefore, the author requested the trainees and QC staff to carefully observe the production floors in the factory before the brainstorming session. Through this process, we found that some of gluing work of shoe parts was outsourced. Hence we divided the sample data of defects to the shoes with the outsourced process and without the process, reanalyzed the defect rates, finding that the outsourced products showed significantly high rate of defects. Before discussing the reason why the products with the outsourced process had a high defect rate, what we needed was site observation. The author, trainees, and QC staff visited the company to which the factory outsourced the gluing process and then understood the reasons for high defects immediately following the inspection of its work process. There are two reasons: one is the use of low-quality glue at a cheap price, and another is the lack of a process to bleed air contained in the adhesive face by tapping on the glued parts after adhesion. Countermeasures derived from these observations were immediately introduced, which halved the defect rate. This case demonstrates that as the reasons for defects exist in the workplace, so too do the hints for countermeasures.

3. Quality oriented by consumer prioritize

There is one principle which should never be forgotten when implementing *Kaizen*. This principle demands that *Kaizen* provide greater customer satisfaction. *Kaizen* which damages customer satisfaction is not *Kaizen* but a change for the worse. Here is an example: a manufacturer may change the required period for delivery of own its products to customers, from 7 days to 15 days, in order to improve their delivery rate within the set period. This change is not *Kaizen* if the manufacture does not consider the convenience of customers. The idea of being customer-oriented may not come naturally on the production floor as front-line workers have hardly any opportunity to have direct contact with customers. In this case, the post-process of production in the factory is like a "customer" because the previous process works as supplier to the next process as buyer. Customer satisfaction should be understood as the ease of work in the post-process, as this line of thinking from one process to the next eventually leads to the real customers who are the users (Hosoya 1984).

Customer satisfaction can be expressed by the value or cost which customers consider appropriate for a product or service that they receive. There could be a change, such as lowering the function or capability of a product or the withdrawal of polite service which may appear to lower the satisfaction of customers at first glance. However, if the price of the products drops more than the lowered customer satisfaction (or any cost increase due to a change can be compensated with other benefits for the customer), this change can be described as an act of *Kaizen*. One example is that of a dry cleaner extending the delivery time from three days to five days while reducing the price by half. In this case, it is essential to carefully determine the reaction of customers to this change. Lowering the product or service value based on prejudice on the part of the seller involves considerable risk.

The quality-first policy means, in fact, the same as the customer-oriented policy even though the phrases used are different. Quality in this case means broadly defined quality which comprehensively covers not only the product quality but also the quality of marketing, after-service and other auxiliary services, and price.

4. Focus on bottleneck

Consider the case shown in Fig. 3.5 that illustrates a production line composed of three processes, that is, cutting, boring, and polishing. The processing time to complete a product is one minute for cutting, three minutes for boring, and two minutes for polishing. The production capacity of this production line is determined by the processing time for boring. To be more precise, 20 products can be produced in 1 hour (60 minutes ÷ 3 minutes). When only the cutting process is looked at, the production capacity is 60 products per hour. Similarly, the production capacity is 30 products per hour for the polishing process. When each process is operated to its full capacity, there is a build-up of 40 products in the process per hour between the cutting process and boring process. Meanwhile, the polishing process incurs idle time of 20 minutes per hour because of the non-forwarding of work in process from the boring process.

It is evident that the boring process constitutes a bottleneck for this production line as the process with the lowest processing capacity determines the production capacity of the production line. If the processing time of the boring process can be shortened from three minutes to two

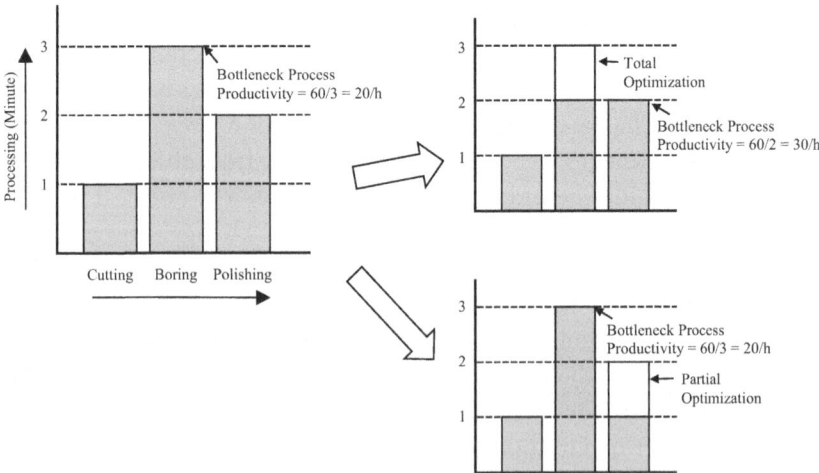

Fig. 3.5 Total optimization and partial optimization. (Source: Created by the author)

minutes, the capacity of the production line will improve by 50% without any *Kaizen* directed toward the other two processes. In contrast, shortening the processing time of the polishing process by 50% will not change the capacity of the production line. In this particular case, *Kaizen* for the cutting or polishing processes is partial optimization as such *Kaizen* does not lead to *Kaizen* of the whole process. However, *Kaizen* of the boring process is almost total optimization to improve the productivity of the production line even though it is only *Kaizen* for one process. To ensure that *Kaizen* leads to improvement of the company performance, *Kaizen* should focus on the bottleneck work, process, or department. If *Kaizen* for partial optimization is found to be helpful for the vitalization and/or capacity development of the workplace, this type of *Kaize*n should receive the first priority. Similarly, the viewpoint of a bottleneck is quite useful for *Kaizen* for the product quality. What is important for *Kaizen* for the product or service quality is to begin with the most serious quality-related problem.

3.3.2 Four Guidelines for *Kaizen* Management

5. Strong commitment by the owner is essential for successful *Kaizen.*

Compared to the Six Sigma and so on, *Kaizen* is believed to be a bottom-up approach, making the best use of the own initiative of front-line workers. This understanding is partly but not completely correct. Let us assume a situation where *Kaizen* activities start in each department following a kick-off meeting at which the owner expresses his expectations for *Kaizen*. If the owner subsequently adopts a stance of waiting for positive results to emerge on the grounds that "*Kaizen* is a bottom-up activity," his expectations will not be met. It must be pointed out that leadership is responsible for the (1) presentation of a vision to be pursued by all employees, (2) promotion of motivation, and (3) achievement of the task. In this context, commitment is a concept congruent with the (2) promotion of motivation. To be more precise, it is essential for the owner to show to the employees constant interests in as well as commitment to *Kaizen* by means of listening to production floor workers about their progress, encouraging their efforts, and, in some cases, making decisions to solve important problems on the production floor. It is also essential for the top executive to personally attend meetings where *Kaizen* achievements are reported, to comment on reports, and to encourage further efforts. This is because there is a strong link between the strength of the commitment of the owner to *Kaizen* and the actual scale of *Kaizen* achievement.

6. *Kaizen* is for both change at the production floor and human resources development.

Kaizen follows a bottom-up approach combined with a gentle top-down approach. However, if *Kaizen* is based on impulse, it is neither very effective nor efficient. *Kaizen* often follows the steps listed below after it has become a familiar practice on the production floor. Those in bold are particularly important activities.

(a) ***Kaizen* kick-off**
(b) **Implementation of the 5S**
(c) **Formulation of a body** (i.e., QCC or cross-functional team) **to implement *Kaizen***
(d) **Training on the basic concept and proceedings of *Kaizen***
(e) Establishment of a suggestion system
(f) *Kaizen* of *Muda* where problems appear easy to solve
(g) Improvement of the work
(h) Change in the layout
(i) **Elimination of seven *Muda***

Out of the above nine steps, (a), (c), and (d) are steps focusing on mind-set change and readiness of the workers. The implementation of 5S in step (b) also promotes a *Kaizen* mind-set as described in (iii) of 3.2.2. Step (c) is the formulation of an implementing body of *Kaizen* that can provide opportunities for mutual stimulation and learning among co-workers, which is an essential process of human development. At step (d), workers can learn the basic concept and proceedings that capture the meaning of *Kaizen*, aims, basic ways of thinking, and methodologies. Step (e) also has the effect of sustaining workers' understanding that the current state can be improved as well as their efforts to find a trigger for improvement. Even in steps (g), (h), and (i), momentum and knowledge on *Kaizen* can be shared among departments of the company if a session on *Kaizen* experience sharing is organized periodically. In these ways, *Kaizen* is a process carried out by a pair of wheels of *Kaizen* focusing on material (quality, productivity, cost, and delivery) and people.

Kōnosuke Matsushita, the founder of Panasonic, a world-famous Japanese manufacturer of household electrical appliances (Matsushita 2006), made a well-known remark, "Our company is where we develop people. We also make electrical appliances." His statement clearly indicates a corporate objective which places human resources development and product manufacturing on the same level. The book *Fundamentals of QC Circle* (JUSE 1980), referred to as the bible for QC circle activities, lists on its opening page the three basic principles of QC circle activities, as shown in Fig. 3.6. QC circle activities aim at encouraging self-development and mutual development to improve the capacity of all circle members (corresponding to No. 1 on the list) by means of independently solving workplace problems related to products and jobs through group activities (No. 3 on the list), thereby creating a pleasant and vital workplace (No. 2 on the list).

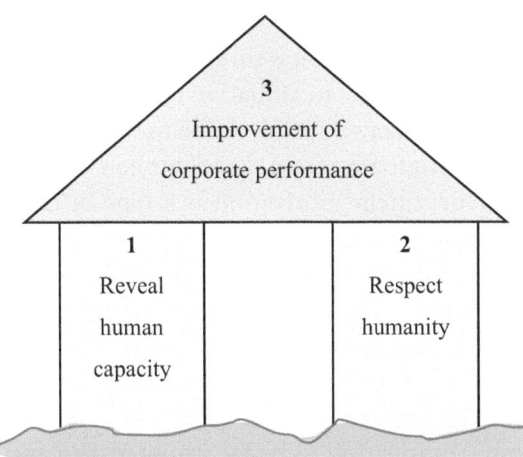

Fig. 3.6 Basic principles of QC circle activities. (Source: Created by the author based on "Fundamentals of QC Circle (1980)," JUSE Press, Ltd.)

7. Once surplus manpower is generated through labor-saving by *Kaizen*, excellent employees should be picked out and assigned to prepare for the launch of a new product and to pursue further *Kaizen*

Kaizen of productivity generates surplus manpower on the production floor. This situation leads to the question of who should be removed. There are typically two options to deal with this situation. One is to make the surplus workers redundant for their inferior work-related competence. This is probably the worst option as the remaining workers are unlikely to further cooperate with *Kaizen*. This option must be avoided at all costs. A better way of labor-saving is to pick out excellent workers from the production floor and to assign them to more creative jobs, such as leaders of *Kaizen* on the production floor and leaders of the launch of a new product. Such assignments make the picked workers realize that they have been assessed as excellent workers, while the morale of other front-line workers is not adversely affected.

8. Motivation to implement *Kaizen*

Sustaining interest in *Kaizen* is essential to ensure the continuity and ultimate success of *Kaizen*. What is important to sustain this interest is the motivation of those implementing *Kaizen*. According to the psychology of learning, motivation has three levels, ranging from economic motivation at the lowest level to affiliation and achievement motivation at the highest level (Ichikawa 1995). Affiliation motivation is a type of motivation which originates from good human relationships in the workplace and achievement motivation is a type of motivation which upholds a relatively high objective, and which tries to overcome obstacles to achieve the objective. Once motivation of a lower level is satisfied, motivation at the next level becomes stronger. Small group activities often used for *Kaizen* play an important role in satisfying affiliation and achievement motivation, but they may not be effective enough to continue *Kaizen*. In developing countries, it is fairly common for economic motivation to be far stronger than anticipated.[10]

---

[10] A public servant who has become a *Kaizen* consultant appears to have strong achievement motivation and intrinsic motivation, but many are seeking the opportunity to change their jobs because

Motivation is further divided into extrinsic and intrinsic motivations. The former is the result of stimulation by means of evaluation, reward, punishment, or imposition by someone other than the person concerned. In contrast, intrinsic motivation is the result of one's own inner interest, attention, and/or drive. Intrinsic motivation is believed to be favorable from the viewpoint of perpetuity or personal growth, but extrinsic motivation has a very strong impact in developing countries.

A system to distribute the effects of *Kaizen* has profound effect in developing countries. This system is related with extrinsic motivation working on economic motivation. One example is as follows:

1. The target of *Kaizen*, for example, is to decrease the amount of defective products by half, which may bring additional income estimated as ($20,000).
2. If the abovementioned target was completed, profit derived by *Kaizen* would be allocated to employees at a predetermined rate, for example, 60% of the yield from decreasing product (actual $21,000 x 0.6 = $12,600).
3. The abovementioned two items are contracted between management and a representative of employees at the kick-off meeting of *Kaizen* as a pre-arranged agreement on how to assess the *Kaizen* effects and how to distribute the increased profit between the management and workers.

3.4 Advantages and Challenges of *Kaizen*

This section explores the advantages and challenges of transferring *Kaizen* to developing countries, particularly in Africa. They are divided into inherent advantages and opportunities.

---

of a salary gap of almost double between the public and private sectors. The more excellent they are, the more readily they move to a private company when the conditions are met. As a result, the job turnover is as high as 15% in some countries in a year ("*Kaizen* Knowledge-Sharing Seminar" sponsored by JICA, First Seminar in Ethiopia in 2016 and Second Seminar in Kenya in 2017).

3.4.1 Inherent Advantages of *Kaizen* Technologies

For the implementation of *Kaizen*, such methodologies and tools as the 5S, 7 QC tools, and QC story are available as easy-to-learn and easy-to-use kits which are of great value for problem-solving. There are also many practical guidebooks on how to apply these methodologies and tools. For example, a guidebook on the 7 QC tools explains not only how to use a control chart, cause and effect diagram, check sheet, histogram, stratification, and scatter diagram but also which seven tools should be used in each step of a QC story.

The 5S is a *Kaizen* methodology which is often used at the beginning of *Kaizen* because it is considered easy-to-start. The 5S can be described as a simple procedure. However, when we understand that the proper implementation of the simple 5S has pervasive effects on improved quality and productivity,[11] surfacing of *Muda*, vitalization of the workplace, and fostering of people's *Kaizen* mind, we understand that the 5S is a technology with an unexpectedly long reach. The next common step is to eliminate *Muda*. The concept of *Muda* is both broad and deep.

Many *Kaizen* technologies do not demand a large fund. In general, the borrowing rate of interest is high in developing countries, and it is not unusual for private banks to charge an annual interest rate of 20%. Although the interest rate charged by public financial institutions is lower than that, the available public funds for lending are usually too limited to meet the entire funding demand of companies for loans. For SMEs, the borrowing procedure is often complicated and time-consuming even before the question of the interest rate coming into play, making it extremely difficult for them to access both private and public financial institutions. The need to increase investment or working capital for the purpose of increasing the production capacity must be met by funds in hand or by borrowing from relatives and friends. This means that SMEs often must pass over immediate business opportunities because of funding constraints. *Kaizen*, however, usually does not require large funding as it seeks rational ways of thinking rather than money. Many companies

---

[11] In the case of SMEs, productivity often increases by 10–30% with positive effects on quality as well.

start *Kaizen* in appreciation of this fact. At those factories where *Kaizen* is thoroughly implemented, old machinery, which has passed its depreciation period, and machinery remodelled to have a higher function than the processing capacity stated in the catalogue are in operation. These are examples of reducing the need for investment by *Kaizen* to implement appropriate TPM and to establish and observe the standard work.

3.4.2 Opportunities for *Kaizen* Transfer

As private initiatives, Japanese companies planning to outsource their production to an East Asian country firstly transfer their production technologies, including Japanese-style *Kaizen* technologies, to a local outsourcing subcontractor. This is followed by direct investment to start production at a factory of its local subsidiary or joint-venture company. Local workers at this factory learn Japanese-style production methods and *Kaizen* technologies through QC circle activities, OJT, and sometimes training in Japan. Some of these workers may become owners of their own businesses and implement previously learned *Kaizen* ideas and methods. The transfer of *Kaizen* technologies often occurs when a Japanese subsidiary outsources production of parts to a local factory. In addition, as described in Chap. 2, there is a long history of assistance for *Kaizen* in developing countries by JICA, an international cooperation agency of Japan.

Kaizen at manufacturing sites has been an important element leading to high economic growth in Japan. Needless to say, it is important to harmonize product development, marketing, business strategy, other innovations, and investment with various policies, including fiscal, foreign exchange, labor, and education policies. When other conditions are harmonized with economic growth in this manner, *Kaizen* can be a powerful leading force for economic growth. The relationship between *Kaizen* and the economy is not solely a causal relationship as the reverse causality of economic growth stimulating *Kaizen* is also possible. Companies that introduce *Kaizen* tend to adopt an assertive business stance, achieving significant growth of their business performance. *Kaizen* is acutely needed by conservative companies whose business performance is declining.

However, the reality tends to be the opposite as these companies tend to be reluctant to introduce *Kaizen*. To summarize, there is a two-way causation between *Kaizen* and economic growth: while the dissemination and expansion of *Kaizen* leads to economic growth, economic growth leads to the dissemination and expansion of *Kaizen*. In other words, *Kaizen* and economic growth proceed in tandem.

3.4.3 Challenges of *Kaizen* Transfer

How to develop capable organization as a promoter of *Kaizen* is a subject issue for examination when *Kaizen* is due for further expansion. Business consulting is an independent professional advisory service aimed at assisting a business owner and his/her organization to achieve the purpose and targets of the organization by means of solving problems of business management, taking opportunities to widen the knowledge possessed by the organization, and implementing any necessary reforms.[12] However, in many cases, consultation service for *Kaizen* promotion to a specific company is implemented in a limited way for reasons of insufficient quality and quantity of consultants in developing countries. Therefore, the development of capable consulting organizations that can respond to wide range of demand is a critical challenge. These organizations should be structured and developed based on the breadth of the anticipated activities and number of consultants, as described below.

Four perspectives must be taken into consideration when determining the desirable form of a consulting organization. The first perspective is to structure an organization based on the type of business as a target. Manufacturing, construction, and services are examples of business types. Manufacturing can be further classified into textiles, garments, agricultural product processing, woodworking, metals, machinery, chemicals, and so on. The second perspective is based on the purpose of technology used for *Kaizen*. To be more precise, the consulting service is classified based on the expertise regarding quality, productivity, or other target areas of *Kaizen*. The third perspective classifies the consulting service

---

[12] The definition given by Kubr (2005, p. 12) is quoted here with some modifications.

based on the size of the client company or organization. What the author's consulting experience in Japan and the survey on consulting demands in Turkey suggest is that the smaller the size (business) of the client, the stronger the demand for a town-doctor type of consultant capable of offering a wide range of advice and assistance. In large companies, there is instead some need for consultants who can act as advisors to the top management. The fourth perspective relates to the idea of establishing a consulting organization as a fixed or flexible organization in response to client needs.

The priority among these four perspectives for the establishment of an actual consulting organization depends on the type of *Kaizen* service to be provided (5S, elimination of *Muda*, etc. with training, diagnosis, guidance, follow-up, etc.) and the number of consultants involved. There are four practically viable forms of consulting organization, as will be explained next (see Table 3.3).

Table 3.3 Forms of consulting organization

Type of organization	Target company	Services/tools to be provided	Number of staff (consultants)
a Start-up	Micro and small (enterprise)	5S	Several – ten
b Business type-specific (developed from research institute)	Medium size	QC, IE, PM (+ 5S)	50 or more (in-house consultants)
c Specialty-based	Large (company)	TQM, TPS, TPM (+ 5S + QC/IE/PM)	100 or more (in-house consultants)
d Flexible (business type-specific and specialty-based)	Medium and large size	(TQM/TPS/TPM + 5S + QC/IE/PM)	50 or more

Source: Created by the author

The specialty-based organization has a system to mobilize highly skilled consultants within the organizations (start-up, business type-specific, and flexible) to form a specialist department. Therefore, specialty-based organization can coexist with other types of organizations

The flexible organization can exist based on the business type-specific or specialty-based organization, which can form project teams in response to needs of clients. The members of the team are selected from staff consultants

- Start-up type organization
  This is a form of consulting organization brought in soon after the commencement of services for *Kaizen*. The targets for consultation are micro and small enterprises and the tool used for *Kaizen* is the 5S in most cases. The number of consultants involved varies from several up to ten, and the form of organization reflects neither the type of business nor the specialist field, such as quality or productivity.
- Business type-specific organization
  When the parent body of the organization assisting *Kaizen* is a research institute for industrial technologies, the form of consulting organization with 50 or more in-house consultants tends to have vertically divided consulting departments following the structure of the parent body designed to correspond to specific business types. The targets for assistance include medium-sized companies and QC, IE, and PM (preventive maintenance) are increasingly used as tools for *Kaizen*.
- Specialty-based organization
  When the targets for services include large companies, more advanced *Kaizen* services such as TQM, TPS, or TPM are required. Apart from a consulting department offering basic *Kaizen* technologies, this type of organization has developed specialist departments with consultants having specialist knowledge of quality, productivity, cost, and so on. At this stage, the number of in-house consultants is likely to exceed 100.
- Flexible organization
  Although both the business type-specific organization and specialty-based organization have their own advantages, they also have major disadvantages. The biggest disadvantage is their inability to respond quickly to clients' diverse needs for *Kaizen* services. For example, assume that company A, a client garment manufacturer, hopes to receive comprehensive assistance for *Kaizen* and that the introduction of advanced *Kaizen* technologies is required for a rapid increase in the company's productivity. Nevertheless, the maintenance of standards as a central tenet is sufficient as far as the quality aspect is concerned. In this case, it may be necessary to form a *Kaizen* project team for company A consisting of four consultants, that is, a consultant familiar with the garment industry, a consultant with rich experience in the sophisticated improvement of productivity, and two

basic level consultants, in order to maintain the quality standards while rapidly increasing productivity. This kind of response becomes feasible when an organization has 50 or more consultants.

In a situation in which a public organization that supports *Kaizen* is active in rural areas in addition to the metropolitan area, the town-doctor type consultants who can cover broad issues are to be assigned in its rural offices. In a head office of the organization, in addition to town-doctor type consultants for basic *Kaizen* activities, a consultant unit that employs experts on specific industry or *Kaizen* methodologies may be established in order to deal with advanced level *Kaizen* needs. In the consulting business field, while there are general consulting firms covering all types of business and specialist fields, there are also consulting firms specializing in specific types of businesses, such as finance and tourism, where viable consulting is only possible with in-depth knowledge of the industry concerned. There are also consulting firms specializing in specific functions, such as production control, marketing, human resources development, and so on. There are also examples of a single consulting firm having internal structures to provide services specializing in certain types of businesses or functions. The general practice is to arrange a flexible project team to cater to the particular needs of individual clients.

3.5 Concluding Remarks

Kaizen refers to a continuous activity to fill the gap between the current state and the ideal state. Japanese people who have a strong sense of *mottainai* or *Muda* imported many management technologies from the US to reduce *Muda*, that is, to proceed with *Kaizen*. These imported technologies were transformed to Japanese *Kaizen* technologies incorporating such small group activities as QC circle activities to make management technologies more effective. TPS, of which Japan is very proud, is quite different, in that its idea is directly opposite to Ford's production system in a number of aspects. There is no question that it has had a significant impact on the idea of *Kaizen*.

The 5S, 7 QC tools, and QC story are basic *Kaizen* tools. Meanwhile, TQM, TPS, and TPM are core *Kaizen* technologies, not unitary technologies but systems combining a number of technologies. Broadly defined, *Kaizen* includes both *Kaizen* using inherent technologies and *Kaizen* using management technologies, but narrowly defined *Kaizen* means *Kaizen* using management technologies alone. However, *Kaizen* for quality or for the preventive maintenance of machinery is difficult to proceed with solely using management technologies as substantial progress cannot be made without knowledge of inherent technologies. Because of this, it is desirable for a consultant team to include a consultant with detailed knowledge of inherent technologies.

Kaizen has four general features: (1) cost reduction through the rigorous elimination of *Muda*, (2) participation of front-line workers in *Kaizen* and enhancement of their morale and capabilities, (3) application of *Kaizen* in correspondence with the level of the company, and (4) prioritization of the rational use of available resources over innovation requiring sizable investment.

There are eight guidelines of *Kaizen* implementation: (1) importance of actual implementation, (2) on-the-spot observation rather than deskbound discussions, (3) consumer orientation and the principle of quality first, (4) focusing on the bottleneck, (5) strong commitment by the owner, (6) *Kaizen* as a process of human resources development, (7) labor-saving coupled with the promotion of excellent employees, and (8) appropriate distribution of *Kaizen* results for motivation.

There appear to be various reasons for the acceptance of *Kaizen* by many countries: (1) availability of easy-to-start *Kaizen* menus corresponding to different control levels, (2) availability of easy-to-use *Kaizen* technologies, (3) no need for large funding, (4) transfer of *Kaizen* technologies by Japanese companies, (5) dissemination of *Kaizen* through Japan's Official Development Assistance (ODA), and (6) tandem progress of economic growth and *Kaizen*. For further effective dissemination of *Kaizen* at an advanced level, the role of a consulting organization is crucial.

We believe that almost all of these reasons are applicable to African countries. The implication seems to be that in all likelihood, a large number of enterprises in Africa will take off by introducing *Kaizen* with a clear understanding of its value in practice.

References

Asahi Shinbun. (2013). *Toyota Shin Genba Shugi Keiei (Toyota New Genbaism Management)*. Asahi Shinbunsha.
Fujita, A. (1978). *IE no Kiso (Fundamental of IE)*. Tokyo: Kenpaku-sha.
Hosoya, K. (1984). *QC teki Monono Mikata, Kangaekata (Point of View and Thinking in Perspective of Quality Control)*. Tokyo: JUSE Press.
Ichikawa, S. (1995). *Gakushu to Kyoiku no Shinrigaku (Psychology of Learning Education)*. Tokyo: Iwanami-shoten.
Ishikawa, K. (1989). *Hinshitsu Kanri Nyumon A (Introduction to Quality Control A)*. Tokyo: JUSE Press.
Japan Management Association. (1980). *Toyota no Genba Kanri (Field-work Management in Toyota)*. Tokyo: JMA Management Center.
JIS Q 9024. (2003). *Keizokuteki Kaizen (Continuous Improvement)*. Tokyo: Japanese Industrial Standards.
Kubr, M. (2005). *Management Consulting: A guide to the profession* (4th ed.). Geneva: International Labour Organization.
Matsushita, K. (2006). *Hito wo Ikasu Keiei (Management to Vitalize Human Resource)*. Tokyo: PHP.
Monden, Y. (1985). *Toyota Sisutemu (Toyota System)*. Tokyo: Kodan-sha.
Nitta, M. (1999). *Kadai Tasseigata QC Story (QC Story for Task Achievement)*. Tokyo: JUSE Press.
Ohno, T. (1978). *Toyota Seisan Hoshiki (Toyota Production System)*. Tokyo: Diamond-sha.
QC Circle Headquarters (Ed.). (1980). *Fundamentals of QC Circles*. Tokyo: JUSE Press.
Shingo, S. (1980). *Toyota Seisan Hoshiki no IE teki Kosatsu (Consideration from IE on Toyota Production System)*. Tokyo: Nikkan Kogyo Shinbun-sha.
Suzuki, T. (1992). *Shin TPM Program: Kako, Kumitate (New TPM Deployment Program for Processing and Assembling)*. Tokyo: Japan Institute of Plant Maintenance.
Wada, K. (2009). *Monodukuri no Guwa (Mythology of Manufacturing)*. Nagoya: The University of Nagoya Press.

Open Access This chapter is licensed under the terms of the Creative Commons Attribution 4.0 International License (http://creativecommons.org/licenses/by/4.0/), which permits use, sharing, adaptation, distribution and reproduction in any medium or format, as long as you give appropriate credit to the original author(s) and the source, provide a link to the Creative Commons license and indicate if changes were made.

The images or other third party material in this chapter are included in the chapter's Creative Commons license, unless indicated otherwise in a credit line to the material. If material is not included in the chapter's Creative Commons license and your intended use is not permitted by statutory regulation or exceeds the permitted use, you will need to obtain permission directly from the copyright holder.

4

Kaizen and Standardization

Tsuyoshi Kikuchi and Momoko Suzuki

There are many methods and concepts of *Kaizen* that can be used to achieve quality and productivity improvements. Most of these originated in the West in line with the desire to improve production management. These were imported to Japan, improved and modified to suit the industrial climate and corporate culture of that country. Together with those aspects independently developed in Japan, they were further developed as *Kaizen*. As this was the driving force for high economic growth in post-war Japan, it became the focus of global attention. Specifically, its components of Quality Control (QC) circle activities, Total Quality

---

T. Kikuchi (✉)
Consulting Division, Japan Development Service Co., Ltd., Tokyo, Japan
e-mail: go-kikuchi@jds21.com

M. Suzuki
Industrial Development and Public Policy Department, Japan International Cooperation Agency, Tokyo, Japan
e-mail: Suzuki.Momoko@jica.go.jp

© The Author(s) 2018
K. Otsuka et al. (eds.), *Applying the Kaizen in Africa*,
https://doi.org/10.1007/978-3-319-91400-8_4

Control (TQC) or Total Quality Management (TQM),[1] Toyota Production System (TPS) and Total Productive Maintenance (TPM) are well-known.

The United States (US) thoroughly scrutinized *Kaizen*, especially in the 1980s, and attempted to improve and modify the parts of the concept originating in Japan to match the industrial climate and corporate culture of the US. Typical examples of such improved and modified methods are the Six Sigma, the Lean Production System and the Business Process Re-engineering (BPR) methods. These have not only resulted in positive achievements among companies in the US but also become widespread in European countries, in Asia and in the rest of the world.

Among these newly developed methods, the problem-solving phases, relevant tools and techniques of the Six Sigma approach gained the status of international standards in 2011 as the Quantitative Methods in Process Improvement—Six Sigma—Part 1: DMAIC Methodology (ISO 13053-1: 2011) and the Quantitative Methods in Process Improvement—Six Sigma—Part 2: Tools and Techniques (ISO 13053-2: 2011). In December 2015, the ISO added further international standards concerning the required specific levels of competency regarding Six Sigma and Lean Production for individuals and their organizations. The title is ISO 18404: 2015 Quantitative Methods in Process Improvement—Six Sigma—Competencies for Key Personnel and their Organizations in Relation to Six Sigma and Lean Implementation.

There seem to be two types of *Kaizen* in the world today: the type that has a background of supporting the post-war industrial development in Japan and the type that incorporates new ideas from Western countries while referring to the principles that originated in Japan. In this chapter, the former is

---

[1] "Total quality management practiced in Japan was conventionally called total quality control. However, control in English originally implies comparison with a standard, and does not mean the establishment of a standard or plan. As TQC deals with all aspects of business operation, it has become increasingly clear that the phrase "quality management" should be used to accurately convey the meaning of the phrase "quality control" in the Japanese language. As such, Japanese total quality control is now commonly called TQM in Western countries. The Union of Japanese Scientists and Engineers (JUSE) which is the primary organization for the promotion of TQC in Japan declared the change of the phrase from TQC to TQM in 1996" (Japan Industrial Management Association 2002/2012).

referred to as "Japanese-style *Kaizen*[2]" and the latter as "Western-style *Kaizen*." Which type is best in terms of suitability and effectiveness depends on the industrial climate and corporate culture of the country in question, or the specific judgment of top executives (Kurosaki and Otsuka 2015, 201; Stern 2016, xvi). This is our own conclusion based on our experience of involvement in various *Kaizen* projects. Accordingly, a comparison is made between the characteristics of Japan's TQM and Six Sigma, between TPS and the Lean Production System and between BPR and *Kaizen* in this chapter, but the relative superiority of one over the other is not discussed.

The important issues to note in this chapter are that there are "Japanese-style *Kaizen*" and "Western-style" *Kaizen* and that the Western-style, incorporating such approaches as Six Sigma and Lean Production, has been taken up by the ISO to develop relevant international standards. It is also important to investigate what impacts these international standards have on *Kaizen* projects assisted by Japan International Cooperation Agency (JICA) or any other international donors and what the desirable future direction for Africa is in relation to this methodology.

4.1 *Kaizen* Modified in the US

Japan originally learned production management technologies (the concepts of which were collectively called *Kaizen* in Japan, even though there was no exact definition of this term[3]) from the West, mainly the US, improved these to suit Japan's industrial climate and corporate culture, redeveloped them, disseminated them throughout Japan first[4] and then

---

[2] Since "*Kaizen*" was originally developed in Japan, there may be no need to say "Japanese-style *Kaizen*" because "*Kaizen*" itself already has the meaning of "Japanese-style" or "Japanese-born." However, one of the intentions in this chapter is to compare "*Kaizen* originated in Japan" with "*Kaizen* modified or redeveloped in Western countries", the term "Japanese-style *Kaizen*" instead of "*Kaizen*" is therefore used to assist readers to easily understand the comparison. In addition to the two types of *Kaizen*, the term "*Kaizen*" has a general meaning as used in this chapter.

[3] A new concept of the definition of *Kaizen* was established in Chap. 1 of this book.

[4] In Japan, private organizations played a prominent role in the learning of production management technologies from the West, improved them to suit the industrial climate in Japan and disseminated them to companies in Japan. Among others, the Union of Japanese Scientists and Engineers (JUSE), Japan Productivity Center (JPC) and Japan Management Association (JMA) fulfilled this role, especially after World War II (Kikuchi 2012).

re-exported them along with the overseas expansion of Japanese companies. Meanwhile, the West took notice of the improved, redeveloped or invented *Kaizen*, and re-learned *Kaizen* in turn, improving or re-arranging it to suit its own industrial climate and corporate culture, or systematizing it to achieve positive results in Western countries, and then spreading it worldwide. Western-style *Kaizen* is of course known in Japan and has been adopted by some Japanese companies. However there appear to have been mixed outcomes from adopting this style, as the performance of some Japanese companies has not necessarily improved. The one thing which is certain right now is that local *Kaizen* methods and concepts have taken deep root among Japanese companies.

Six Sigma, Lean Production System and Business Process Re-engineering (BPR) are typical *Kaizen* methods which have been improved, redeveloped or systematized in the US. Each of these is briefly described below, and then a comparison of the characteristics of Western-style and Japanese-style *Kaizen* is attempted.

4.1.1 Six Sigma

Six Sigma is a problem-solving method developed by Motorola, Inc. of the US in the early 1980s, when the company was trying to find a way to reduce the number of defective products it was making.[5] It is said that this method was invented with reference to Japan's QC circle activities, factory floor *Kaizen* activities and TQC, TQM[6] and TPS.[7] According to

---

[5] In 1979, Motorola was planning to enter the pocket bell market in Japan but was surprised to find that the level of defects in its own products was much higher than that of Japanese manufacturers. Six Sigma is said to originate from Motorola's subsequent intensive quality improvement activities (Ito 2001).

[6] TQM (Total Quality Management) is a system used to economically produce goods or services where the quality meets the demands of purchasers. For the effective implementation of quality management, the participation and cooperation of all members of a company, ranging from the top executives to managers, supervisors and workers, are essential at all stages of business activities, including market research, R&D, product planning, design, preparation for production, purchasing and subcontracting, manufacturing, inspection, sales and after-sales service as well as finance, personnel affairs and education. Quality management implemented in this manner is called total quality management or company-wide quality management (Japan Industrial Management Association 2002/2012).

[7] TPS (Toyota Production System) is a general term to describe the production management system developed by Toyota Motor Corporation. As it emphasizes the maximum elimination of *muda*

the Six Sigma method, the problem-solving process is divided into four phases, that is, "measure," "analyze," "improve" and "control," and is called MAIC by combining the initial letters of these four phases. A team of experts, which is unique to Six Sigma, works to solve a problem or task. For the formation of such a team, the top executive is the supreme leader, but the key members of the team are experts with specific education and training. These experts have the titles of Master Black Belt (MBB), Black Belt (BB) or Green Belt (GB) depending on their capability. The overall approach characterized by these features is called Six Sigma.[8]

Using the Six Sigma method, Motorola improved its business performance and was awarded the Malcolm Baldrige National Quality Award (MBNQA) in 1988. This award, given by the President of the US, was established by Congress in 1987 to raise awareness of the importance of quality management and to acknowledge that US companies were successfully implementing a quality management system.[9] The granting of this prominent award to Six Sigma made the method known throughout the US. The General Electric (GE) Company, in particular, showed much interest in it.

John Francis Jack Welch, Chairman of GE, introduced Six Sigma to the company at the end of 1995 to successfully carry out GE's wide-ranging quality program. Six Sigma was introduced not only in the manufacturing departments but also in the non-production business departments throughout the company (Financial Times 2001). What was emphasized during the application process was the clear definition of who their customers were and what the focused problems and issues for improvement were. This approach led to the establishment of the DMAIC method, with the addition of D (define) before MAIC. The Six Sigma

---

(waste), it is sometimes called "Lean Production" (Japan Industrial Management Association 2002/2012).
[8] Sigma (σ) or standard deviation (SD) is a statistical term to indicate variation in the distribution of a set of data values, meaning the probability of the occurrence of errors or mistakes. Six Sigma is the level of the occurrence rate of errors or mistakes of 3.4 times per million. In practice it is difficult to achieve this level; therefore, Six Sigma should be understood as a name based on an ideal target of reducing errors or mistakes infinitely close to zero.
[9] The award is named after Malcolm Baldrige, who proposed the program and was the US Secretary of Commerce at the time. The award targets six sectors, that is, manufacturing, service, small business, education, health care and non-profit (https://www.nist.gov/baldrige/baldrige-award).

method of GE was systematized as a method to solve problems faced by all departments of GE. In other words, it became a *Kaizen* method to deal with the business challenges faced by GE and greatly contributed to enhancement of the company's business performance. The achievement of Six Sigma at GE became widely known not only in the US but also in Europe and Asia, accelerating its worldwide diffusion. We compare the characteristics of Six Sigma with TQM. As Six Sigma is said to have originated from TQM, there are obviously similarities between them as well as differences, as shown in Table 4.1, which is self-explanatory.

4.1.2 Lean Production System

The Lean Production System (or simply "Lean") was developed in the US as a method to thoroughly eliminate *muda* (waste) with reference to the Toyota Production System (TPS). This method was popularized by James P. Womack, Daniel T. Jones and Daniel Roos in 1996 (Pepper and Spedding 2010; Womack and Jones 1996). It has since become widely known and used by not only American companies but also European companies.

Lean is said to hardly differ from TPS. For example, the Glossary of Production and Manufacturing Management Terms edited by the Japan Industrial Management Association (2002/2012) explains that "the Lean Production System is a synonym for the Toyota Production System or Kanban System which puts just-in-time (i.e., the production or supply of what is needed when it is needed, and in the quantity needed) into practice." Even the Home Page of Toyota Motor Corporation treats them as the same system.[10] However, some researchers claim that these systems differ in several respects. Nakano (2017)[11] is one such researcher and he explains the differences between TPS and Lean as outlined below (see also Figs. 4.1 and 4.2).

---

[10] Toyota Motor Corporation's vehicle production system is a way of "making things" that is sometimes referred to as the "Lean manufacturing system" or "just-in-time (JIT) system," cited from Toyota's Home Page, on 1 June 2017.

[11] Nakano worked at Toyota Central R&D Labs., Inc. for 25 years and has conducted research on production management and production systems in different countries (Nakano 2017).

Table 4.1 Similarities and differences between Six Sigma and TQM

Similarities and differences	Six Sigma	TQM
Similarities	Systematic improvement of quality for growth Action guidelines for quality management, including the importance of a top management and customer-oriented approach Use of statistical data Essence of implementation steps (both have their own steps for improvement)	
Organization of improvement activities	Organization formed by dedicated members: <Six Sigma system> Champion (president) Promotion manager (director) Sponsor Master Black Belt Black Belt (practical team leader) Green Belt Yellow Belt	Everyday organizational set up as the basis: <QC circle (small group)> Leader (selected from the circle members) Circle members (front-line workers)
Customer satisfaction	Seeking customer satisfaction to achieve a profit (profit oriented)	Achievement of customer satisfaction leads to profit (customer oriented)
Decision on implementation theme	Top-down approach	Bottom-up (+ top-down) approach
Steps of implementation	Standard phases of implementation: DMAIC 1. Define: define the problem 2. Measure: collect data to determine the current situation 3. Analyze: identify causes through data analysis 4. Improve: devise and test hypothetical solutions 5. Control: sustain successful solutions	Self-motivating *Kaizen* process: <problem-solving type QC story>[a] 1. Select the theme 2. Establish the current situation and target 3. Formulate an action plan 4. Analyze causes 5. Examine and implement solutions 6. Verify the effects 7. Standardize and establish a control 8. Reflect and identify future tasks

Source: Prepared by the author following Yamada (2006/2015) for the framework of this table, and following Yamada et al. (2012), Uchida (1995/2006), Japanese Standards Association (2017) and Union of Japanese Scientists and Engineers (2001)

[a] There are three types of QC story, that is, "problem-solving QC story," "task-achieving QC story" and "policy-implementing QC story" (Yamada et al. 2012)

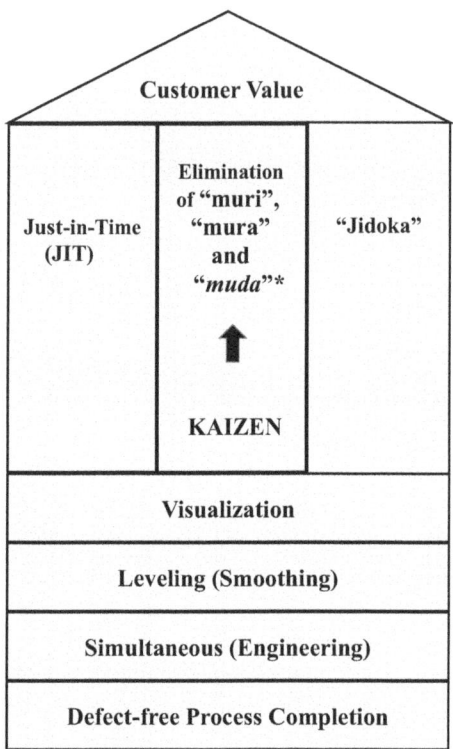

Fig. 4.1 Basic concept of the Toyota Production System (TPS). (Source: Nakano (2017, 13)). *Elimination of "muri," "mura" and "muda": Toyota has identified as "mudas" seven types of non-value-adding waste in business or manufacturing process, that is, *overproduction, waiting (time on hand), unnecessary transport or conveyance, over-processing or incorrect processing, excess inventory, unnecessary movement* and *defects*. Liker (2004, 28–29) added an eighth waste to the abovementioned seven wastes, that is, *unused employee creativity*)

According to Toyota's home page, the Toyota Production System was established based on the two concepts of "just-in-time" and "*jidoka*" (automation with a human touch).[12] The former means "making only what is needed, when it is needed, and in the amount needed." The latter

---

[12] Kiichiro Toyoda established Toyota Automotive Company on the philosophy and management approach of his father, Sakichi Toyoda, but added his own innovations. "For example, while Sakichi Toyoda was the father of what would become the *jidoka* pillar of the Toyota Production System, Just-in-Time was Kiichiro Toyoda's contribution (Liker 2004, 18).

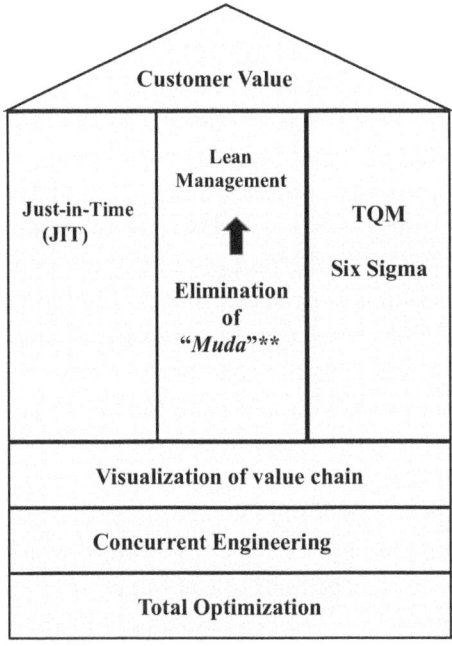

Fig. 4.2 The basic concept of a Lean Production System. (Source: Nakano (2017, 17). ** Elimination of *"muda"*: Womack and Jones (1996) add one more *"muda"* to the seven that Toyota identified as non-value-adding wastes, that is, *service which does not meet the customer's requirement*)

means that "if any equipment malfunctions or defective part is discovered, the affected machine stops automatically, and the operators cease production and correct the problem." Under TPS, daily *Kaizen* efforts are made to eliminate "muri, mura and *muda*." There should be no "muri" or unrealizable task in work practices, any "mura" or unevenness in production activities and their results and no *"muda"* which means a lack of customer value or added value. TPS adopts such methods as "visualization," "smoothing," "simultaneous engineering" and "defect-free process completion" to produce concepts, policies, activities and results related to "just-in-time," "jidoka," "muri, mura and *muda*" and *"Kaizen"* (Nakano 2017, 13–14).

"Visualization" is a powerful method to make stakeholders share a common understanding by clarifying problems and factors on the production floor. "Smoothing" means the elimination of variations by means of making the work load of each process of a production system even and is also called "levelling." "Simultaneous engineering" means simultaneous merchandise planning, product design, production system design and marketing planning activities in-house or in cooperation with companies in the supply chain. The purpose of this method is to shorten the development period, to lower the cost and to develop high-quality products and services. "Defect-free process completion" means the concept as well as activity of upholding the creation of a process whereby inferior products are neither produced nor sent to the following process. In other words, it treasures the idea of "completing the quality within a process" (Nakano 2017, 14–15).

Compared to Fig. 4.1 for TPS, the pillar "jidoka" in TPS is replaced by TQM and Six Sigma in Fig. 4.2 for Lean, both of which were developed in the West. In Lean management, the elimination of *muda* takes precedence over the elimination of muri and mura. To materialize Lean, the value stream mapping method[13] is frequently used to make "the value chain visualized." "Concurrent engineering" is an approach then used to shorten the development period by making several sections work concurrently.

One special characteristic of TPS worth mentioning here is that Toyota heavily invests in the education and training of not only future leaders but also shop-floor workers. Toyota applies its production system used at home, that is, TPS, to all its factories throughout the world, regardless of the different industrial climates or corporate cultures in other countries. A thorough understanding of the methods and tools of TPS among all employees, ranging from top executives to front-line workers, is the result of focused and unsparing investment in education and training. One phrase which is often heard at Toyota is "Toyota makes people before making cars" (Liker 2004). In other words, Toyota may represent an exceptional case where it has successfully exported its own corporate culture to countries with different industrial climates and corporate cultures from Japan.

---

[13] The value stream mapping method is designed to visualize value chain from the beginning of product or service through the customers (Nakano 2017, 54).

4.1.3 Business Process Re-engineering (BPR)

The basic idea of BPR is for an organization to identify its key business processes and to shed any excess fat from these processes to make them efficient. The background of this idea is the discovery of the necessity to fundamentally review and re-design the business organization whereby business processes are segmented and to carry out a series of reforms to produce value for end customers.

BPR spread throughout the world with the publication of "Re-engineering the Corporation" by James Chamy, co-founder of the consulting company CSC Index, and Michael Hammer, an electrical engineer and former professor of computer science at the Massachusetts Institute of Technology (MIT). They defined re-engineering as "the fundamental rethinking and radical redesign of business processes to achieve dramatic improvements in critical measures of performance such as cost, quality, service and speed." Its roots lay in the research carried out by MIT from 1984 to 1989 on "Management in the 1990s" (Financial Times 2001). It is said that these two authors referred to many fashionable business ideas, such as TQM, just-in-time, customer service, time-based competition and Lean manufacturing, at the time to come up with the idea of BPR, but it is clear that many of these ideas were derived from the *Kaizen* methods and concepts that had originated in Japan.

What then are the similarities and differences between BPR and the *Kaizen* that originated in Japan? One similarity is that both set out a target to be achieved. As described later, however, the concept and the method for setting out the target are different. The crucial aspects of the target are that both BPR and *Kaizen* are approaches to enhance customer satisfaction, and thus both aim at eliminating *muda* in business activities and business processes to improve efficiency. However, one important difference is that while BPR has a strong connotation of fundamentally reviewing and improving the business process or reforming the business process at once, *Kaizen* involves gradual and continual improvement with the existing business process being largely maintained. For the setting of a target, while BPR designs the ideal situation, *Kaizen* identifies the gap between the reality and the ideal (target) as a problem to be solved. The approach is thus strongly conscious of the need to improve quality along with the elimination of *muda*.

BPR's handling of workers can be harsh, as illustrated by the phrase used by its proponents: "peripheral processes (and, therefore, peripheral people) must be discarded. Don't automate; obliterate."[14] In contrast, the basic of *Kaizen* is to respect people.[15] The proponents of BPR also state that "scoping to scale" in re-engineering means more than the simple change in individual business processes and that true re-engineering targets the entire organization or is a recipe for company reform (Financial Times 2001). In this sense, BPR aims at achieving total optimization. In contrast, *Kaizen* can be described as an attempt to achieve total optimization through the piling-up of partial optimization successes. Table 4.2 summarizes the above descriptions of BPR and *Kaizen*.

4.1.4 Background of Japanese-Style *Kaizen* and Western-Style *Kaizen*: Differences in Industrial Climate and Corporate Culture

At the outset, it must be asserted that whether *Kaizen* methods or concepts are suitable or effective for a company depends on the industrial climate of the country involved, and its corporate culture, as well as judgment by the executives of the company in question. Both Motorola and GE became aware that Japan's TQM which was born in a different industrial climate and its corporate culture did not easily fit with the industrial climate and corporate culture in the US. Because of this, it is essential to clarify the differences between the industrial climate and corporate culture in Japan and those in the US and the background for the emergence of Western-style *Kaizen*.

Compared to Japanese top executives, those in the US are said to be required to produce results in a shorter time. Because of this, they are reluctant to resort to a bottom-up approach to accumulate small *Kaizen* achievements to ultimately produce a substantial result, as in the case of

---

[14] One of the problems of BPR was "that re-engineering appeared inhumane. In some cases, people were treated appallingly in the name of re-engineering" (Financial Times 2001).
[15] *Kaizen* activities are led by a QC circle (small group). One of the basic principles of a QC circle is "to respect humanity to create a meaningful and buoyant workplace" (QC Circle Headquarters 1970/2012).

Table 4.2 Similarities and differences between BPR and Kaizen

	BPR	Kaizen
Similarities	Setting of a target	
	Enhancement of customer satisfaction	
	Improvement of efficiency and effects of business activities and business processes	
	Elimination of *muda* (non-added value), that is, in particular to improve efficiency	
Process	Completely reviewed at once, that is, re-engineering and re-design	Continuous improvement of existing processes
Viewpoint of reviewing processes	Re-engineering of processes from the viewpoint of customers	Quality improvement and cost reduction to enhance customer satisfaction
Involvement of management and front-line workers	Re-engineering is conducted with the decision taken by and under the strong leadership of the top executive. In this sense, BPR is management-led task achievement or a top-down approach	*Kaizen* activities are implemented by a QC circle comprising employees although these activities follow the philosophy and policy expressed by the top executive. In this sense, *Kaizen* is a bottom-up with a top-down approach
	Participation of front-line workers are limited	Front-workers' participation is emphasized
Optimization target	Total optimization	Total optimization through accumulation of partial optimization

Source: Prepared by the author with reference to the Financial Times (2001) and Stern (2016)

Japan. Instead, top executives in the US tend to aim at finding a breakthrough as quickly as possible.[16] Therefore, they have little choice but to employ a top-down business approach. Moreover, the educational standard of factory workers in the US is not particularly high, and top executives therefore do not expect these workers to have the ability to propose solutions or to solve problems. This situation is also assumed to strengthen the preference for a top-down approach.

There is another reason why American executives take a top-down approach. Dynamism in the labor market works in the US more than in Japan, where a lifelong employment system still exists. Thus, American executives seem to have no other choice to take a top-down approach with strong decision-making due to large turnover of labor.[17] On manufacturing floors in Japan, QC circle activities by workers (small group activities) are trusted as well as respected by top executives. The high educational standard of workers and strong sense of loyalty among workers to their own company due to the lifelong employment system[18] are some of the reasons for the strong trust of top executives in their workers. Nevertheless, even though there is a strong trend among Japanese companies to opt for the bottom-up approach, this does not mean that workers practicing QC circle activities conduct them arbitrarily, or away from the framework of company policies. In short, the seemingly independent activities of workers are performed within the framework of company policies with the understanding of the top executive. Presentation meetings for the results of QC circle activities are attended by the top executives who commend or even give a special reward to those groups achieving excellent results. Therefore, it is safe to say that the business

---

[16] "Because Western firms tend to focus on breakthrough innovation and are weak at continuously improving in small amounts, this has been the focus of teaching *Kaizen* to Western firms" (Liker 2004, 26).

[17] According to Liker (2004, Preamble to Japanese version), it is very difficult for Americans with strong individualism to standardize their works. They prefer to be treated as independent individuals who decide their own approach by themselves. Efforts and a sense of discipline to learn excellent approaches or manners from others are therefore lacking in most American work places. In contrast, it is very natural for Japanese to follow the best approach which the whole team believes or selects in their companies. It is one of the teamwork processes in Japan.

[18] Japan is a country with a high educational standard and very high literacy rate. Its lifelong employment system nurtures a sense of loyalty to the company (Nakano 2017).

activities of these Japanese companies are performed with company-wide full participation from top to bottom.[19] It may thus be more apt to describe corporate management in Japan as being based on both the bottom-up and top-down approaches.

Six Sigma activities are conducted in a top-down manner, and the principal body for the implementation of these activities is a Cross-Functional Team (CFT) made up of members from different departments. In the case of QC circle activities (small group activities) which are the mainstay of *Kaizen* activities in Japan, the group members continually find new problems every day at the same production floor and solve such problems internally using their combined wisdom. While a CFT in Six Sigma disbands when the problems are solved, QC circle activities continue all the time. However, it must be noted that a CFT is formed even in Japan when there is a need to solve inter-departmental problems.

As shown by the Six Sigma activities, *Kaizen* activities in the US emphasize original data and quantification; however, it would not be correct to say that such activities in Japan ignore statistical data. Rather, it is simply that *Kaizen* activities in Japan strongly emphasize facts (at the production floor).[20] Such activities in the US, especially Six Sigma activities, use detailed instructions to employees along with strict manuals. In contrast, in Japan they demand that workers tackle new problems almost daily that cannot be dealt with by the available manuals. To do this, all group members must rack their brains compared to their US counterparts, who conduct their *Kaizen* activities as instructed or as shown in manuals. For example, ISO 18404 specifies the methods and tools to be used for different stages of *Kaizen* or, more specifically, each phase of

---

[19] "Top executives and managers consider QC circle activities to be important activities for human resources development and vitalization of the workplace, practice such company-wide activities as TQM themselves and provide guidance and assistance aimed at the full participation of all while respecting their human qualities so that QC circle activities can contribute to improvement of the quality as well as development of their companies" (QC Circle Headquarters 1970/2012).

[20] According to Ohno (1978), the founder of TPS, "Data is of course important for manufacturing, but I place the greatest emphasis on facts." Liker (2004, 226) wrote that "To Ohno, the big difference (between data and facts) is that data is one step removed from the process, merely 'indicators' of what is happening. What you want to do is to verify the on-the-scene facts of a situation. Mr. Ohno's approach is very much like that of a forensic scientist investigating a crime scene."

DMAIC. In contrast, *Kaizen* activities in Japan generally demand the development of a new method or technique for each problem or task, even though some activities may follow a manual exactly. In other words, such activities in the US can be described as ready-made activities, and those in Japan can be described as custom-made activities.[21]

4.2 ISO and *Kaizen*

4.2.1 Internationally Standardized *Kaizen*

As described at the beginning of this chapter, the International Organization for Standardization (ISO) published ISO 18404 as a new international standard in December 2015. The full title of this standard is "Quantitative methods in process improvement – Six Sigma – Competencies for key personnel and their organizations in relation to Six Sigma and Lean implementation." This standard clarifies the requirements for an organization to implement Six Sigma as a process improvement method and establishes the required competencies for key personnel to implement Six Sigma and Lean. There are different titles for key personnel for Six Sigma implementation as shown in Table 4.3. ISO 18404 specifies the experience and competencies required of each key person. All key personnel must undergo training organized by a specified body (an accredited body in the future) to equip themselves with the required standard competencies (Ishiyama 2017b).

Prior to ISO 18404 (2015), the ISO published ISO 13053-1 and ISO 13053-2, making Six Sigma an international standard in 2011. The full title of ISO 13053-1 is "Quantitative methods in process improvement – Six Sigma – Part 1: DMAIC methodology" and that of ISO 13053-2 is "Quantitative methods in process improvement – Six Sigma – Part 2: Tools and techniques." According to the DMAIC methodology, *Kaizen* activities subject to Six Sigma are divided into Define, Measure, Analyze,

---

[21] A similar discussion is seen in the paper "The Quality and Productivity Improvement in Tunisia: A Comparison of Japanese and EU Approaches" (Kikuchi 2013).

Table 4.3 Six Sigma (SS)/L(Lean)/L&SS methods and key personnel

Methods	Title of key personnel
Six Sigma (SS)	Master Black Belt (MBB)
	Black Belt (BB)
	Green Belt (GB)
Lean Production System (L)	Lean Expert
	Lean Leader
	Lean Practitioner
Lean & Six Sigma (L&SS)	L&SS-MBB (MBB + Lean Expert)
	L&SS-BB (BB + Lean Leader)
	L &SS-GB (GB + Lean Practitioner)

Source: Prepared by the author with reference to Ishiyama (2017a)

Improve and Control Phases (ISO 13053-1), and the tools and techniques used in each phase are set out in ISO 13053-2 (Stern 2016).

Another widely known ISO related to *Kaizen* is the ISO 9000 series (or ISO 9000 family), which consist of a set of international standards for quality management and quality assurance published by the ISO in March 1987. ISO 9001 was revised in 2000 and on 23 September 2015 as ISO 9001:2015, which is the latest version. The purpose of this latest version is to provide a core set of requirements which can be used for the next ten years or longer in a stable manner, taking changes in the implementation methods and techniques regarding Quality Management System (QMS) since 2000 into consideration (Nakajyo and Suda 2015). In short, the revisions made in 2015 aim at enhancing confidence in the competency of organizations providing conforming products and services, thereby increasing confidence in QMS based on ISO 9001 among customers (Nakajyo and Suda 2015). ISO 18404 specifies the competencies required of experts (key personnel) for Six Sigma and Lean and the requirements for organizations promoting these approaches. Accordingly, ISO 9001 and ISO 18404 are considered to have a complementary relationship, whereby the latter supplements the former.[22]

---

[22] This statement is based on the materials distributed at the "International Symposium on Trends of ISO 18404" held by the Japanese Standards Association (JSA) on 10 February 2017. At this symposium, a JSA person stated that "for organizations which already operate QMS based on ISO 9001, the introduction of Six Sigma as a business *Kaizen* technique should prove effective, even though the introduction of Six Sigma alone is possible."

Currently, ISO 9001 certification is widely obtained regardless of company size, public or private sector or business fields. Users of this standard are not restricted to the manufacturing sector but include such diverse business fields as engineering and building construction, information and communication, electricity and gas, transportation, wholesale, retail, restaurants, hotels, medical care, welfare, education, finance and public administration. While ISO 9001 certification is relatively easy to obtain even for a small organization, ISO 18401 Certification is much more difficult unless the organization concerned is fairly large. Because of this, the likely way forward for a small manufacturer is to obtain ISO 9001 certification to start with, in preparation for ISO 18404 certification in the future. It is highly unlikely that any organization wishing to obtain *Kaizen*-related ISO certification can obtain quality management or *Kaizen*-related ISO 18404 certification prior to ISO 9001 certification.

4.2.2 Significance of International Standardization

What then is the significance of international standards, such as the ISO standards? In general, the purposes of standardization are those listed below. In the past, the principal purposes of standardization were (1) through (4) but have been broadened in recent years to include (5) through (9) (Takayama 2011). The intention of the ISO to make Six Sigma and Lean international standards will require the achievement of most of the purposes listed below, especially (2) through (7):[23]

1. Securing interchangeability and interface consistency;
2. Improvements in production efficiency;
3. Setting of appropriate quality for a product;
4. Promotion of mutual understanding;
5. Dissemination of technologies (outcomes of R&D);
6. Strengthening industrial competitiveness and development of a competitive environment;

---

[23] *Kaizen* projects assisted by JICA aim at improving the the productivity of individual companies as stated in (2), improving quality as (3), disseminating *Kaizen* technology to industries in general in recipient countries as (4), and strengthening the industrial competitiveness of recipient countries through the dissemination of *Kaizen* as (5).

7. Promotion and facilitation of trade;
8. Securing of safety and pace of mind (consumer protection, consideration of the elderly and handicapped, and so on); and
9. Environmental consideration (energy saving, recycling, etc.).

While the above list spells out the general advantages of international standardization, the advantages at the company level, industry level and country level are listed side by side. The revised list shown below focuses on the company level with some supplementary adjustments:

- Improvement of the quality of operation of an organization;
- Improvement of the quality of goods and services provided for customers by an organization;
- Improvement of the image of an organization (including the public image);
- Improvement of the credibility of an organization (especially for existing and potential partners for business transactions);
- Advantage in terms of international transactions; and
- Contribution to the national and regional economy as well as trade.

However, standardization does not always bestow advantages. "Whether or not an internationally established standard is the best standard is a different matter" (Hashimoto 2013/2015). Such a statement makes sense when we look at the history of the revisions made to the ISO 9000 series. Thus, for ISO 18404, it is planned to periodically review the ranking of the techniques used at each stage of DMAIC (Ishiyama 2017b). The ISO is an independent international non-governmental organization. Its head office is in Geneva, Switzerland, and its membership consists of 163 national standards bodies. Accordingly, the international standards published by the ISO are not necessarily binding. As far as *Kaizen*-related ISO standards are concerned, neither ISO 18404 nor ISO 9001 demand the compliance of individual organizations. It is up to the judgment of each organization or top executive to try to obtain ISO 18404 or ISO 9001 certification.

However, there can be situations where it is necessary to obtain ISO certification to support a certain business transaction. One example is ISO 9001, which is said to be a hit product of the ISO. Even if an organization can offer a product or service with a high level of customer satisfaction through its own quality management system without obtaining ISO 9001 certification, possession of ISO 9001 certification can help it to gain the trust of even a new customer (business partner or general consumer) in its products or services. In recent years, there appears to have been an increasing trend both at home and abroad to add the possession of ISO 9001 certification to the trading conditions set by a business partner or customer when placing an order. This trend shows that ISO 9001 is becoming the benchmark for measurement of the trustworthiness of a new trading partner. However, it is said that obtaining and maintaining (periodic inspection, etc.) ISO 9001 certification is hugely expensive. In fact, many organizations, especially SMEs even in Japan, are reluctant to have ISO 9001 certification for this reason, even though they acknowledge the advantages of this certification.

On 10 February 2017, an International Symposium on the Trends in ISO 18404 was held in Tokyo with the sponsorship of the Japanese Standards Association (JSA). At this symposium, it was disclosed that while ISO 18404 was published by the ISO in December 2015, the UK is currently the only country working to further elaborate this standard.[24] The UK is said to be planning the introduction of a certification system based on ISO 18404 with the leadership of the Royal Statistical Society (RSS) and the United Kingdom Accreditation Service (UKAS). British speakers were invited to the symposium and one of them explained: "the UK's efforts regarding ISO 18404 are currently at the pilot project stage but the intended certification system would attract some EU countries to follow, with possible expansion to the world if the pilot project proves to be successful." The sponsor of the symposium took the view that ISO 18404, which has systematized and standardized methods for the improvement of manufacturing and business processes, will follow the historical development of ISO 9001.[25]

Has any African company obtained ISO 18404 certification? There is a future possibility that African companies will be required to obtain ISO

---

[24] Both Six Sigma and Lean were originally systematized in the US with reference to Japanese *Kaizen* methods. However, the UK is said to be the country which put them on the stage of the ISO with a view to making them international standards.

[25] Many *Kaizen* consultants in Japan take the view that while the number of Japanese companies obtaining ISO 9001 certification is large, the number of those obtaining ISO 18404 certification may be small.

18404 certification, or to appoint a black belt expert of a Western partner company or other for international transactions. However, there is speculation that SMEs in Africa are hesitant to voluntarily obtain ISO 18404 certification, presumably because of the following reasons. First is the question of company size. The companies which developed Six Sigma are such international companies as Motorola and GE. Japanese companies which have introduced it to Japan are also large companies, including Toshiba, Sony and NEC. There is a suspicion that Six Sigma may only be applicable to large companies. In the case of the *Kaizen* projects assisted by JICA, the companies selected for guidance[26] are mainly small and medium enterprises (SMEs) with up to 100–200 employees, including the president and factory manager; with those with ten employees or less not being unusual. Therefore, there is no possibility of African SMEs introducing Six Sigma because of their size.[27]

A second reason relates to human resources development. Most developing countries do not have a human resources development body for Six Sigma.[28] However, it is possible that individual consultants with Six

---

[26] Strictly speaking, one of the main purposes of a JICA *Kaizen* project is to foster and train personnel who can then disseminate *Kaizen*. Local companies offer their actual production floors as training venues. In other words, *Kaizen* guidance for local companies is not the direct purpose. Nevertheless, the themes to be dealt with on the production floors used for training are selected from the problems faced by host companies, and the fostering and training of *Kaizen* dissemination personnel are conducted with the participation of the owner, factory manager and workers of each host company.

[27] JICA *Kaizen* projects occasionally feature local large companies. In Ethiopia, in line with the policy of the Ethiopian government to foster model companies for *Kaizen*, large state-owned sugar factories have been selected as the subjects for *Kaizen* guidance along with large private metal processing, textile, garment and other factories in the private sector (see Chap. 5). It is conceivable that there will be requests for fostering model companies or factories for *Kaizen* from other developing countries. The possibility remains that in some cases, the introduction of or guidance on Six Sigma or Lean may also be requested. International diffusion of ISO 18404 in the future may lead companies of a certain size to opt for the introduction of Six Sigma as these companies aiming at exporting or increasing the export of their products may conceive that the possession of ISO 18404 would be beneficial for their business.

[28] One report submitted at the symposium held in Tokyo on 10 February 2017 suggested that there are only three training bodies for Six Sigma in Japan. The number is nearly 100 in the UK, more than 100 in the US, and there are several dozen in China. Such bodies are said to also exist in France, but the number is unclear. When the author asked a British speaker about the dissemination situation of Six Sigma in Africa at the symposium, the reply was that "although the identities of companies which have introduced Six Sigma are unclear, they are likely to be multi-nationals, if any. One training course on Six Sigma existed at Nairobi University in Kenya where a friend taught the course."

Sigma training experience abroad and experience of providing guidance on Six Sigma will emerge. It is also theoretically possible that foreign experts could be invited to provide training at home. Also, a company can dispatch its staff abroad to undergo training but may find the cost and duration of training problematic.[29] It is likely therefore that the subject SMEs of JICA *Kaizen* projects in developing countries do not have the financial ability to pay for the training of Six Sigma experts (black belt or green belt, etc.). If so, is there any top executive who can decide on human resources development as an anticipatory investment for future profit? This is the problem faced by companies in developing countries, especially by the top executives or owners of SMEs. While the people who can be considered candidate members of a Six Sigma project are, by definition, capable people in their companies, the top executive of every company is haunted by the risk of employees with a black belt or green belt qualification being head-hunted by another company (including multi-nationals) willing to pay a higher wage.

The third is the problem of developing an organizational structure. In general, JICA *Kaizen* projects aim at fostering staff members capable of transferring *Kaizen* technologies (methods and concepts) to local companies (human resources development), and developing or strengthening those organizations receiving JICA assistance, usually the counterpart organization, that are developing an organizational structure. However, it is not easy to successfully develop human resources capable of providing guidance on Six Sigma as well as an organizational structure for *Kaizen* dissemination during the project period,[30] as described earlier, let alone

---

[29] The training duration and cost differ depending on the country and training body. In the case of Toshiba Sigma Consulting Corporation, for example, the Master Black Belt course lasts for 10 days at a cost of ¥600,000, the DMAIC Black Belt course for 20 days at ¥1,200,000, the Lean Six Sigma Black Belt Course for 9 days at ¥540,000 and the Lean Six Sigma Green Belt Course for 6 days at ¥360,000 (https://www.toshiba-sigma.com/education, 14 September 2017).

[30] A JICA *Kaizen* project usually lasts for one to three years. There have been one-year projects (Argentina 2009–2010) and a two-year project (Tunisia 2006–2008), while the *Kaizen* project in progress in Ethiopia at present is a ten-year project and an exceptional case (Phase I for 2009–2011, Phase II for 2011–2014, Phase III for 2015–2020; see Chap. 5). The main activities during the project period are human resources development (fostering of *Kaizen* dissemination personnel) and the development of an organizational structure. Guidance for specific local companies is provided during these activities but the time available is quite limited. Meanwhile, guidance for local companies (transfer of *Kaizen* technologies) takes place simultaneously with the fostering of dissemination personnel.

successfully guide SMEs to develop an organizational structure capable of introducing Six Sigma given the time constraints.

The fourth reason is the difficulty in mastering advanced methods. Six Sigma uses difficult and advanced techniques, such as statistical tools (e.g., multivariate statistics and multivariable analysis), probability distribution tests (normality test, etc.), design of experiment (DOE), project risk analysis and measurement systems analysis (Ishiyama 2017b). Most companies participating in JICA *Kaizen* projects are SMEs in developing countries and the educational background of top executives or factory managers is not necessarily high. Therefore, it is safe to assume that they do not possess sufficient skills to use these complex and advanced methods.[31]

The four reasons described above suggest that SMEs in developing countries, especially in Africa, are unlikely to show interest in Six Sigma. It may be possible for them, however, to examine the possibility of introducing Six Sigma once they have developed to the stage where their products or services are about to enter the international market. In any case, obtaining ISO certification is not compulsory. It is up to individual organizations whether they employ the methods standardized by the ISO. Six Sigma and the Lean Production System may prove to be suitable and effective methods for some organizations. However, other *Kaizen* methods, such as TQM and TPS, may be better suited to other organizations.

4.3 What Kind of *Kaizen* Methods and Concepts Are More Appropriate for African SMEs?

Here, we approach the question of what kind of *Kaizen* methods and concepts are more appropriate for African SMEs. The first viewpoint is to examine under which conditions *Kaizen* is likely to be accepted by SMEs in Africa. This is an examination from a relatively short-term viewpoint in contrast to the second viewpoint to be discussed later. African SMEs

---

[31] Six Sigma is armed with an arsenal of sophisticated technical methods. At Toyota, they keep things simple and use very few sophisticated statistical tools. The quality specialists and team members have just four key tools: (1) go and see, (2) analyze the situation, (3) use one-piece flow and "and lamp on" to expose problems and (4) ask "why" five times (Liker 2004, 135).

may pursue more advanced *Kaizen* activities when their size as well as business activities are expanded in the future. When this happens, they will face the decision of needing to select either TQM or TPS that originated in Japan, or Six Sigma or Lean that was developed in Western counties. In preparation for this decision, it is essential to explore what should be done now. This decision has implications for the way JICA as well as other international donor agencies assist *Kaizen* diffusion in Africa.

4.3.1 More Acceptable Conditions for *Kaizen* (First Viewpoint)

In the last ten years, JICA has assisted *Kaizen* projects in eight African countries.[32] The contents of this assistance are the development of human resources capable of disseminating and guiding *Kaizen* and the transfer of *Kaizen* methods and concepts to local companies (mostly SMEs), along with practical training on the production floor. The outputs of both human resources development and implemented *Kaizen* at SMEs participating in a JICA project have been generally praised by the governments of recipient countries (see Chaps. 2 and 5). Here, the appropriate conditions for the introduction of *Kaizen* to African companies (not limited to SMEs but including large companies which would be introducing *Kaizen* for the first time) are examined by focusing on *Kaizen* methods and concepts. Based on the first author's experience of involvement in such projects,[33] the authors would like to argue that the following conditions can make *Kaizen* more acceptable to African SMEs. The first condition is that the methodology must be "easy to understand." Any *Kaizen* method or concept should be easy to understand for both the top executive and employees involved. The top executive or owner of an African SME may not necessarily have a high educational background. In fact, there are many with only basic education. Moreover, many employees have not even had sufficient basic education. In consideration of this situation, it is essential for any *Kaizen* method or concept to be easy to understand.

---

[32] Cameroon, Egypt, Ethiopia, Ghana, Kenya, Tanzania, Tunisia and Zambia.

[33] For the last ten years or so, the first author has been involved in JICA *Kaizen* projects as the project team leader in four countries: Tunisia (two years: 2006–2008), Argentina (one year: 2009–2010), Ethiopia (three years: 2011–2014) and Mexico (one and a half years: 2014–2015).

The second is to be "not so difficult to implement." It is desirable for any *Kaizen* method not to be complex but easy to implement on the production floor in addition to its ease of understanding by the top executives and employees of African SMEs. Preparatory work is required for the introduction of *Kaizen*. For a company planning to introduce this approach for the first time, it is essential to deploy someone who is responsible for its implementation. This means that the company concerned must train or secure the services of such person(s) and, therefore, a company may be reluctant to implement *Kaizen* because of the time and cost involved.

The third is "results in a short time." For the successful introduction of *Kaizen*, a methodology that does not require much preparation time and which produces results in a relatively short period of time after its introduction is desirable. Although some *Kaizen* results take some time to emerge, there are many methods capable of producing visible results in a relatively short time. What is important is that not only the top executive but also employees feel and verify the results at an early stage of implementation even if these are only small. Such results then lead to an increased level of recognition of the approach, thereby becoming the driving force towards the next stage of *Kaizen*.

The fourth is that it must be "inexpensive to introduce." There are many *Kaizen* methods and concepts which can contribute to quality improvement (e.g., reduction of defective products) or productivity improvement (e.g., productivity improvement per employee or unit of machinery) without much investment and using existing machinery. Even if investment is required to introduce *Kaizen* for the first time, it is desirable that the amount of investment does not constitute a burden on a SME.

The fifth is "low risk." Although it is possible to initiate *Kaizen* on a large scale, it is also possible to begin small. Such efforts mean lower costs if such efforts fail or do not produce the expected results. The sixth is that it should not "be difficult to train employees." Whichever *Kaizen* activity is to be implemented, the training of a person(s) implementing the activity is required regardless of whether the approach originated in Japan or was redeveloped in the West. It is desirable for this training not to become a burden on African SMEs in terms of time and cost. If possible, the preferred course of action is to develop the ability of employees to educate themselves,[34] and to solve problems by gaining experience through the process of implementation, even if the level of theoretical knowledge of *Kaizen* is not high to start with.

These are the six conditions which would make *Kaizen* more acceptable for African SMEs. Which *Kaizen* methods and concepts can meet these conditions in a concrete manner? Table 4.4 compiles the basic methods and concepts based on the experience of JICA *Kaizen* projects. Many of the methods and concepts listed in the table generally satisfy the six conditions discussed above.[35]

In JICA *Kaizen* projects, most of the methods and concepts listed in Table 4.4 have been transferred to developing countries through classroom lectures. Meanwhile, the number of methods experimented with on the

Table 4.4 Basic *Kaizen* technologies (methods, tools and procedures)

Categories of basic *Kaizen*		Basic *Kaizen* methods, tools and procedures
Basic *Kaizen* technologies	Fundamental methods and tools of *Kaizen*	Process analysis, motion study, time study, work analysis, work sampling, line balancing, layout improvement, direct costing, cost accounting and so on
	Common methods and tools of *Kaizen*	5S[a], 7QC tools, new 7QC tools, why-why analysis, brainstorming, TWI, visualization, *muda* elimination, QC circle and cross-functional team, suggestion system and so on
	Basic procedures of *Kaizen*	PDCA, QC story, problem-solving procedure, task-achieving procedure, project management and so on

Source: Prepared by the author with reference to Chap. 3
[a]Strictly speaking, the 5S constitute the entry point for *Kaizen* activities

[34] In recent years, there has been emphasis on the self-learning ability of workers for corporate growth or development among scholars, researchers, policy planners and business people (Hosono 2016). Japanese-style *Kaizen* contains methods conforming to this emphasis.
[35] Toyota is one of the companies which have produced the best *Kaizen* results. One independent consultant who obtained his experience at Toyota emphasizes that "80% of the problems on the production floor can be solved by basic *Kaizen* methods. *Kaizen* leaders and trainees in developing countries often want to learn advanced *Kaizen* but should concentrate on mastering basic *Kaizen* methods instead."

production floor is limited because of the constraints posed by the limited duration of each project. In this chapter, the methodology is discussed in terms of "Japanese-style *Kaizen*" versus "Western-style *Kaizen*." The methods and concepts shown in the above table are commonly included in both styles (Ishiyama 2017b; Stern 2016; Nakajyo and Yamada 2006).

4.3.2 Direction for *Kaizen* Promotion in Africa (Second Viewpoint)

The discussion in this chapter is based on the idea that the suitability of *Kaizen* methods and concepts for companies planning to introduce these depends on the industrial climate of the country concerned, the culture of each company planning such introduction and the judgment of the top executive of the company concerned.[36] Let us now explore the question of how African countries should deal with *Kaizen* in line with the expansion of their business activities and organization from different viewpoints.

Technology transfer under the *Kaizen* projects assisted by JICA so far targets the methods and concepts listed in Table 4.4. In short, the methods and concepts for transfer are the basic ones common to both Japanese- and Western-style *Kaizen*. To be more precise, JICA's assistance helps the target companies to build foundations that can be used for either style in the future. This approach can be upheld as being desirable for international cooperation, because it allows those companies (mostly SMEs) that have received JICA's guidance to opt for not only Japanese-style *Kaizen* (TQM and TPS, etc.) but also for Western-style *Kaizen* (Six Sigma and Lean, etc.) when they decide to introduce such activities in the future. While it may sound repetitive, the key point here is that JICA's assistance does not force only Japanese-style *Kaizen* on recipient countries.

After the completion of a JICA *Kaizen* project in Tunisia in which the first author was involved, it was learned that one of the Tunisian companies assisted by JICA had obtained ISO 9001 certification. In other words,

---

[36] There are cases, such as Toyota, where exactly the same TPS as employed at the head office in Japan is successfully introduced in foreign countries or regions with a different industrial climate and corporate culture. However, in all likelihood, such success is only made possible because Toyota's creed of "Before we make cars, we make people" is thoroughly implemented at Toyota's plants in various countries across the world.

JICA's assistance had made it easier for this company to obtain ISO 9001 certification. This may also mean that there could be cases in the future where participation in a JICA *Kaizen* project facilitates the obtaining of ISO 18404 Certification for participating companies in developing countries. In short, JICA *Kaizen* projects contribute to the development of the basic capacity of the target companies so that these companies can adopt appropriate *Kaizen* methods, including such Japanese-style methods as TQM and TPS, and such Western-style methods as Six Sigma and Lean, and can also obtain ISO 9001 and ISO 18404 certification.

JICA may not have consciously sought this kind of outcome, but it can be said that the approach it has adopted has ended up achieving something desirable in terms of international cooperation. Any future *Kaizen* project assisted by JICA should be formulated to make such potential a reality. At present, JICA is implementing a research project on the required level of the standardization of *Kaizen* for Africa. In its standardization efforts, JICA should consider the desirable contribution of these efforts to the development of the basic *Kaizen* capacity of companies in the target countries to enable them to opt for either style, and meet the challenge of obtaining ISO 9001 and ISO 18404.

Figure 4.3 outlines an image of the future direction of African enterprises (MSEs), based on the above discussion. It is hoped that JICA's research project on this issue is expected to show the standard contents and direction for future *Kaizen* assistance for African companies. At the result of the research project implementation "African-style *Kaizen*," which paves the way for more advanced methodologies (Japanese style or Western style) for African SMEs, may be suggested. The significance and outline of such standardization of *Kaizen* for Africa are discussed in the next section.

4.4 Standardizing *Kaizen* Approaches in Africa

JICA's current research study on "Standardizing *Kaizen* Approaches in Africa" aims to produce a handbook to guide policy makers and practitioners who intend to promote and implement these procedures in their country to enhance its competitiveness and productivity. The handbook will consist of

Kaizen and Standardization

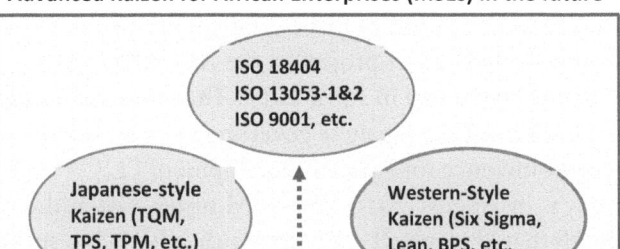

Fig. 4.3 An image of future *Kaizen* for African enterprises (MSEs). (Source: Prepared by the author)

definitions of *Kaizen*, recommendations and methods for dissemination and deployment approaches, as well as standard curricula, a syllabus and textbook lists for *Kaizen* facilitators.[37] Recommendations for the certification system

---

[37] *Kaizen* facilitators is a generic term used in this book to refer to lecturers, trainers and consultants, who disseminate it through providing training and consultancy services to an individual and organizations. See Chap. 3 for details.

will also be made. The guidelines will also contain key success factors and lessons learned from case studies in 14 different countries.[38]

This research study is a sub-project of the *Africa Kaizen Initiative* that JICA and NEPAD launched in April 2017. The initiative was also one of the commitments from the Japanese government made during the Tokyo International Conference for African Development (TICAD) VI, held in Nairobi, Kenya, in August 2016. Prime Minister Abe addressed in his opening speech that "Japan will cooperate with NEPAD to spread *Kaizen* throughout Africa. We will aim to increase the productivity of factories by 30 percent where *Kaizen* is introduced."

The core strategies of the initiative are (1) advocacy at policy levels, (2) standardizing *Kaizen* in Africa, (3) identifying and strengthening the functions of centers of excellence and (4) networking with *Kaizen* promoting institutions in Africa and around the world. The initiative aims to disseminate *Kaizen* through centers of excellence utilizing *Kaizen* facilitators trained under a standard training program and certified by a regional accreditation system, while extracting buy-in from policy makers, and connecting *Kaizen* promoting institutions around the world. The next section will elaborate on the ideas behind standardization and the key features of the initiative's *Kaizen* standards.

4.4.1 Why Is Standardization of *Kaizen* Necessary?

The purpose of standardizing *Kaizen* in Africa is to speed up the process of scaling up. There is no doubt that African firms need to upgrade their capacity to compete in the global market. As mentioned in Chap. 1, many firms in Africa do not possess the very basic skills for management. Cirera and Malony (2017) introduce *Kaizen* as an approach Japan took during the post-World War II years to successfully upgrade its business capacity. They argue that *Kaizen* enhances the production capability of firms, which serves as the basic layer of firm capability. To this day, *Kaizen* has spread throughout the world through Foreign Direct Investments (FDIs) or through consultants who have studied or practiced *Kaizen* and contributed to upgrading firm capability. Japanese firms operating overseas are also of great assistance in disseminating

---

[38] The research team conducted studies of Tunisia, Ethiopia, Kenya, Ghana, Tanzania, Zambia, Cameroon, Egypt, Costa Rica, Argentine, Singapore, Malaysia, Thailand and Japan.

Kaizen. However, in areas where FDI and experienced consultants are limited, a push from the public sector and international donors may be needed.

So far, JICA has implemented *Kaizen* projects in eight countries in Africa and has developed few hundred *Kaizen* facilitators in partnership with government agencies in each country. However, the number is not enough to meet the huge demand that exists in Africa. We need to have many more *Kaizen* facilitators on the continent and to accelerate the process. Partnerships with various organizations and bringing in forces from the private sector should be sought. To do so, we need to have a common understanding of *Kaizen*.

Unfortunately, the complex aspect of *Kaizen* makes it difficult to grasp what it really is. The knowledge of *Kaizen* has been continuously developing through trial and error, and each company in Japan has their own unique way of implementing and conducting *Kaizen*. Through dissemination around the world, new knowledge has been created and boundaries have been expanded. Some of the knowledge may be externalized and have become explicit knowledge but much still resides within the people. People have different understandings of *Kaizen* and sometimes this may be misleading. Thus, we need to have a common understanding of what *Kaizen* is and understand how it can be effectively implemented in African firms. Furthermore, we need to rephrase it in the context of today's Africa. We thus hope that the standardization of the *Kaizen* approach serves as the cornerstone for common understanding of what *Kaizen* is in Africa.

4.4.2 Key Features of the Initiative's *Kaizen* Standard

Although the research study for "Standardizing *Kaizen* Approaches in Africa" is continuing and the results are not yet finalized, there are five key features that are expected in the outcome. First, the initiative's *Kaizen* standard is a regional standard that should be designed to fit the needs of the African continent. Africa's ownership is essential. The standards will be drafted by the research study team but in consultation with major *Kaizen* promoting institutions in and out of Africa.[39] Finally, when the standard is set out, it should be approved by the African nations.

---

[39] It is planned to consult with *Kaizen* promoting institutions in Cameroon, Ethiopia, Ghana, Kenya, Tanzania, Tunisia and Zambia where JICA projects are on-going and South Africa, where

Second, the standards will be set to develop qualified *Kaizen* facilitators. The study will formulate a standard training program (curricula and a syllabus) and develop a certification system. On the other hand, we should not attempt to impose a standard towards firms because we think it is unrealistic in Africa. Imposing such standards may overburden the firms especially if they are Micro, Small and Medium Enterprises (MSMEs). Our objective is not to standardize the firms but to upgrade their capability. We want more firms to be implementing *Kaizen* rather than feeling overburdened.

Through focusing the standards for developing qualified *Kaizen* facilitators, we hope to amplify the number of facilitators substantially. These facilitators can provide the firms with advice that targets their specific problems in more efficient way without overburdening them with standards. When the firms develop the capacity to implement more systemized and advanced *Kaizen* such as TPS, TQM and TPM, the facilitator can guide the firms to implement these approaches. Furthermore, this may also increase the number of facilitators. Until now, most of these facilitators were trained under a JICA project. However, if the standard curricula become open knowledge and the certification system is open to the public, more people from the business side may join and become *Kaizen* facilitators. We need many more facilitators in Africa than we have now. In Africa, developing firm capability is more necessary than standardizing them. Thus, standardization of qualified facilitators may be more practical and efficient approach in the continent.

Third, the scope of *Kaizen* knowledge tackled by the standard approach should respond to the needs of today's Africa by taking into account its future. Thus the knowledge and skills that will be dealt in the standard may be broader than the conventional knowledge associated with *Kaizen*. For example, those managerial skills that are usually not classified as *Kaizen* skills, such as business planning, marketing and accounting, will be also included in the initiative's standard. Likewise, Western-style *Kaizen* should not be discriminated against but observed and incorporated if deemed beneficial for African firms. We should keep the good aspects of Japanese-style *Kaizen* but also be aware of the criticisms made of it.

---

the Secretariat of PAPA resides. The initiative will also consult with Japanese *Kaizen* promoting institutions such as the Japan Productivity Center.

In fact, in the interviews conducted by our research study team, interviewees from Malaysia and Singapore commented that Lean and Six Sigma are much easier to implement compared with *Kaizen*. When the interviewer asked why, the answer was "*Kaizen* is philosophical, Lean is more technical." "*Kaizen* depends on individual capacity. It is not sustainable." Regardless of the correctness of their comments, we need to be aware of these notions. As mentioned earlier, much of *Kaizen* knowledge is tacit knowledge that resides in the people. This makes it difficult for people to understand. We need therefore to convert their tacit knowledge into explicit knowledge.

The fourth feature is flexibility. A word of caution that may appear to contradict the concept of standards is needed in Africa's case. Although this is a regional standard, the African continent is made of more than 50 countries with different economic levels and policies. Even within the seven countries where JICA is currently implementing *Kaizen* projects, the context, purpose and means are different. In Ethiopia, the Ethiopia *Kaizen* Institute (EKI), a government agency which is the core *Kaizen* promoting institution in the country, is providing services to large and medium enterprises and to the public sector. The majority of EKI consultants are recruited from new graduates (see Chap. 5 for further detail). On the other hand, in Cameroon, the SME agency utilizes private consultants to provide *Kaizen* as part of its business development service to SMEs. The curriculum needed to train facilitators in Ethiopia and Cameroon may therefore differ. To respond to these different circumstances, dividing the curriculum into modules is suggested by this research study. In this way, each country can choose the modules needed according to their targets and the background experience of the consultants. Different levels of certification, such as basic level consultant to advanced level consultant, should also be considered depending on the modules taken, level of knowledge and the years of experience a consultant has.

Likewise, we need to understand that customization is one of the essential features of *Kaizen* as argued in Chaps. 2 and 5. For effective application in country, customization has had a great role in the past. As US developed Lean and Six Sigma to adjust *Kaizen* to their corporate culture, Asian countries have also practiced customization. In Vietnam, Nguyen Dang Minh (2017), Chairman of the Advisory Board of the GKM Lean Institute, introduced a managerial philosophy called TAM

THE to help Vietnamese understand the concept of Lean management. Here Minh acknowledges Lean management as equivalent to TPS. TAM THE is a "Made in Vietnam" Lean management philosophy that teaches that working seriously with good intentions will develop the firm's capacity and that this is beneficial. African firms and communities should be able to customize and create their knowledge for themselves. Thus, the initiative's standard should focus on transferrable knowledge and skills so that customization can be attempted in each country.

Finally, the standard should be subject to periodical revision. *Kaizen* knowledge is something that constantly evolves through continuous conversion of tacit knowledge to explicit knowledge and through customization. Furthermore, considering the current transformation of industries through digitalization and AI, the knowledge used today may not be relevant in the future. In order to accommodate these changes, periodical revision is needed.

In a nutshell, the initiative's *Kaizen* standard is a regional standard for developing qualified facilitators. The set of knowledge and skills that will be dealt in the standard will be adjusted to the current challenges that African firms are facing. Though the bulk of the knowledge will be derived from conventional *Kaizen* knowledge, a broader set of skills will be incorporated. Furthermore, the standard will be periodically revised to accommodate new knowledge created within and out of Africa.

4.4.3 Significance of Standardizing *Kaizen* in Africa

As previously mentioned, the purpose of the initiative's standard is to accelerate the catch-up process in African firms through the implementation of *Kaizen*. Up until now, aside from the counterpart organizations in JICA's projects, only few organizations provide *Kaizen* or Lean services to firms in Africa. Since the few private firms that do exist provide services mostly for large or multi-national companies, local SMEs do not have a place to turn to. Even within JICA's projects inefficiency can be seen. In each country where JICA has implemented a *Kaizen* project, the experts dispatched to those countries had to develop curricula and textbooks from scratch. If a standard curriculum and textbooks were available, there would be no need to develop these from the beginning.

Furthermore, if a qualification system for *Kaizen* facilitators is in place, more personnel from the private sector can be expected to join the force. There is no need for them to be trained in the standard training program if they already have experience in *Kaizen* applications. They could simply pass the exam and become qualified *Kaizen* facilitators, but if they wished to enhance a particular skill they could choose from the modules and receive training.

However, to really accelerate the process, standardization of *Kaizen* is not enough. That is why the initiative has four main strategies. However, other strategies need to be put in place to give it real effect. First, government support from each country is needed. Many enterprises still do not realize what they lack in their management capabilities. Therefore support from the government is needed, especially for MSMEs with limited capital. In this way we can stimulate the potential demand in Africa.

Second, we need to have core partner organizations that have the capacity to provide standard training and accreditation for qualified facilitators. Of course, the seven organizations in our partner countries are candidates but there can be other organizations that provide this training. For example, the Pan-Africa Productivity Association (PAPA), a regional organization promoting and encouraging member countries[40] to develop productivity cultures that can assure better living standards, can be one of the candidates. Productivity South Africa, where PAPA locates its secretariat, has experienced consultants. These organizations are expected to become Centers of Excellence that can also provide assistance to neighboring countries through providing training or dispatching their facilitators. Together with a standard curriculum, the initiative aims to develop a database where materials and case studies are stored. Any country can access and read, listen and watch to see how *Kaizen* can be implemented in different environments.

Third, creating a network of *Kaizen* promoting institutions within Africa and globally is also expected to boost the process. The *Kaizen* network is also expected to facilitate the process of converting tacit knowledge residing within people and each country to explicit ones that can be shared on a borderless basis.

---

[40] Botswana, Burkina Faso, Ghana, Kenya, Mauritius, Namibia, Nigeria, South Africa, Tanzania, Zambia, and Zimbabwe.

The initiative will also attempt, at the policy level, to promote awareness of this approach. All African politicians recognize that they must enhance the productivity of their economy, firms and workers. Choosing what policy measures to adopt and implement is the hard task. Fortunately, the development of a basic *Kaizen* capability is compatible with other advanced methods, as we argued in the previous section. Furthermore, implementation can be achieved without large investment. The most basic factor for successful development is cultivating *Kaizen-oriented* minds and the *Kaizen* culture. It is also expected that eventually, this dissemination system will work on its own. The duration of the initiative is for ten years starting from 2017, and there will be a periodical review, which will make it possible to assess the extent to which our purposes are fulfilled. The challenge is whether we can create *Kaizen*-oriented minds and culture in Africa that will not only develop firm capacities but also create a learning society so that the continent can adapt to the future challenges that they may face.

4.5 Concluding Remarks

There appears to have been a somewhat ironic cycle of development in this area. Japan learned technologies (methods and concepts) from the West and developed them in its own way. In turn, the US learned technologies that had been successfully developed in Japan and redeveloped them in its own way to produce successful examples of these technologies. The technologies developed in the US then spread to the rest of the World, and the UK pushed some of them to gain the status of international standards (ISO standards). Following this cycle, the question may be immediately raised as to whether Japanese companies are affected by ISO standards, such as ISO 18404; however, there is no way of knowing at present how they will be affected in the coming years.

The more important question for us in this chapter was what impact will ISO 18404 have on African companies? The possibility that some multi-nationals based in Africa and large African companies operating in the international markets will opt to obtain ISO 18404 certification cannot be denied. However, ISO 18404 does not appear to have much impact on most African SMEs that are operating within the local market. In short, it is currently inconceivable that African SMEs will move to obtain ISO 18404 certification.

Needless to say, African SMEs should eventually advance their *Kaizen* methods such as to TQM, TPS, Six Sigma, Lean and so on so that they could compete within the global market. They may even be challenged to obtain not only Japanese-style *Kaizen* but also Western-style *Kaizen*. In consideration of such prospects, international cooperation for African SMEs should start from the implementation of basic *Kaizen* to enhance their firm's capability so that the opportunity to challenge these styles of *Kaizen* and ISO standards can be seized where and when appropriate. To achieve this outcome, the standardization of these activities at the current level in Africa must contribute to "the development of a basic *Kaizen* capability" for African SMEs.[41] This is precisely the direction that JICA's current research study on "Standardizing *Kaizen* Approaches in Africa" is heading towards.

References

Cirera, X., & Maloney, W. (2017). *The Innovation Paradox, Developing-Country Capabilities and the Unrealized Promise of Technological Catch-Up*. Washington, DC: World Bank Group.

Financial Times. (2001). *Handbook of Management* (2nd ed.). London: Pearson Education.

Hashimoto, T. (2013/2015). *Monodukuri no Kagakushi (Scientific History of Manufacturing: Standardization Revolution Which Changed the World)*. Tokyo: Kodan-sha.

Hosono, A. (2016). Industrial Strategies: Toward a Learning Society for Quality Growth. In A. Norman & J. E. Stiglitz (Eds.), *Efficiency, Finance, and Varieties of Industrial Policy*. New York: Columbia University Press.

---

[41] The World Bank (2008) assumes that foreign trade, foreign direct investment and contacts with diaspora are major channels of technology transfer for developing countries. The Bank gives scant weight to international technical assistance as an important channel of technology transfer. We would like to stress that standardization and transfer of management technology like *Kaizen* for SMEs in developing countries is a challenging topic, even for the Bank.

Ishiyama, K. (2017a). Six Sigma to Kokusaikikaku ISO 18404: Hyoujunka to Hinshitsukanri (Six Sigma and International Standard ISO 18404: Standardization and Quality Management). *Journal of Japanese Standards Association, 70*(2), 45–46.

Ishiyama, K. (2017b). Six Sigma Sainyumon: Hyojunka to Hinshitsu Kanri (Re-introduction to Six Sigma: Standardization and Quality Management). *Journal of Japanese Standards Association, 70*(6), 6–17.

Ito, K. (2001). Six-Sigma no Igi to Kadai (Signification and Theme of Six Sigma). *Journal of Japan Society for Production Management, 8*(2), 77–82.

Japan Industrial Management Association (Ed.). (2002/2012). *Seisan Kanri Yougo Jiten (Glossary of Production and Manufacturing Management Terms)*. Tokyo: Japanese Standards Association.

Japanese Standards Association. (2017). International Standards for Certification of Kaizen Personnel and Their Organizations: Symposium on the Trends of ISO 18404, Unpublished Material, February 10, 2017.

Kikuchi, T. (2012). *The Role of Private Organizations in the Introduction, Development and Diffusion of Production Management Technology in Japan*, GRIPS Development Forum. Tokyo: National Graduate Institute for Policy Studies.

Kikuchi, T. (2013). The Quality and Productivity Improvement Project in Tunisia: A Comparison of Japanese and EU Approaches. In K. Ohno & I. Ohno (Eds.), *Eastern and Western Ideas for African Growth: Diversity and Complementarity in Development Aid*. Oxford: Routledge.

Kurosaki, T., & Otsuka, K. (Eds.). (2015). *Korekara no Nippon no Kokusai Kyoryoku (Japan's International Cooperation in the Coming Years)*. Tokyo: Nippon Hyoron-sha.

Liker, J. K. (2004). *The Toyota Way*. New York: McGraw-Hill.

Minh, Nguyen Dang. *Kigyo no seisanseikoujyou to jizokuhatten no tameno made in Viet Nam Lean Management (Made in Viet Nam Lean Management for Enhancing Firm Productivity and Sustainability)*. National Graduate Institute for Policy Studies, Tokyo, January 24, 2017.

Nakajyo, T., & Suda, S. (2015). *ISO 9001:2015 Shin-kyu Kikaku no Taisho to Kaisetsu (ISO 9001:2015-Targets and Explanations of Old and New Standards)*. Tokyo: Japanese Standards Association.

Nakajyo, T., & Yamada, S. (Eds.). (2006). *TQM no Kihon (Basics of TQM)*. Tokyo: JUSE Press.

Nakano, M. (2017). *Ima Sekai deha Toyota Seisan Hoshiki ga donoyoni Shinka shiteiruka (How Is the Toyota Production System Evolving in the World?)*. Tokyo: Nikkan Kogyo Shinbun-sha.

Ohno, T. (1978). *Toyota Seisan Hoshiki (Toyota Production System)*. Tokyo: Diamond-sha.
Pepper, M. P. J., & Spedding, T. A. (2010). The Evolution of Lean Six Sigma. *International Journal of Quality & Reliability Management, 27*(2), 138–155.
QC Circle Headquarters. (Ed.). (1970/2012). *QC Sakuru no Kihon (Basics of QC Circle)* Tokyo: JUSE Press.
Stern, T. V. (2016). *Lean Six Sigma*. Boca Raton: CRC Press.
Takayama, J. (2011). *Kokusai Hyojunka no Genjo to Wagakuni no Kadai (Current Situation of International Standardization and Challenges for Japan)*. (Reference No. 725, June, 2011). Tokyo: National Diet Library of Japan.
Uchida O. (1995/2006). *Hinshitsu Kanri no Kihon (Basics for Quality Management)*. Tokyo: Nikkei Publishing.
Union of Japanese Scientists and Engineers. (2001). JUSE Special Japan-US Joint Seminar: Six Sigma and TQM, Unpublished Material, August 29 and 30, 2001.
Womack, J. P., & Jones, D. T. (1996). *Lean Thinking: Banish Waste and Create Wealth in Your Corporation*. London: Simon and Schuster.
World Bank. (2008). *Global Economic Prospects: Technology Diffusion in the Developing World*. Washington, DC: World Bank.
Yamada, S. (2006/2015). *TQM: Hinshitsu-Kanri Nyumon (Introduction to TQM Quality Management)*. Tokyo: Nippon Keizai Shinbun-sha.
Yamada, Y., Shimoda, T., & Niikura, N. (2012). *QC Sutori no Kihon to Katsuyo (Basics and Application of QC Story)*. Tokyo: JUSE Press.

Open Access This chapter is licensed under the terms of the Creative Commons Attribution 4.0 International License (http://creativecommons.org/licenses/by/4.0/), which permits use, sharing, adaptation, distribution and reproduction in any medium or format, as long as you give appropriate credit to the original author(s) and the source, provide a link to the Creative Commons license and indicate if changes were made.

The images or other third party material in this chapter are included in the chapter's Creative Commons license, unless indicated otherwise in a credit line to the material. If material is not included in the chapter's Creative Commons license and your intended use is not permitted by statutory regulation or exceeds the permitted use, you will need to obtain permission directly from the copyright holder.

5

Kaizen as Policy Instrument: The Case of Ethiopia

Getahun Tadesse Mekonen

This chapter reports on the experience of Ethiopia in transferring and disseminating the Japanese concept of *Kaizen*, philosophy of continuous improvement. *Kaizen* was introduced to Ethiopia by Japan International Cooperation Agency (JICA) in 2009 and has since become a mainstay instrument of reform. It has been widely accepted and implemented by many companies. There are concerns over the transferability of *Kaizen* to developing countries, particularly to African countries. Issues raised by those who claim *Kaizen* to be unique to Japan are mostly related to its Japanese religious and cultural background. The differences between the homogenous social fabric of Japan and the diversified ethnicities of Africa are one factor raised as an impediment to *Kaizen* transferability. However, while these characteristics may have certain impacts, they have not hampered the transfer and dissemination of *Kaizen* to Ethiopia, where there are multiple ethnicities, religions, and cultures.

Three consecutive *Kaizen* projects, supported by JICA, have been implemented in Ethiopia since October 2009. The first pilot project was

G. T. Mekonen (✉)
Principal Kaizen Consultant, Addis Ababa, Ethiopia

undertaken to confirm the transferability of *Kaizen* and study how use of the concept could be expanded after the JICA project was completed. The initial introduction of *Kaizen* into selected pilot companies proved the receptiveness of Ethiopian companies to new initiatives and showed encouraging results in improving quality and productivity. Encouraged by the results of the project, the Ethiopian government established the Ethiopia *Kaizen* Institute to disseminate and expand on the results attained during the pilot project.

The second project was aimed at training Ethiopian *Kaizen* consultants in order to build the capacity of the institute. In this project, 57 *Kaizen* consultants and 133 trainers from Technical and Vocational Education and Training (TVET) Institutes received training. The Ethiopia *Kaizen* Institute enthusiastically launched the *Kaizen* movement in large-scale sugar, textile, and leather companies using trained consultants. Highly promising quantitative and qualitative changes were recorded. The change in attitudes and the creation of smooth relationships in situations where there was strong conflict between management and the workforce were the most outstanding results. The monetary values of achievements attained each year amounted to hundreds of millions of birr.

The third project, currently underway, is designed to transfer advanced-level *Kaizen* knowledge, with 90 *Kaizen* consultants passing through this project. Around 30 companies that previously disseminated *Kaizen* during the pilot and second projects will be introduced to advanced *Kaizen*. Ethiopia designed its own local capacity-development program in collaboration with local universities, and 18 *Kaizen* consultants from the institute have now graduated with MSc degrees in *Kaizen*, 16 are in second year, and 22 are in their first year.

Ethiopia *Kaizen* Institute has conceived its own *Kaizen* transfer and development roadmap, prepared models, and crafted strategies. The roadmap plots the transfer of *Kaizen* from Japan over 15 years—from 2011 to 2025—in three phases that correspond to the growth and transformation plan of the country. It has completed the first phase and the second phase will be completed in 2020.

Overall, the Ethiopian experience has proved that differences in religion, culture, and diversity are not impediments to the transfer of the

Kaizen concept to Africa and that *Kaizen* could bring about dramatic changes in companies and public institutions.

This chapter consists of five sections. Section 5.1 explains how *Kaizen* transfer to Ethiopia was initiated, followed by Section 5.2, which illustrates the formation of the Ethiopia *Kaizen* Institutes. Section 5.3 discusses the Ethiopia *Kaizen* roadmap and strategies. The major achievements, success factors, and ongoing challenges are presented in Section 5.4. Finally, lessons that can be drawn from the Ethiopian experience are outlined in Section 5.5.

5.1 The Landmark

During the summer of 2008, the late Prime Minister of Ethiopia, H.E. Meles Zenawi, was discussing development issues with scholars from the Western and Eastern worlds (GRIPS 2016). Contact with Japanese academics provided him with an opportunity to learn about *Kaizen*. In search of better understanding, he requested that JICA provide further explanation regarding *Kaizen* projects and the experience of African countries. JICA honored his request by providing information and progress concerning JICA-assisted *Kaizen* Projects in Africa. After hearing about the productivity and quality improvement impacts of *Kaizen* as well as its contribution to the industrial development of Japan—initially based on small and medium-sized enterprises (SMEs)—he extended his request to JICA for further assistance. In addition to these contacts, *Kaizen* was frequently discussed in High level Policy Dialogue forums assisted by JICA and the professional contributions of Professors Kenichi Ohno and Izumi Ohno, from the GRIPS Development Forum.

A project entitled "The Study on Quality and Productivity Improvement (*Kaizen*) in the Federal Republic of Ethiopia" was designed by JICA in consultation with an Ethiopian counterpart and signed by the Ministry of Industry and JICA on June 4, 2009. The project time frame was from October 2009 to May 2011 and it incorporated the following three major objectives (JICA 2011a):

1. Formulate a national plan to enhance activity on quality and productivity improvement (*Kaizen*) for Ethiopian enterprises in the industrial sector;
2. Formulate a manual which can be used for quality and productivity improvement activity (*Kaizen*); and
3. Transfer relevant skills and techniques to the staff members of the *Kaizen* Unit of the Ministry of Industry.

The Ministry of Industry established a *Kaizen* Unit (KU) consisting of ten members and assigned a team leader. The members were drawn from the Ministry and Institutions affiliated to it, and the new team was given a written mandate to work with JICA consultants to realize the project objectives. The project was hosted by the Metal Products Development Center, which provided offices, as well as conference and training rooms for JICA consultants and the unit. JICA deployed a team of experts and their first task was to explain the concept of *Kaizen* by opening discussions between the unit members and JICA experts.

When the project started, the Ministry and all institutions affiliated to it, including the Metal Products Development Center, were preoccupied with business process reengineering (BPR) projects. BPR is a change tool developed in the USA that helps to define processes, identify value-adding and non-value-adding activities, and reduce or eliminate those non-value-adding activities from processes of production and services to improve efficiency. In Ethiopia, BPR was introduced by the government to improve the efficiency of public services.

The pre-eminent place of BPR, with its goals of fundamental, drastic, and dramatic change, meant that it took us some time to be convinced of the merits of *Kaizen*. We were told the meaning of *Kaizen* as 'a small incremental change' or 'continuous improvement' by JICA experts. On top of that, none of us in KU had experience of working with Japanese people. The discussion took us a few weeks and, over time, the commitment of the JICA experts to enlightening us about *Kaizen*—along with their discipline, well-preparedness, art of mining information, and punctuality—convinced us. The more we came to know the secret of *Kaizen*, the more we were convinced and buried ourselves in *Kaizen* activities and literature.

The first objective of the project was to transfer *Kaizen* knowledge and skills from JICA experts to KU members. In line with this, course modules were prepared by JICA experts and delivered with the help of classroom demonstrations, videos, and games. The major course contents were the definition of *Kaizen*, elimination of waste, visual management, quality control circles, problem-solving steps, seven quality control tools, operation standards, and time study. A month-long classroom training (CRT) was followed by five months of in-company training (ICT).

To select the 30 companies for the pilot project, a long list of medium and large manufacturing companies was prepared. Among the major selection criterion were that the participating companies needed to be situated within a radius of 100 km of the capital city. They needed to make contributions to export/import substitution, possess scale of capital, have a diverse range of products, and avoid duplication of support with other donors. The interest and commitment of management and workers was another important criterion. A national conference was held to introduce the project, to assess the interest of companies, and to facilitate registration of those who expressed a willingness to participate. The initial long list was shortened from 180 to 60 companies. Through visiting the companies, the JICA expert team and KU members identified 30 pilot companies from 5 sub-sectors, namely, (1) 10 companies in basic metal and engineering, (2) 6 in agro-processing, (3) 6 in chemical manufacturing, (4) 4 in leather, and (5) 4 in textiles. These companies were divided into three groups and each group of ten companies undertook training for a duration of six months.

The ICT had two components. The first one was to invite the owners and top management members of companies to the Metal Development Center for a one-day seminar with the objective of creating awareness on *Kaizen* and introducing the ICT plan. This was followed by training of *Kaizen* core members consisting of top and middle managerial staff, selected work stations for trial, and frontline workers in each company. The trainings were conducted by both JICA experts and KU members, based on the following steps (JICA 2011b):

Step 1. Overview of *Kaizen*

Step 2. Understanding standardization of workplace environment and operations

(a) Theme-1 5S
(b) Theme-2 Operation Standard and Time Study
(c) Theme-3 Elimination of Waste (*MUDA*)

Step 3. Implementing *Kaizen* Activities at the Company

(d) Action-1 Organizing Sort Activity
(e) Action-2 Understanding '3S' activities in Eliminating *MUDA*
(f) Action-3 Standardizing Operations at the Selected Workplace

Step 4. Understanding and Overview of QC Circles

(g) Theme-1 How to Organize a QC Circle/What is the QC Story?
(h) Theme-2 QC 7 Tools and QC Circle Presentations

Step 5. Organizing QC Circles at the Company

(i) Action-1 Conducting QC Circles Meetings
(j) Action-2 Conducting QC Circles Presentation Meetings

Step 6. Preparatory Work for Companywide *Kaizen* Activities

Checklists and formats were prepared to be used by the KU members and companies throughout their *Kaizen* activities. Side by side with CRT and ICT, a training program was arranged and conducted in Japan for 30 company owners and managers as well as 10 KU members. This training program offered an important chance to observe and learn in the actual environment of Japanese companies, workers, and people. Many participants shared their judgment that *Kaizen* is not only a management philosophy but is also a part of Japanese 'culture'.

There were regular mini-conferences between the JICA experts and KU members to discuss issues requiring clarification and the challenges that periodically arose within companies. KU members took different topics, prepared presentations, and delivered them at mini-conferences as part of their self-education process. The objective of skill transfer comprised the major part of the project and it was concluded by developing a consultant skill matrix for KU members and future *Kaizen* consultants. The skill matrix was prepared based on local participant experiences of the pilot project, while also incorporating Japanese experiences. The matrix comprises Grade I (Junior Consultant), Grade II (Assistant Consultant), Grade III (Consultant), Grade IV (Senior Consultant), and Grade V (Lead Consultant). The competence requirements were improved during the second and third JICA projects, and incorporated into the Ethiopia *Kaizen* Institute (EKI) Strategic Roadmap and Model, which will be discussed later in this chapter. KU members were evaluated by JICA experts and ranked into Grade II (Assistance Consultant) and III (Consultant). The matrix was further developed and used during the establishment of the Ethiopia *Kaizen* Institute.

Quantitative and qualitative assessment criteria,[1] as shown in Table 5.1, were designed to determine the effects of *Kaizen* activities on companies. The impact of *Kaizen* on 28 out of 30 companies was assessed using the above assessment criteria and the results are summarized in Table 5.2. The pilot project raised quality and productivity consciousness in the pilot companies. It was clear that introducing *Kaizen* into these companies improved quality, productivity, and safety, reducing costs and lead time.

Those companies with Grade III and above, which constitute 65% of the total population, are characterized by strong management commitment and good management-employee relationships, while those below Grade III that accounts for 35% lack these commitments. The impact of *Kaizen* activity on 65% of the companies constitutes satisfactory achievement, thereby confirming the success of the project. In addition, this result indicates the high transferability and high acceptability of *Kaizen* to Ethiopian companies.

The second objective of the project was to develop a manual to be used by KU members and the proposed Ethiopia *Kaizen* Institute, which was under consideration by the government at that time. The manual contains procedures, steps, and a sequential flow of *Kaizen* activities. The

---

[1] *Kaizen* results are counted on two levels. The first level consists of qualitative results such as changes in attitude, improvement of industrial culture, and improvements in work relations between management and employees. The second one comprises quantitative results calculated before *Kaizen* activity implementation to set targets and after implementation to observe the changes. Usually calculations are based on *Kaizen* elements (quality, productivity, cost, delivery, safety, environment, and morals).

Table 5.1 Assessment criteria

Area	Indicator	Formula	Data required and other notes
1. Quality	(1-1) defect rate	(Quantity of defects)/(quantity of product produced)	Either one of the two should be used depending on the nature of production process
	(1-2) yield	(Quantity of good products produced)/(quantity of material input)	
2. Cost	(2-1) cost by product	Cost by product per unit	
	(2-2) gross profit ratio	(Revenue − cost of goods sold)/(revenue)	Gross profit ratios by product, as well as total company
3. Delivery	(3-1) delivery schedule non-adherence count	Number of occurrence of delivery schedule non-adherence	Associated records: description including reason/background of each non-adherence case
4. Safety	(4-1) labor injury count	Number of labor injuries	Associated records: description of incidence including reason/background
5. Productivity	(5-1) machine utilization rate	(Actual time machine utilized)/(planned machine utilization time)	Associated records: time/duration and reason for each facility stoppage occurrence
	(5-2) production capacity	Quantity of products produced per unit time	
6. Morale	(6-1) absentee ratio	(Number of absent employees)/(total number of employees)	(HR data)

Source: JICA (2011a)

Table 5.2 Assessment results of pilot companies

	Grade					
Sub-sector	1	2	3	4	5	Total number of companies
1. Metal	1	2	2	2	1	8
2. Textile	1	1	1	1	1	5
3. Agro	1	2	1	1	1	6
4. Chemical		1	2		3	6
5. Leather	1		2			3
Total	4	6	8	4	6	28

Source: JICA (2011a)

sequence primarily consists of (1) acquisition of *Kaizen* knowledge, (2) rapid assessment of the workplace environment and operations at companies for identification of problems, (3) selection of model workplaces, (4) application of *Kaizen* activities at selected model workplaces for examination, (5) self-organization of *Kaizen* activities through conducting QCC activities, (6) preparatory work for companywide *Kaizen* activities, and (7) self-evaluation of *Kaizen* activities for continual *Kaizen* dissemination. This sequential flow comprises an actual application of PDCA modality (i.e., 'Plan-Do-Check-Act' cycle). Thus, the manual provides not only the operational and procedural guides for carrying out *Kaizen* activities but also enhances opportunities to customize the application methodology revealed in the manual into various workplaces and companies. The manual is accompanied by audio-visual[2] materials.

The *Kaizen* knowledge components and the steps moving from the base to the top with the help of PDCA cycle were depicted as a *Kaizen* tree to clearly show the *Kaizen* system in action in five sequential steps from simple to complex. This concept has been used in crafting the Ethiopia *Kaizen* Model and Roadmap, which will be discussed in Section 5.3.

The third objective of the pilot project was to develop a National Plan, which was comprised of objectives and strategies for dissemination, institutionalization, and establishment of a *Kaizen* movement. However, the latter two were not covered by the project. JICA recruited additional experts to undertake an institutionalization study. The study of the *Kaizen* movement and extraction of best experiences relevant to Ethiopia was done as part of the High level Policy Dialogue.

The dissemination plan was incorporated into the manual. The *Kaizen* dissemination plan took into consideration synchronizing the implementation of *Kaizen* with the National Development Plan. During the final stage of the project, Ethiopia was crafting the Growth and Transformation Plan (GTP I) and revising the Micro and Small Enterprise Development Strategy. It was an opportunity to streamline *Kaizen* dissemination into the national plan and to formulate the modalities for reaching various scales of companies.

---

[2] The audio-visual materials are DVDs elaborating *Kaizen* components using simulations by KU members. They show company experiences of customizing *Kaizen* activities to Ethiopian situations and interviews.

The awareness and quick decision to adopt *Kaizen* by the government of Ethiopia, the rapid response by JICA in designing the project and deploying experts, and the success of the project became a landmark for subsequent JICA assistance and the benefits were harnessed by Ethiopian companies. It provided the impetus for the Ethiopian government to establish a strong and vibrant *Kaizen* Institute, thereby nurturing hundreds of *Kaizen* consultants and making Ethiopia *Kaizen* a flagship project for JICA. As a landmark, it contributed to the upgrading of KU into the Ethiopia *Kaizen* Institute, where it could craft its vision as "a center for transformed working cultures and innovation management skill," thus spearheading its place as a center of excellence in Africa.

5.2 Institutional Development

The remarkable success of the pilot project increased the Ethiopian appetite for knowledge. During the wind-up of the pilot project, the Ethiopian government, delighted with the results and setting its sights on establishing the Ethiopia *Kaizen* Institute, and incorporating KU members as its core staff, requested that JICA undertake a study of the institutionalization framework. JICA was also satisfied with the performance of the project and was ready to help. KU members had been introduced to *Kaizen* and had recognized its potential. The objective of the study of institutionalization was mainly to draw lessons from different countries assisted by *Kaizen*. An expert in the field who participated in the Singapore JICA Quality and Productivity Project was appointed. Sato (2011) explored the experiences of 13 countries in different regions: in Asia (Singapore, Malaysia, Thailand, and Vietnam), Latin American (Chile, Argentina, and Mexico), and Eastern Europe (Poland, Baltic countries, Armenia, Bosnia and Herzegovina, and Serbia).

The experiences of these countries have been summarized below in a way that shows how key insights were helpful in establishing an institute that met the needs of Ethiopia. During the study, there were frequent discussions with the experts and the conclusion we arrived at was that many things could be learned from both the success and failure cases of other countries.

5.2.1 Learning from Success Factors

5.2.1.1 Approach to *Kaizen* Activities

Most of the countries included in the study tried to implement *Kaizen* activities at the level of a national movement; however, only Asian countries were able to successfully realize the approach. A major factor identified for success is the commitment of political leadership. For instance, in Singapore, the Prime Minister undertook initiatives toward promoting *Kaizen* activities. Top management commitment was not limited only to political leadership but also applied to enterprises and institutions involved in disseminating *Kaizen*.

5.2.1.2 Vision, Mission, and Objectives

Those countries that promoted their own quality and productivity movements and succeeded have crafted their own visions, missions, and objectives suitable to their specific conditions. This is very important because no two countries are alike in every aspect.

5.2.1.3 Organizational Frameworks

The experiences of each country show that there is no blueprint or standard organizational framework. In most cases, it depends on political will, as well as the policy and strategy environment within each country the institution is intended to serve. The experiences of different countries show that they have different institutional set-ups, commonly known as organizational structures. Some organizational structures are simple while others are complex. Although, in most of the studied cases, governments use the same name, 'productivity center', to describe the institution, the functional structure, the courses delivered, the scope of activities, and target groups served differ.

5.2.1.4 Importance of Customization

The experience of countries covered by the study showed that some countries failed to persevere, while others succeed. The difference between success and failure depends, by and large, on materials' development for training and consultancy services. In most cases, those countries that did not make good progress were those using teaching materials they had obtained from other countries without any modifications. Those who succeeded expanded implementation in their own countries and even abroad. Some modified teaching materials and developed certification bodies to match their own needs. To achieve the need of a country, customizing teaching materials, methods, and ways of dissemination must receive the attention of local staff. It could be said that preparing custom-made teaching materials is a key factor in successful activities.

5.2.1.5 Creating a *Kaizen* Mindset

As discussed in Chap. 1, continuous improvement is one of the principles of *Kaizen*. However, normally, people tend toward keeping the status quo and maintaining prevailing conditions without change. This is mainly due to comfortable familiarity with existing circumstances, fear of the unknown, and desire to preserve a peaceful life. *Kaizen* activities cannot be implemented with such an attitude. Changes in attitudes or receptiveness to new ideas for improvement are a result of basic *Kaizen* and a prerequisite for advanced *Kaizen* and further progress. The case studies showed how experts faced enormous challenges in changing people's mindsets in some countries.

5.2.1.6 The Need for Commitment and Leadership

As has repeatedly been noted, the commitment of top management is the most crucial element in the success of *Kaizen* activities. No success has been made without commitment from top management. For instance, in the case of Singapore, the success of their quality and productivity movement was the outcome of the commitment of Prime Minister Lee Kuan

Yew. In Japan, the success of *Kaizen* activities depends entirely on the commitment of institutions like the Japan Productivity Centre, Japan Union of Scientists and Engineers, Japan Management Association, and companies' top management. It can be concluded that success is the result of top-level commitments at all levels. Leaving *Kaizen* activities entirely to foreign experts is unlikely to bring about the desired results. The participation of local staff in all activities and taking on leadership to meet local needs is very crucial.

5.2.1.7 Expanding *Kaizen* Activities

The experience of some successful countries shows that they were trying to extend their activities to other countries. Some were trying to become centers of *Kaizen* activities in their region. This indicates that success could create opportunities to excel and become a center of excellence, thus broadening *Kaizen* activities beyond their own borders.

5.2.2 Learning from Cases of Failure

One can learn not only from success factors but also from cases of failure as well. Factors contributing to failure, among other things, are implementing *Kaizen* only to meet short-term goals, leaving *Kaizen* activities to foreign experts, and not being sufficiently involved from the beginning, thereby creating gaps after the experts have left. Using a 'copy-and-paste' approach or depending exclusively on foreign-made teaching materials without customizing these to meet local needs, lack of a clear vision, mission, and strategy are also major factors leading to failure in some countries.

These successes and failure cases were taken as an input while designing the organizational structure of the Ethiopia *Kaizen* Institute and crafting strategies to successfully transfer and develop *Kaizen* in Ethiopia. One important concept of institutional development is human-oriented management. This concept is unique compared to others developed in Western countries. In Japan, it is common for top management to encourage employee improvement. There is a saying, "if you do not have money, you need to use your brain, and if you do not have a brain, you should make your maximum effort through toil at your work". The literal meaning of this saying is to make work improvements without spending money or by investing time (without using money).

5.2.3 The Ethiopia *Kaizen* Institute

Taking into account the dissemination plan prepared by the project (JICA 2011b) and lessons learned from the experience of other countries (Sato 2011), a Formation Paper explaining (1) the concept of *Kaizen*, (2) the experiences of successful countries including Japan and Singapore, (3) the achievements of the pilot project, (4) the survey of the positive response of participants in the discussion on the institutional development study, (5) the role of the institute, and (6) the scope of its activity in launching a countrywide movement as well as the Gazette were prepared by KU and presented to the Council of Ministers for a decision. The Ethiopia *Kaizen* Institute was established by the proclamation of the Council of Ministers 256/2011 (FDRE 2011). The objectives of the institute as stipulated in the gazette are to initiate a countrywide broad-based quality and productivity movement and thereby enhance industry competitiveness. The major powers and duties of the institute are as follows:

1. formulate and implement as approved; policies, strategies and programs that assist in the dissemination of the *Kaizen* knowledge and implementation tools, create a countrywide quality and productivity movement that could enable the effective implementation of government policies and strategies;
2. prepare, review, and distribute *Kaizen* training and consultancy manuals customized to micro, small, medium, and large enterprises and follow up their performances; provide training of trainers on Technical and Vocational Education and Training Institutes' industrial extension experts to enable them to be capable to provide *Kaizen* training and consultancy to micro and small enterprises and provide *Kaizen* training and consultancy to medium and large companies;

3. coordinate, consult, and support *Kaizen* concepts and tools to disseminate them at any level of service and educational institutes, establish and perform a system that induces organizations to implement *Kaizen*, support organizations to establish quality control circles and/or continuous improvement circles, and register their performances;
4. conduct studies, collect, organize, and disseminate information to observe improvements made because of *Kaizen*; prepare key performance indicators to measure *Kaizen* implementation results, establish evaluation and certification systems for *Kaizen* trainers and consultants, accumulate best *Kaizen* practices, disseminate and produce *Kaizen* model companies; and
5. prepare recognition and incentive systems and implement them upon approval of organizations; recognize quality control circles that have excelled in *Kaizen* training and consultancy performances; designate a quality month and perform countrywide discussion forums.

The institute is presently accountable to the Ministry of Public Service and Human Resource Development. The Joint Coordination Committee of the JICA project is chaired by the Minister. The institute submits to the ministry monthly, quarterly, and annual performance reports and is evaluated by the management team of the ministry chaired by the minister. The leadership tier consists of a council, ministry, director general, and deputy director generals. The Prime Minister is the Chairperson of the Council and members are drawn from appropriate government offices, the private sector, and professional associations. The number of members is determined as required. The duties of the council are mainly to:

1. advise the institute on its activities;
2. evaluate and forward its recommendations on *Kaizen* strategies, plans, studies, and research formulated with a view to facilitating the development of manufacturing and service-rendering organizations;
3. forward its opinions on capacity-building programs; and
4. evaluate the implementation of the plans of the Institute.

JICA commissioned the second project to train *Kaizen* consultants recruited by the institute. The project duration was for three years from November 2011 to December 2014. The outputs of the project were:

1. The institutional and organizational foundation of Ethiopia *Kaizen* Institute (EKI) is established as the core and lead organization for the dissemination of quality and productivity improvement, that is, *Kaizen*;
2. The system of HRD for dissemination of quality and productivity improvements to large and medium enterprises is functionalized in EKI; and
3. The model system for EKI to foster TVET trainers' trainers (TTTs) is developed for quality and productivity improvement (*Kaizen*) for micro and small enterprises (MSEs) (JICA 2014a).

JICA deployed an expert group and EKI continuously recruited consultants to be trained by the project. Six consultants who were former KU members were permanently attached to the project. The modalities of training were one-month classroom training (CRT) and five-month in-company training (ICT) for medium and large industries and two-week CRT and eight-week ICT for micro and small enterprises. The Japanese experts provided classroom trainings to EKI consultants and to TVET trainers of trainers. TVET trainers of trainers were selected from all regions and they were expected to expand *Kaizen* activities in their respective regions. In each batch, large and medium enterprises as well as micro and small enterprises were selected. The selection was followed by a reconnaissance survey by JICA and EKI consultants. Based on the survey results and commitments of the company, a one-day awareness creation program was conducted mainly for managers and *Kaizen* representatives to further stimulate their motivation. EKI consultants were deployed to enterprises supervised and assisted by JICA experts.

The project plan called for the training of 60 EKI consultants over three years of the project, while the actual achievement was 57 trained consultants. The difference was mainly due to EKI's limited capacity to supply trainees as per the plan in each batch. The plan also called for the training of 170 professional TVET trainers, with 137 TVET trainers' trainers actually achieved. The difference of 33 TVET trainers was due to the failure of some regions to send a satisfactory number to EKI for the training in each batch. This problem was observed at a later stage and the reason was that the newly trained TVET trainers' trainers were leaving their respective institutions and regions because they were offered better salaries when they returned with their certificates showing they had completed *Kaizen* training. The issuing of such certificates became a problem and was discussed among JICA experts and EKI. Through in-company training, *Kaizen* was introduced to 51 large and medium enterprises and 129 micro and small enterprises.

The consultant training program was comprised of two parts. In addition to the training in Ethiopia discussed above, ten top management members and those consultants attached to the project were trained in Japan. A further 36 consultants received training in Malaysia. As part of the strengthening of the institute, 3 vehicles, 1 big copy machine, 8 projectors, 11 notebook personal computers, and 6 video cameras were provided to EKI through the project.

During the final stage of the project, training materials and the supporting manual (JICA 2014b) were developed to be used by EKI after the project. The manual consists of two volumes, with volume one comprising the various concepts and principles of *Kaizen* technologies with detailed explanations, while volume two deals with practical examples of how to use each technique. In addition to these, a manual on best practices of QCCs in Japan was prepared by Professor Hiroshi Osada (Professor Emeritus of Tokyo Institute of Technology) at the request of EKI to provide more information about QCC activities and problem-solving methodologies. The request was accepted by JICA and a manual consisting of 12 cases of best practice on quality control circles—originally published in Japanese language by Union of Japanese Scientists and Engineers (JUSE)—was translated and published (Osada 2013).

The number of consultants increased during the course of the second project. When the project started in 2014, the institute was staffed by 123 employees, with 82 consultants (44 male and 38 female). Out of this total, 57 were trained by the project. As of 2017, the institute has 153 employees including 107 consultants—65 males and 42 females—an increase of 30% within two years. A comparison between 2014 and 2016 is given in Table 5.3.

Table 5.3 Growth of consultants from 2014 to 2017 at EKI

S.N.	Job title	2014			2017		
		M	F	T	M	F	T
1	Director General	1	–	1	1	–	1
2	Deputy Director General	1	–	1	2	1	3
3	Director	4	3	7	8	3	11
4	Lead Consultant	4	0	4	7	1	8
5	Senior Consultant	5	1	6	22	7	29
6	Consultant	3	1	4	7	2	9
7	Associate Consultant	12	23	35	8	19	27
8	Junior Consultant	15	9	24	10	9	19
Total		44	38	82	65	42	107

Source: Compiled from EKI data (2016c)
Note: *S.N.* serial number, *M* male, *F* female, *T* total

The second project was considered to be success and the JICA evaluation report concluded that its achievements were satisfactory. With EKI growing in strength over time, a request was placed for JICA for a third assistance project. The goal of the assistance is for intermediate *Kaizen* capacity building based on the long-term strategy proposed in the report and in the framework of the Second Growth and Transformational Plan. *Kaizen* is well reflected in this plan and EKI has designed its own five-year plan corresponding to the GTP II period 2015–2020 (FDRE 2015). The request was accepted, and it is expected that 90 consultants will be trained in intermediate *Kaizen* with the help of this project. The organizational structure of the institute has been changed twice within a four-year period. The major cause of the change is the expansion of EKI's activities. The current structure is organized around 5 major sectors and 21 Directorates (EKI 2016a) as indicated in Fig. 5.1.

The change was not only in structure but also in motivating the consultants by raising their salaries and providing benefits. For comparison, Table 5.4 shows the original and current job grades, salary scale and benefits (gross pay before tax deduction in terms of nominal income) and percentage changes. The changes in payroll for different job grades are about 32% on the lower side and 41% on the higher side.

EKI's recruitment policy is to employ young graduates from universities with high grades, train them in-house for six to ten months on the theory and practice of *Kaizen* (CRT and ICT), and deploy them to provide

Kaizen as Policy Instrument: The Case of Ethiopia

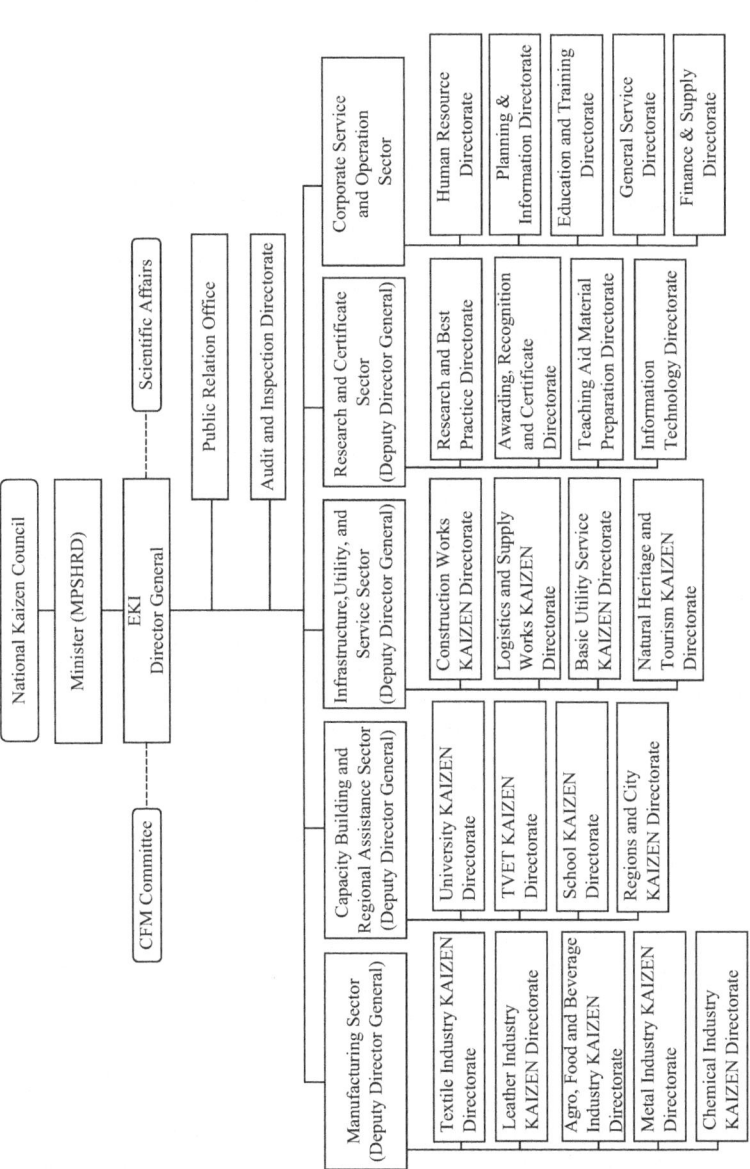

Fig. 5.1 Organizational structure of EKI. (Source: EKI 2016a, b, c)

170　G. T. Mekonen

Table 5.4 Enhanced job grade and remunerations

	Base salary		Additional benefits				
Job title	First structure	New structure	House allowance	Position allowance	Fuel allowance	Total	Change in %
Director General	8946	14,116	5000	5000	Car and fuel	24,116	37.12
Director	6708	11,872	4000	5000	Car and fuel	18,720	32.14
Lead Consultant	5718	9834	4000	–	2402	16,236	35.22
Senior Consultant	4845	8069	3000	–	2402	13,471	35.96
Consultant	4056	6529	2000	–	1601	10,130	40.04
Associate/Assistant Consultant	3359	5207	2000	–	1601	8808	38.14
Junior Consultant	2774	4075	1000	–	1601	6676	41.55

Source: EKI (2016a)

Table 5.5 Budget of EKI in million birr

S.N.	Budget line	2011(4 months) (2004)	2012–2013* (2005)	2013–2014 (2006)	2014–2015 (2007)	2015–2016 (2008)	2016–2017 (2009)
1	Salary and working capital	4.6	15.5	18.8	18.9	26.2	30.0
2	MSc training				2.4	2.4	2.5
	Total	4.6	15.5	18.8	21.3	26.6	32.5

Source: EKI Annual Reports (2011–2016)

Note: US$1=21 birr on average for conversion

*It shows progressively increasing allocation of budget for EKI which shows the commitment of the government in action support for the movement. At the management level, EKI employs senior people by following stringent selection procedures. Ensuring gender balance is an important consideration because in the textile, leather, and food areas, by and large, the proportion of females is very high, and gender mainstreaming is a development policy of the Ethiopian government.

Creating a strong and vibrant institute cannot happen without the required resources, particularly finance. The Government of Ethiopia showed its commitment right from the beginning. EKI was established in the fourth quarter according to the Ethiopian calendar. The fourth quarter is usually time for clearing backlogs, not a time to request new budgetary allocations. However, the government allocated 4.6 million birr for four months to start up the institute. So far, the budget has never been a limiting factor for its activities. From 2014/2015 onwards, the government allocated budget to provide not only working capital but also money for local training for MSc degrees in *Kaizen*. Table 5.5 indicates the growth of the EKI budget over time in nominal values.

In summary, the first project confirmed the transferability of *Kaizen* to Ethiopia and led to the birth of EKI. The second project trained 57 EKI consultants and helped EKI to develop autonomous capacity for launching a *Kaizen* movement using basic *Kaizen* knowledge without the help of Japanese experts or other foreign assistance. The third project is to raise the capacity of EKI to an intermediate level (JICA 2016). By the end of this project, EKI hopes to achieve an advanced level of *Kaizen*, which is the apex of *Kaizen* knowledge. It has planned for this venture to be undertaken in the years 2020–2025.

5.3   Ethiopian *Kaizen*: Roadmap and Strategies

At the end of the pilot project, KU raised questions concerning the scope of *Kaizen* knowledge and how quickly we would be able to learn. The more we discussed *Kaizen* with the JICA experts and the more we read literature on matters related to *Kaizen*, the more we came to understand the difficulties involved in learning and applying all of the concepts and technologies in a short period of time. In response to this difficulty, the JICA team developed the *Kaizen* tree concepts, articulated in Chap. 1.

The tree approach stratifies *Kaizen* knowledge into five layers (JICA 2011a). KU members were given an overview of *Kaizen* and exposed to knowledge on 5S, standard operations, QCC, and *MUDA*. Complex concepts and systems such as total quality management (TQM), total productive maintenance (TPM), and analytical tools such as 7QC tools and basic industrial engineering (IEs) were introduced briefly at the end of the project to provide participants with a very basic awareness of the terms. During the first and second round of classroom sessions and the company trainings of the second project, the challenges this posed for participants became obvious. There was enormous complexity in high-level concepts such as TQM (Umeda 2001), TPM (Suzuki 1994), policy deployment, process capability, quality diagnosis, cost management, delivery management, Toyota Production System (TPS) (Liker 2004; Kato and Smalley 2011), the whole system, and the methods of the problem-solving approach (Hosotani 1989). This prompted us to recall the lessons that we had drawn from the experiences of other countries: not to leave everything to foreign experts and the need to customize *Kaizen* knowledge, training materials, and dissemination methodology to the local context. We started thinking about how to develop a roadmap and strategy of our own—the Ethiopian way. In particular, the sharing of the history of QCC development in Japan in three stages—that is, junior, medium, and high level—opened our eyes and unlocked our potential to generate ideas on how to categorize *Kaizen* into different levels ranging from simple to complex.

From the readings of various books written on *Kaizen*, EKI has borrowed from the ideas of Masaaki Imai (1986), who described *Kaizen* as "…the unifying thread running through the philosophy, the systems, and the problem-solving tools developed in Japan over the last 30 years". The 30 years Imai refers to run from the 1950s to the 1980s, a period when Japanese people vowed to learn Western scientific management and quality control. They also customized, improved, and developed new concepts, systems, and tools. A comprehensive definition of *Kaizen* is given in Chap. 1.

After collecting the training course materials in the pilot and second projects, EKI assembled them into three components (management/principles, systems, tools) according to the difficulty of learning and implementation in companies. The idea of classifying *Kaizen* into three levels was presented for discussion to EKI staff and JICA experts. This was incorporated into *Kaizen* overview training courses by EKI consultants and continuously improved based on feedback collected from companies and consultants.

EKI top management produced a paper, the *Kaizen* Movement Strategic Directions and Action Plan from 2015 to 2025 (EKI 2014a), which was circulated among JICA Tokyo and JICA Ethiopia, GRIPS Development Forum, Policy Dialogue Forum members in Ethiopia, ministries, JICA project experts, and institutions established to assist different industrial sub-sectors. The paper has two parts, with the first part providing a historical overview and definition of *Kaizen*, offering a brief review of the introduction of *Kaizen* to Ethiopia, and discussing the customized approach of Ethiopian *Kaizen* and *Kaizen* infrastructure—that is, how to structure *Kaizen* institutions nationwide.

Part two of the paper presents the long-term action plan, mission and vision, goals, objectives and actions, resources required, and major support programs. The action plan details major activities during 2012–2025 in three stages, with each stage to be completed in five years. The plan also articulates the desired outcomes of consultant development at different levels, the impacts of *Kaizen* dissemination in improving quality and productivity and enhancing the competitiveness of companies, as well as the resources and technical support required. Japanese experience shows the importance of the strategic involvement of their scholars, organized under Japan Union of Scientists and Engineers and Japan Management Association, in developing improved and new tools, manuals, and procedures. In recognition of this fact, and seeking to lay the foundations for the creation of local capacity to enhance the conceptual and analytical capability of consultants and creating linkage with universities, EKI initiated MSc and PhD programs on *Kaizen* in 2014.

As part of the local customization effort, three books have been written in local languages[3] (Mekonen 2014, 2015a, 2017). The first book discusses the four steps of *Kaizen* transfer and ownership modality. The first three steps refer to the transfer of *Kaizen* from the source, Japan, to Ethiopia over the next 13 years (2012–2025). The year 2025 is the deadline set by the government for transforming Ethiopia from a low middle-income country and EKI therefore also set this year as the target for

---

[3] These three books are written by the author of this chapter, who is the former Director General of EKI.

completing the transfer of *Kaizen*. The fourth step is ownership of total *Kaizen*, customizing it to the Ethiopian situation and crafting an Ethiopian management version. This book fostered discussions within EKI and the public, and the feedback was encouraging.

The second book explores the Toyota way from three perspectives—lean management, lean leadership, and lean manufacturing—and extracts lessons relevant to the Ethiopian situation in a simplified way. The third book comprises a simplified approach to integrating TQM, TPM, and TPS principles and draws up a framework on how to synchronize and implement them. Several MSc papers and studies were conducted on different aspects of *Kaizen* by different universities. In addition, 18 MSc papers were produced by the first graduates of MSc on *Kaizen* by EKI consultants. EKI has also produced a *Kaizen* song emphasizing the importance of quality and productivity improvement, along with the resulting benefits, citing the results of *Kaizen* implementation as examples. This song has been broadcast on various public and private media outlets, most often in the month of September (the *Kaizen* month).

EKI top management produced a paper, the "Comprehensive Understanding of *Kaizen* and Implementation Strategy" (EKI 2014b), which primarily focused on creating a common language, the components of the three levels, the three development stages of *Kaizen* promotion teams (KPTs)[4] equivalent to QCCs (JUSE 1985), and the role of industrial development institutes in disseminating *Kaizen*. This paper was circulated among different institutions and finally became a government policy.

Although the roadmap for transferring *Kaizen* over a 15-year period in three stages and the direction set is doable, EKI felt that its knowledge of *Kaizen* was still incomplete. One morning in July 2014, EKI top management asked if one of the JICA experts, namely Mr. Seiji Sugimoto, could provide a complete list of *Kaizen* concepts, systems, and tools. After two days, he came up with a list of 82 elements or courses of *Kaizen* on A-3 paper—some of which were unheard of within EKI. After some discussion about the list, he was requested to categorize them into the three levels of components EKI had generated previously. Simple criteria

---

[4] KPTs are a customized approach to QCCs, the 5S committee, TQM committee, SOP committee, and TPM committee, by which the activities of all these committees are undertaken from within the same KPTs organizational structure step by step.

were developed for differentiating these concepts into levels based on the difficulty of learning and the ability of consultants and companies, given their absorptive capability, to comprehend the terms. Finally, with the help of Professor Hiroshi Osada, the Strategic Framework of Ethiopia *Kaizen* Version One was crafted (EKI 2014c). From this framework, the Ethiopia *Kaizen* Model was designed. The model comprises a three-level-knowledge, three-level-qualification, three-level-organization, and three-term-transfer model.

Three-level knowledge refers to the categorization of *Kaizen* into three stages, depending on learning and implementing complexity. Three-level qualifications indicate that the professional requirement for the first level is BSc/BA, the second level MSc/MA and the third level is a PhD in *Kaizen* management. Three-level organizations refer to EKI at the federal level, regional *Kaizen* institutes, and *Kaizen* units organized in *Kaizen* implementing organizations, and the synergy between them. Three-term transfer is the time that it took Ethiopia to complete the knowledge transfer of and 'own' *Kaizen*. The first term occurred between 2012 and 2014, whereby the first level was transferred, and this has thus been achieved. The second term is from 2015 to 2020, with the goal of transferring and owning the second level of *Kaizen* with the assistance of JICA through the third project for the same period. The third term will be from 2020 to 2025, as per the strategic framework of Ethiopian *Kaizen*. The components of *Kaizen* that apply to each level are also defined (see Tables 5.6, 5.7, and 5.8).

Level one (Table 5.6) consists of basic *Kaizen*, which can be managed by first degree holders and junior KPTs (junior QCCs). As indicated above, EKI is capable enough of training its newly recruited consultants as part of internal consultancy development and also of providing training and consultancy to companies, without the assistance of foreign experts.

Level two (Table 5.7) is relatively advanced compared to level one. This level can be handled by second degree holders or highly experienced consultants and medium KPTs (medium QCCs). As discussed above, this level is planned to be attained between 2015 and 2020.

There might be some overlaps of concepts and technologies within the levels depending on the absorptive capabilities of implementing companies and, whenever such conditions emerge, the consultants can adjust to the situation. Each one of these levels passes through 5 steps and 20

Table 5.6 First-level *Kaizen*

Kaizen management	*Kaizen* systems	*Kaizen* tools

1. Brief history of the development of scientific management from 1850 to 1950
  i. The emergence and development of *Kaizen* (Japanese model), the role of JPC, JUSE, and JMA in knowledge transfer and productivity movement
 ii. Toyota *Kaizen*
iii. Principles of *Kaizen* management and the development of *Kaizen* from 1950 onwards
2. Experience of Singapore in *Kaizen* transfer (Singapore model)
3. Ethiopia *Kaizen* model and strategies
	1. PDCA—SDCA
	2. Junior KPTs
	3. Autonomous maintenance
	4. Problem-solving methodologies
	5. *Kaizen* costing
	6. *Kaizen* consulting procedure
		1. 3Mus
		2. 5S
		3. Soft problem-solving/*MUDA* identification, elimination, and standardization tools
		  i. Brainstorming
		 ii. 5 M+1I analysis
		iii. QPCDSEMG analysis
		iv. Value analysis—process evaluation
		 v. Why-Why analysis
		vi. 5 W+2H

Expected outcome—organized workplace		
1. A comprehensive understanding of *Kaizen* 2. Mindset change	1. Implementing first-level K-system 2. Standard process	1. Practicing first-level K-tools 2. Work standard

Source: EKI (2014c)

major activities known as the TIISO Model (Mekonen 2017). TIISO stands for testing, institutionalizing, implementing, sustaining, and ownership. Testing refers to the learning and trial period of any new concepts and technologies. Institutionalization is customizing the curriculum and teaching materials and producing capable consultants. Implementation refers to the widening and deepening of dissemination activities in companies. Sustaining is making a brake not to slide back, while standardization and ownership refer to the complete transfer of the concepts, technologies, and management without foreign assistance. The TIISO Model is presented in Figs. 5.2 and 5.3.

Detailed activities need to be performed for each step. For instance, testing has two activities: learning from abroad—that is, Japan—and building local capability. The rest are indicated in Fig. 5.3.

Table 5.7 Second-level *Kaizen*

Kaizen management	*Kaizen* system	*Kaizen* tools

1. *Kaizen* management
  i. Productivity management
  ii. Quality management
  iii. Cost management
  iv. Delivery management
  v. Policy management
  vi. Cross-functional management
  vii. Daily management
2. Basics of *Kaizen* leadership—lean leadership
	1. Medium KPTs
	2. TPS
	3. Intermediate TQM
	4. Intermediate TPM
	5. Appropriate costing system
	6. MRP
	7. Production scheduling
		1. SOP
		2. 7 QC tools/QC story
		3. Value stream mapping
		4. Quality control process chart
		5. Basic IEs
		  Time study
		  Motion study
		  Line balancing
		  Process analysis
		  Operation analysis
		  Control charts
		  Process capability index
		  Ergonomics
		  Layout
		6. Multi-activity analysis
		7. Ratio-delay study
		8. Shortening set-up time

Expected outcome—system innovation		
1. A comprehensive understanding of intermediate *Kaizen* management 2. Strategic leadership	1. Implementing second-level K-system 2. Standard systems	Practicing second-level K-tools Operation standard

Source: EKI (2014c)

The activities in each step are self-explanatory, and we believe that readers will understand them as they are set out here. As noted above, the first 18 consultants have already graduated with an MSc in *Kaizen*, 16 consultants are in second year, and 22 are in first year. EKI has also plans to introduce a PhD program in *Kaizen* in 2018 with the support of JICA. This will further increase local capacity.

5.3.1 GTP II Plan (2015–2020)

EKI has developed a second growth and transformation plan corresponding to the national growth and transformation plan (EKI 2015a, b, c). The two major areas of focus are transferring the second-level *Kaizen* and

Table 5.8 Third-level *Kaizen*

Kaizen management	*Kaizen* system	*Kaizen* tools
1. Advanced *Kaizen* management	1. IKT (Innovative *Kaizen* Team)	1. TRIZ
2. Innovation management	2. Advanced TQM	2. Offshoring
3. Global production management	3. Advanced TPM	3. Production sharing
4. Value management	4. Advanced analytical systems	4. Value engineering
5. Advanced KAIZEN leadership—lean leadership	i. Competitive analysis	5. Quality function deployment
	ii. Financial analysis	6. Failure mode effect analyses (FMEA)
	iii. Value analysis	7. Fault tree analysis (FTA)
	iv. Business modeling	8. Reliability engineering
	v. Business systems analysis	9. Single-minute exchange of die (SMED)
	vi. Idea generation methods	
Expected outcome—innovation management		
1. Excelled management	1. Implementing third-level K-system	1. Practicing third-level K-tools
2. Lean leadership	2. Company model and brand	2. World standard

Source: EKI (2014c)

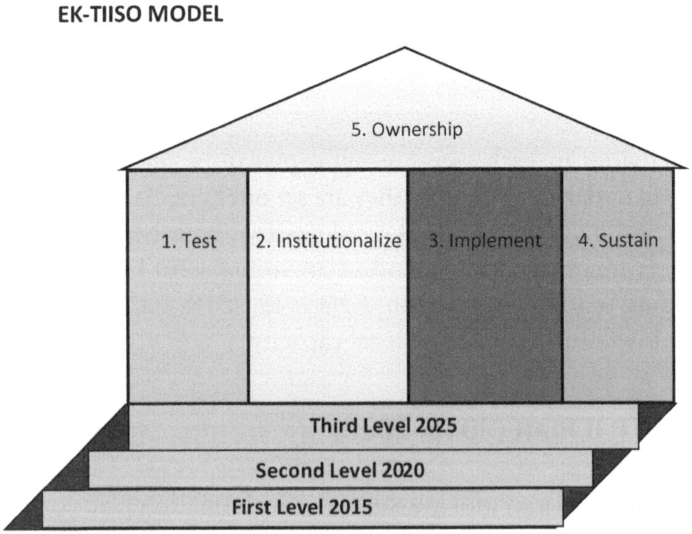

EK-TIISO MODEL

Fig. 5.2 TIISO Model. (Source: Mekonen 2015b)

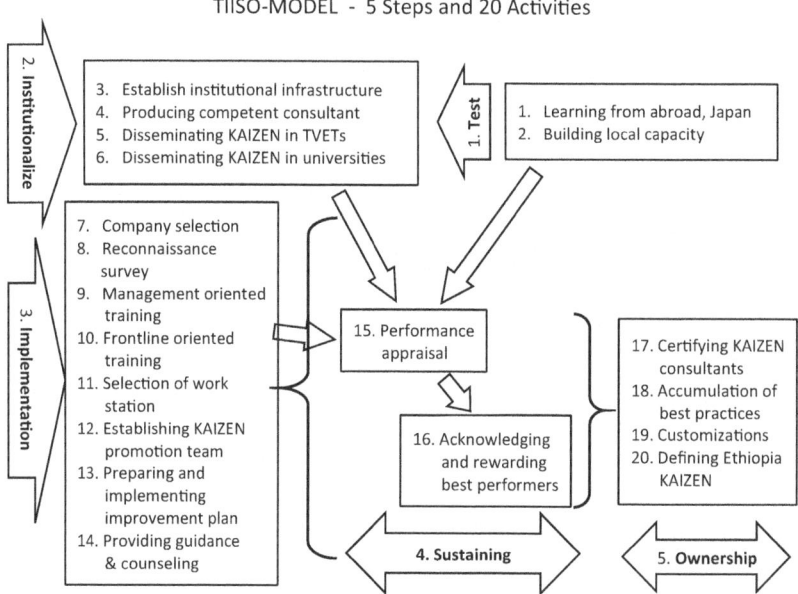

Fig. 5.3 TIISO Model—5 steps and 20 activities. (Source: Mekonen 2015b)

disseminating *Kaizen* in the priority areas stipulated in GTP II. This plan is also taken as a reference to provide support for the building of a center of excellence for *Kaizen*. A summary of the plan is presented below.

5.3.2 Vision of EKI

The EKI vision is "being a center of excellence for transformed working culture and innovation management skill." Specifically, the goals are as follows:

1. Introducing *Kaizen* in the export and import manufacturing industries by training management and frontline workers and organizing them in KPTs with the ultimate goal of improving quality and productivity, reducing waste and defects, improving work safety, and satisfying international buyers' requirements to develop competitiveness for export earnings and substituting imports.

2. Support the Human Resouce Develpment (HRD) objective of producing a competent workforce by introducing *Kaizen* thinking and principles starting from kindergarten and continuing throughout the education system to produce a transformed future generation of citizens.
3. Introducing *Kaizen* in the construction industry and infrastructure development to improve the quality of work, reducing waste in working processes, and standardizing every activity.
4. Implementing *Kaizen* in major service organizations directly influencing the competitiveness of the manufacturing industry.

5.3.3 Basic Direction of *Kaizen* Movement

1. Promoting and maintaining a comprehensive understanding of *Kaizen* and improving the quality of capacity building by transferring *Kaizen* philosophy from the source, that is, Japan, step by step, based on the learning capability of *Kaizen* consultants and absorptive capacity of companies.
2. Giving top priority to the manufacturing industry and associated organizations directly contributing to manufacturing competitiveness.
3. A long-term vision to lay the foundation for longer time spans focusing on producing transformed generations.

5.3.4 Objectives

The overall objective of the *Kaizen* movement during GTP II is to improve the quality of products and services, enhance productivity and competitiveness by providing training for management and frontline workers, and organizing them into KPTs. The goals are to train 98,000 workers and create 10,500 KPTs in the manufacturing industry, 17,140 workers and 2450 KPTs in HRD, and 20,000 workers and 2000 KPTs in construction and basic services. The overall figure will be 135,140 management and frontline workers and 14,950 KPTs.

5.4 Counting the Results: Achievements, Success Factors, and Challenges

The achievements of Ethiopian *Kaizen* can be viewed from two perspectives. These are the results achieved by the three JICA-supported projects, discussed in Sects. 5.1, 5.2, and 5.3, and EKI's own efforts, which are considered in more detail here.

At the time when EKI was first established, two activities were running side by side: CRT programs in the second project and CRT sessions run by KU members for the newly recruited EKI consultants. EKI started owning the dissemination of *Kaizen* from the very beginning. Following every six-month training, each new batch of participants joined the *Kaizen* movement led by EKI management. The *Kaizen* movement began by working with large-scale companies like the sugar and textile industries as well as huge construction projects. It was a challenge and an opportunity for the fast-track development of EKI consultants. EKI reached 458 institutions between 2012 and 2016. The details of institutions reached, number of trainees, and KPTs formed are given in Tables 5.9 and 5.10 (EKI 2012, 2013, 2014d, 2015c, 2016c).

Table 5.9 Different institutions reached by EKI

S.N.	Institutions		Number
1	Manufacturing		80
2	Services		12
3	Construction		11
4	Universities		16
5	TVETs	Institutions	9
		Regions	7
6	Schools		10
7	Kindergartens		5
8	City-based movement	Cities	4
9	Towns		2
Total by EKI			166
10	Projects	MSEs	198
		LMEs	109
Grand total			473

Source: Compiled from EKI Annual Reports (2012–2016)

Table 5.10 Number of trainees and organized KPTs

S.N.	Year	Trainees M	F	Total	KPTs
1	2012–2013 (2005 E.C)	9363	2633	11,996	1315
2	2012–2014 (2006 E.C)	2275	9923	12,198	2275
3	2014–2015 (2007 E.C)	6944	5171	12,115	1789
4	2015–2016 (2008 E.C)	9034	6059	15,093	1790
5	2016–2017 (2009 E.C)			17,552	2489
		27,616	23,790	68,954	9658

Source: Compiled from EKI Annual Reports (2012–2016)

EKI has developed criteria to collect data before and after implementation of *Kaizen*. Every month, implementing companies provide reports to EKI on the progress of improvements using reporting formats developed by the institute. The reporting formats have two parts, namely quantitative and qualitative achievements.

During 2012–2013 and 2013–2014, improvements within 48 companies were assessed using specific *Kaizen* elements. The range of improvements before and after *Kaizen* implementation are summarized in percentages as follows (EKI 2015b):

1. Secured from 52.6 to 9053 square meters of additional workspace after sorting and set-in-order (reorganization);
2. Improvements in labor productivity ranging from 1.29% to 60%;
3. Improvements in capacity utilization of machinery from 25% to 75%;
4. Reductions in defects from 57.1% to 5.0%;
5. Reductions in costs ranging from 6% to 33%;
6. Reductions of occurrences of accidents in companies from the rate of 49.5% to 14.3%.

At the lower end of the scale of improvements in labor productivity are high-tech industries, while much greater improvements were experienced by textile and leather companies. The labor productivity and capacity utilization levels indicate how the companies were disorganized and resources were underutilized before the implementation of *Kaizen*. The gains of up to 9053 sq. m in workspace mean additional free space for investment or expansion without incurring any costs—something that has happened in many companies. Although the gains in all cases are impressive, reductions of defects from 57.1% to 5.0%, reductions in costs in the range of 6% to 33%, and reductions in accidents from 49.5% to 14.3% are drastic changes that motivated implementing companies to continuously pursue *Kaizen*. This has further generated demand by many companies for *Kaizen* activities.

One example of a *Kaizen* activity in a big company is offered here as a brief case study to show the magnitudes of changes that can occur. Metehara Sugar Company (Metehara 2016) was established by Dutch H.V.A in 1970. Its crushing capacity is 17,000 quintals of sugar cane, which should produce 1700 quintals of sugar. It has 2461 permanent, 776 permanent contract, 113 contract, and 3524 temporary employees—6874 employees in total. Out of this large number, there are only 186 professional and 830 semi-professional workers, while the remaining 5858 are semi-skilled. The sugar estate experienced sharp declines in production from 2009 to 2012. It was unable to fulfill its annual plan and its performance compared to attainable capacity fell from 92.3% in 2009, 78.4% in 2010, 71.6% in 2011 to 61.3% in 2012. All the benefits of management and workers had been suspended, and the industrial culture was characterized by heavy confrontations between management and workers. In short, it was a totally demotivating environment. In 2013, EKI conducted a massive training program and many KPTs were formed. Almost all company employees were given multiple rounds of training for over three months and organized into KPTs (see Table 5.11).

After the introduction of *Kaizen*, annual production of sugar increased from 61.3% in 2012 to 88.4% in 2013 compared to the factory's attainable capacity. Similarly, ethanol production increased from 69.5% in

Table 5.11 Number of KPTs organized in Metehara Sugar Industry

S.N.	Departments	No. of KPTs
1	General Manager	16
2	Agricultural Operation	747
3	Factory Operation	158
4	Human Resource Development	19
5	Finance	8
6	Supplies and Facility Management	64
	Total	1012

Source: Metehara (2016)

2012 to 74.6% in 2013. Sugar production grew by 43.98% and daily sugar cane crushing capacity increased by 23%. The improvements in daily sugar production capacity and overall time efficiency were 35% and 20%, respectively. From each quintal of sugar, production costs were reduced by 23 birr and annual fuel costs were reduced by 1.2 million birr (both in nominal value).

In 2014, compared to the performance in 2013, working hours wasted were reduced by 30%, sugar production waste was reduced by 2.4%, annual sugar crushing capacity improved by 5%, daily sugar production capacity increased by 3%, and sugar cane yield increased by 5%. The two-year performances indicate the continuous improvements by the company. The overall improvement in monetary value is provided in Table 5.12, indicating the percentage improvement and monetary gains for this one company. To present the bigger picture, the total monetary values or gains in improvement in each year since *Kaizen* was introduced to Ethiopia are summarized in Table 5.13.

The most important change, over and above these quantitatively explained results, has been the attitudinal change, which is highly significant. Developing confidence in bringing change, bridging the gap

Table 5.12 Monetary value (nominal) of *Kaizen* achievement in Metehara Sugar Estate

Year	Improvements in millions birr
2013	35
2014	275
2015	423
Total	733

Source: Metehara (2016)

Table 5.13 Monetary gains (nominal value) of *Kaizen* in Ethiopia

S.N.	Year	Amount in million birr
1	2011–2012 (2004 E.C)	25
2	2012–2013 (2005 E.C)	75
3	2013–2014 (2006 E.C)	500
4	2014–2015 (2007 E.C)	1121
5	2015–2016 (2008 E.C)	448.5
Total		2169.5
USD equivalent		$105 million

Source: EKI (2016c)

between management and workers through total participatory activities by involving the whole workforce was a far-reaching result in maintaining the momentum of continuous improvement. Most companies that introduced *Kaizen* have continued to improve their workplace in terms of (1) orderliness and cleanliness, (2) worker safety, (3) worker motivation by increasing salaries and providing bonuses, (4) product quality improvements by reducing defects and the need for repairs, (5) productivity improvements by reducing waste, and (6) delivery time improvements in meeting the requirements of their customers. Although the magnitude of change differs between companies, all implementing companies have attained such results.

EKI has developed an annual *Kaizen* award system to motivate companies, KPTs, and individuals. Companies that have implemented *Kaizen*, along with KPTs and individuals, compete every year for the National *Kaizen* Award. The award, presented by the Prime Minister, is issued each year to three companies/institutions, three KPTs, and three individuals from each category of manufacturing, education, services, construction, along with three overall winners across all of the categories.

A review of the various reports issued by JICA and EKI shows that *Kaizen* in Ethiopia is considered to be a successful and flagship project. EKI's roadmap and strategies are now taken as a model for many African countries. Parliament members and high-level officials from the Government of Japan, high-level officials from JICA—including the presidents, vice presidents, and other officers—have visited EKI to observe its performance. EKI received the JICA President's award for successful accomplishments of the projects in 2015.

What are the secrets—if any at all—behind such successes? What are the limitations despite the success stories? Eleven major factors were identified by EKI and discussed nationwide (EKI 2016b). These factors are explored both from the observed positive and negative effects where applicable.

(i) *Continuous support of JICA*

JICA's support is responsible for the lion's share of the success, as discussed intensively in this chapter. The support includes building the capacity of the consultants, providing vehicles and equipment. EKI has wisely and strategically optimized the resources provided by JICA for the benefit of the project. There was a continuous dialogue with experts on how to transfer *Kaizen* concepts and technologies that eventually led EKI to craft a roadmap and detailed time-framed long-term strategy. The efforts made by EKI to successfully realize each project motivated JICA to provide continuous support. EKI was careful about ensuring that it succeeded in every aspect of JICA's stringent evaluation by providing evidence and facts. This created a sense of trust and mutual benefits between JICA and EKI.

(ii) *Commitment of political leadership*

While *Kaizen* was initiated by the late Prime Minister Meles Zenawi, the current Prime Minister Hailemariam Desalegn has also paid significant attention to it. The National Council of *Kaizen* is chaired by the Prime Minister, and the budget of EKI has been approved by Ministry of Finance and Economic Development annually with no or little remarks. The Ministry of Public Service and HRD, to whom EKI is presently accountable, is highly enthusiastic and supportive of *Kaizen* based on the belief that it is an important reform tool not only for manufacturing but also to improve public service delivery.

(iii) *Clear vision, road map, and strategy*

EKI has developed clear vision to become a center of excellence for *Kaizen* in Africa and it has shared its vision with JICA and other African countries, which have tried to learn from the experience of EKI through participation in forums and conferences. It has also successfully promoted its vision during the nationwide *Kaizen* month in September. EKI has designed a clear roadmap over a 15-year period to transfer *Kaizen* from its origins in Japan. The roadmap is presented in detail in the TIISO Model of 5 steps and 20 activities. Clear strategies are designed that are now part of the growth and transformation plan.

(iv) *EKI management commitment and young* Kaizen-*cultured consultants*

The top management leads through learning, directly participating in trainings, implementation, evaluation, and continuously discussing the process with JICA experts. It is also conceptualizing the roadmap, model, and strategies and making it open for discussion for all. The management has followed a democratic leadership style since EKI is not a bureaucratic institution but is instead reform and knowledge-based. All members of the institution, regardless of their status and position, have a full right to demonstrate and air their ideas, comment on anything that seems wrong, and suggest better ideas for improvement. EKI consultants are energetic and always eager to know more.

Daily, weekly, monthly, quarterly, and annual evaluation system and procedures have been put in place. A team of two or three consultants is deployed to each company and they stay for a month and a half in companies that are often far away from Addis Ababa. They evaluate their daily activities as a team and through individual performances. A weekly report is generated and sent to EKI by each team. The concerned directorate compiles a monthly report that is discussed at the working unit and management meeting levels and sent to the ministry. The reports focus not only on activities but also on results by comparing planned against actual accomplishments. The results are presented in terms of qualitative and quantitative values to show changes before and after implementation, as discussed above. For any shortfalls there must be a compensating plan. The performance evaluation of each management member and consultant is based on all these processes.

(v) *Motivating career structure, pay, and benefits*

Although salary is not the only factor in job satisfaction, it is an important element for recruiting and maintaining capable consultants. EKI is a public organization and its pay and benefits are in the highest category of public service salary ranges.

5.4.1 Challenges

Although EKI benefits from these encouraging factors, there are also a number of challenges. Six such factors that were identified and discussed by EKI on many occasions are presented here:

(vi) *Mindset*

It is obvious that any change program has quick recipients, laggards, and resisters. Some companies are reluctant to start activities after they are selected and the plan is prepared. They fear that the training and implementation may take time away from production or routine activities. They tend to believe that the way they are operating is fine, and they are comfortable with the status quo. Due to the fact that local markets absorb whatever is thrown at it, there are no consequences for poor quality or low productivity. If export products produced under subsidies through different incentives do not meet the expected quality, they can still be sold in local markets.

Two tendencies can be observed in some companies. The first one fears EKI consultants who, as public employees, may take some damaging information to government agencies—particularly tax authorities. The second issue is that they become totally reliant on EKI consultants to do everything for them while they wait. In some cases, the different change tools tried were not as productive as expected and there was a tendency toward reluctance to try new ones. Despite the positive effects of BPR on improving service delivery, the way it was implemented in some organizations—in terms of restructuring, placement, and layout—has created suspicion over reform tools. In some factories, particularly export-led ones, the practice of benchmarking has not delivered results to the expected level or investment. Both lack employee participation at the Gemba level[5] and fail to develop the knowledge and skills of workers for the job.

EKI management and consultants make extended efforts to convince company managers and workers regarding the unique character of *Kaizen* and its benefits to all. They explain the main principles of *Kaizen* as continuous improvement, as fully participatory, as beneficial to all members of the company—even for self-improvement—and as creating opportunities for business expansion, thereby benefiting all members of society.

It is through these considerable efforts that changes of attitude are brought about. Some companies are quick to comprehend and become committed early on in the process.

---

[5] Gemba is a Japanese word to represent a workplace.

(vii) *Securing the commitment of owners and managers*

In all countries—including Japan—*Kaizen* has succeeded where the commitments of owners and managers have been secured. The same is true in Ethiopia. Where owners and managers committed themselves to implementation, sustainable improvements were guaranteed. By contrast, there are some companies that are either reluctant to start or quick to withdraw.

(viii) *Frequent turnover of managers and* Kaizen *leaders*

EKI has nurtured strong managers and *Kaizen* leaders in most companies that implemented *Kaizen*. These managers and leaders are in-demand from many other companies. In large public enterprises, strong managers and *Kaizen* leaders are transferred to other departments or promoted internally. The causes of staff turnover might be considered healthy in a competitive market environment. However, when it happens without a clear succession, or handover of responsibilities, or disrupts the sustainability of improvement efforts, it can become counterproductive. This has been noticed in several companies. EKI has developed a succession plan that it tested on itself first and is now promoting it to implementing companies to counteract the negative impacts of turnover.

(ix) *Distorted understanding of* Kaizen

Kaizen is one of the most frequently misunderstood of all change-management concepts and management philosophies. Different literature gives different meanings to it and, even in a single volume, one may find different definitions. EKI has discussed the concept with Japanese experts and professionals for over three years but consensus on a universal definition is yet to be reached. For instance, two different ways of defining the term can be observed in the two manuals developed by the two projects. Some definitions underplay the philosophical aspects and reduce the process to mere technical activities. Others divorce their definitions from the concepts and systems developed in the context of *Kaizen*, making it a part of a system, instead of the system being part of it. For example, the basis for the idea of total quality management system is companywide quality control or total quality control (Ishikawa 1985) developed in Japan between the 1960s and 1980s. In the 1980s, the USA explored these principles and crafted TQM in their own way. In the 1990s, Japan came up with a TQM system based on its experiences, incorporating Quality Control Circle (QCC)s, as well as problem-solving steps and tools (Umeda 2001). This fact is well illustrated in the *Handbook[6] of TQM and QCC* (IADB 2003). Hence, while Japanese TQM is part of *Kaizen*, Western thinkers tend to view *Kaizen* as part of TQM. One limitation of Western TQM is its separation from quality-control activities and problem-solving tools, which are also the products of *Kaizen*. Now this problem is believed to be solved by the definition and explanations provided in Chap. 1 of this book. This provides an opportunity to create a common language among JICA officers, JICA experts, and recipient countries.

(x) *Limitations of quick learning and expanding knowledge*

One issue that is frequently discussed at EKI during quarterly and annual evaluations is the limitation of learning quickly from the JICA experts and the need to broaden knowledge through local customization and reading. One of the prerequisites for *Kaizen*, as learned from JICA experts, is having full knowledge of *Kaizen*. While most people try to do this, some management members and consultants do not progress beyond the PowerPoints provided by the experts without further improvement or customizing them to suit to different audiences. JICA experts have developed their own methods from their experiences in different courses and there is no standard training on a given course, for example, on 5S. Although learning from the experiences of different experts might be good, this has sometimes created confusion and at times become a point of difference between consultants. As explained above, there is a tendency by few consultants to be satisfied with what they know and a reluctance to read and learn more to expand their knowledge, customize, and write about their own cases, and so on.

---

[6] In December 2003, a workshop for knowledge exchange between Japan, Asia, Latin America, and Caribbean was organized at the Inter-American Development Bank (IDB) headquarters on the topic of quality control. As a follow up activity, to develop and disseminate TQM and QCC, a team was formed by the Development Bank of Japan (DBJ) and a handbook on TQM and QCC was prepared.

(xi) *Information management*

One of the *Kaizen* principles is basing decisions on facts. Ensuring that there are complete and accurate data both before and after implementation is indispensable for evaluation. Sometimes, in the processes of training before kickoff, some people start implementing what they have learned every day. Moreover, it can be difficult to get data on productivity, defects, and delivery delays, mainly due to lack of registering these issues in a log book. KPTs (QCCs) forget to register improvements they made, meetings, ideas generated, and so on. Marketing departments lack data on the number of customers, frequency of orders, lost markets, the number of lots or product types, and so on. In some cases, it is difficult to obtain financial data. Although companies have to protect their secrets, and this is acceptable, in some cases there is an extreme view about withholding all data.

5.5 The Ethiopian *Kaizen* Model: A Shopping Arcade for Africa?

Drawing lessons from the experience of a given country is not an easy task. Eight 'takeaway' determinants for success from this research are offered. These are:

(i) Strong commitment of top leadership at all levels;
(ii) Establishment of a national organizational framework with a clear vision, mission, and leadership;
(iii) Optimum utilization of *Kaizen* projects;
(iv) Grassroot-level promotion;
(v) Customization and standardization of training programs and materials;
(vi) Development of capable consultants;
(vii) Establishment of systems of recognition and awards; and
(viii) Sustaining *Kaizen* activities.

Considering these determinants while exploring the Ethiopian case is believed to be helpful in drawing tangible lessons. A brief discussion on each of these points, while referring to the supporting evidence, is offered below without or with little repetition of previously explored points.

5.5.1 Strong Commitment of Top Leadership at All Levels

In different parts of this chapter, the commitment of the late Prime Minister to initiating the transfer of *Kaizen* and the current Prime Minister to sustaining political leadership have been discussed. Such commitments are confirmed by the following facts:

(a) It was the late Prime Minister who requested the support of JICA for the *Kaizen* project and who provided support for the establishment of EKI.
(b) It is the current Prime Minister who has established and chaired the National *Kaizen* Council and supported the expansion and benefits of EKI.
(c) There were frequent exchanges of letters between the Ethiopian government and JICA as well as GRIPS Development Forum to discuss issues related to *Kaizen* and prepare an agenda for discussions.
(d) The budget requested by EKI has been fully endorsed each year.
(e) The success of EKI is partly due to committed company managers and *Kaizen* leaders.
(f) Attention from the minister and state ministers on supervising and receiving reports on its performance.

5.5.2 Establishing a National Organizational Framework with a Clear Vision, Mission, and Strong Leadership

EKI is an outcome of KU and the successful execution of its pilot project. If the project had not been successful, government commitment might have been halfhearted. However, the government and JICA followed up with frequent visits and evaluations of performance reports right from the beginning. The dissemination plan indicated the necessity of having a strong institution to expand on results attained during the pilot project. To establish the institute on a concrete foundation, the experiences of 13 countries were explored and customized to meet the needs of Ethiopia.

This process helped KU to acquire knowledge to prepare a Formation Paper and Gazette. The Gazette explicitly outlined the far-reaching duties of EKI. The commitment of the Prime Minister easily convinced the Council of Ministers to accept and adopt it. The first Director General assigned to EKI has been able to lead the project and has already established a basic knowledge platform. The central belief was to lead by knowledge and not to repeat mistakes that had occurred elsewhere. This was done by exploring the institutionalization study and careful consideration of the direction set in that study for successful accomplishment. Engagement in the project began not only by waiting for the experts but also under the assumption of equal leadership. Systems and procedures were designed that helped with the acquisition of knowledge on *Kaizen* rapidly, and EKI cultivated a learning organization culture. Young and talented staff members were selected as members of EKI and they have been trained continuously. EKI always attempts to create a motivating working environment and team culture.

EKI has carefully learned from the models of Japan and Singapore. However, since these two cases are quite different from the Ethiopian situation, EKI developed its own vision, roadmap, model, and strategies. It has shared these with JICA experts and officials, discussed them with government officials and institutions and popularized them among the public through different media networks. This has helped to create broad-based awareness and develop confidence in the sustainability of *Kaizen* activities. This is what EKI learned, practiced, and succeeded in sharing with others.

5.5.3 Optimum Utilization of *Kaizen* Projects

Among many factors that make EKI successful is strong project management. In all projects, EKI's management is heavily involved. These projects were not left to JICA's experts. There was continuous discussion on the preparation of the project design matrix (PDM), work plan, detailed activities, feedback and evaluation on the CRT and ICT, interim and final project evaluations, as well as the contents of teaching materials and manuals. EKI took the initiatives to customize *Kaizen* for the Ethiopian situation.

5.5.4 Grassroot-Level Promotion

The cases of successful countries like Singapore show that creating nationwide awareness is one of the most important factors for success. In Ethiopia, *Kaizen* was introduced not only in the manufacturing industry but also in different service organizations, including schools. In some cities and towns where big companies like sugar and textile companies implemented *Kaizen*, workers took the ideas home to their families. Many public and private media channels were mobilized to introduce the concept of *Kaizen* and disseminate the results attained to the public. Training was given to communicators and journalists. High-level officials including the prime ministers and frontline workers were interviewed and broadcast on NHK in Japan, the BBC, and CNN. Other foreign broadcasting channels have also covered Ethiopian *Kaizen*.

5.5.5 Customization and Standardization of Training Program and Materials

Kaizen itself is an outcome of customization. No two countries are similar enough for copy-and-paste-style projects to be successful. The unique features of each country should be taken into account in the implementation of *Kaizen*; however, its novelty and quality should be maintained. For instance, the concept of 5S and *MUDA* cannot be changed, but the way it is presented in training and the manner of implementation could differ from factory to factory, country to country, and so on. From the study of the experience of 13 other countries, EKI has learned that customized and standardized teaching materials are one of the key factors for success. EKI has consistently modified and customized teaching materials offered by JICA consultants. This customization takes two forms: firstly, the development of one set of customized master teaching materials and, secondly, to further customize the materials to suit each sub-sector like textiles, leather, metal, construction, and so on.

What EKI has learned from the failure cases of other countries is that a focus on the techniques and short-term targets does not lead to full-fledged success. Particularly, for a country like Ethiopia, attitudinal change is very important, and it must receive high priority. This could be realized through comprehensive understanding of *Kaizen*, strong team work, integrated companywide activities by top and middle management, and frontline workers. In EKI's training materials, this has been emphasized. The results attained so far bear witness to the importance of attitudinal change to sustain improvements.

5.5.6 Developing Capable Management and Consultants

To maintain the continuity and sustainability of the *Kaizen* movement, the presence of strong management and skilled consultants is indispensable. EKI is supported by JICA to develop its consultants. It has also initiated its own programs in collaboration with universities to develop local capacity-building capability. This has two advantages: it enhances the conceptual and analytical capacity of consultants and creates opportunities for university instructors to gain some experience of Gemba. EKI has developed a succession plan to nurture leaders from inside. The plan consists of developing two layers of management; top management and middle management. The overall plan is handled by the director general for top management and by deputy director generals for middle management. EKI's cross-functional KPTs are sources for cultivating middle-management staff. The leaders of cross-functional KPTs are the first layers for recruitment and promotion to fill the vacancy of middle management. As has been indicated above, EKI consultants are always eager to learn and know more, and are motivated to provide training, consultancy, and follow-ups throughout the year, usually staying in companies for a month or two and paying frequent visits every quarter. EKI pays allowances and the cost of accommodation for its consultants.

5.5.7 Establishing a System of Recognition and Award

One of the duties of EKI, as stipulated in the proclamation, is to establish recognition and award systems. As noted above in the discussion about the development of the new organizational structure, this activity has been given due regard. The Department of Certification, Registration, and Awards is led by a Deputy Director General. Every year there is a competition among companies, KPTs and outstanding individuals for *Kaizen* awards. There is also strong competition among EKI consultants to produce excellent companies and KPTs. The award is covered by major media companies and it is an important aspect of promotion.

5.5.8 Sustaining *Kaizen* Activities

JICA's approach to *Kaizen* promotion, regardless of country, is to raise awareness of *Kaizen* activities through the creation of model companies. This was true in Ethiopia. Demand for *Kaizen* was created by the pilot project and sustained in subsequent projects and ownership of EKI. The results that have been achieved and popularized through the media have resulted in increased demand from other companies, and EKI is now being inundated by many requests. Continuous and sustained demand is secured by the quality of training, consultancy, and follow-up services.

In a nutshell, ensuring political commitment, establishing an institutional infrastructure that owns and leads a national *Kaizen* movement, developing qualified and devoted local consultants, securing the commitment of implementing institutions, generating demand through grassroot-level promotion for *Kaizen* activities, and motivating high performers are among the major factors in sustaining *Kaizen* activities.

To conclude, while the above points are the key factors to be considered in terms of *Kaizen* programs, this should not limit readers' freedom to delve more deeply into the chapter. To answer the question of the title of this section: yes, this study demonstrates that EKI's approach can be considered as a useful way for Africa.

References

Ethiopia Kaizen Institute. (2011). *Proclamation on the Formation of EKI Number 256/2011*.
Ethiopia Kaizen Institute. (2012). *Annual Reports*.
Ethiopia Kaizen Institute. (2013). *Annual Reports*.
Ethiopia Kaizen Institute. (2014a). *Strategic Direction of Ethiopia Kaizen Movement*.

Ethiopia Kaizen Institute. (2014b). *Comprehensive Understanding of Kaizen and Implementation Strategy.*
Ethiopia Kaizen Institute. (2014c). *Strategic Framework of Ethiopia Kaizen.*
Ethiopia Kaizen Institute. (2014d). *Annual Reports.*
Ethiopia Kaizen Institute. (2015a). *EKI Growth and Transformation Plan (GTP II) 2015–2020.*
Ethiopia Kaizen Institute. (2015b). *Compiled Best Experience.*
Ethiopia Kaizen Institute. (2015c). *Annual Reports.*
Ethiopia Kaizen Institute. (2016a). *EKI Revised Organizational Structure.*
Ethiopia Kaizen Institute. (2016b). *Discussion Paper Prepared on the Occasion of Kaizen Month.*
Ethiopia Kaizen Institute. (2016c). *Annual Reports.*
Federal Democratic Republic of Ethiopia. (2011). *Proclamation 256/2012.*
Federal Democratic Republic of Ethiopia. (2015). *Second Growth and Transformation Plan.*
Hosotani, K. (1989). *QC-teki Mondai Kaiketsuho (The Quality Control Problem Solving Approach).* Tokyo: JUSE Press.
Imai, M. (1986). *Kaizen: The Key to Japan's Competitive Success.* New York: McGraw-Hill.
Inter-American Development Bank. (2003). *Handbook for TQM and QCC Volume I and II.*
Ishikawa, K. (1985). *What Is Total Quality Control? The Japanese Way* (trans. Lu D.J.) Englewood Cliffs: Prentice Hall. Originally published as a Japanese book entitled *Nihonteki Hinshitsu Kanri* in 1981. Tokyo: JUSE Press.
Japan International Cooperation Agency. (2011a). *The Study on Quality and Productivity Improvement (Kaizen) in the Federal Republic of Ethiopia,* JICA ILD-JR 11–011.
Japan International Cooperation Agency. (2011b). *Ethiopia Kaizen Manual.*
Japan International Cooperation Agency. (2014a). *The Project for Capacity Building for Dissemination of Quality and Productivity Improvement (Kaizen) in the Federal Republic of Ethiopia,* JICA IL-CR (10) 14–129.
Japan International Cooperation Agency. (2014b). *The Project for Capacity Building for Dissemination of Quality and Productivity Improvement (Kaizen) in the Federal Republic of Ethiopia Kaizen Manual.*
Japan International Cooperation Agency. (2016). *The Project on Capacity Development for Kaizen Implementation for Quality and Productivity Improvement and Competitiveness Enhancement,* JICA Progress Report (NO.1).
JUSE (QC Circle Headquarters). (1985). *How to Operate QC Circle Activities.* Tokyo: JUSE Press.

Kato, I., & Smalley, A. (2011). *Toyota Kaizen Methods, Six Steps to Improvement.* New York: Productivity Press.

Liker, J. K. (2004). *The Toyota Way.* New York: McGraw Hill.

Mekonen, G. T. (2014). *Kaizen ltqnajena Asetemamagn lwete (Kaizen for Integrated and Sustainable Change).* Addis Ababa: Messele Multimedia and Printing Works.

Mekonen, G. T. (2015a). *Kaizen ltqamawi lwete, lamrare leheqtena ltewdadarinte (Kaizen for Institutional Transformation, Leadership Excellence and Competitiveness).* Addis Ababa: Messele Multimedia and Printing Works.

Mekonen, G. T. (2015b). EKI Annual Booklet edition 3 number 3: *On Three Generations of Kaizen Transfer and Development Model,* pp. 11–20.

Mekonen, G. T. (2017). *Kaizen Yegna Model (Our Kaizen Model).* Addis Ababa: Mega Printing and Distribution Company.

Metehara Sugar Factory. (2016). *Annual Report.*

National Graduate Institute for Policy Studies. (2016). *Records of Ethiopia-Japan Industrial Policy Dialogue, Vol. II,* GRIPS Development Forum. Tokyo: National Graduate Institute for Policy Studies.

Osada, H. (2013). *Kaizen Best Practices of Quality Control Circles.*

Sato, K. (2011). *Framework of Ethiopia Kaizen Institute.*

Suzuki, T. (1994). *TPM in Process Industries.* New York: Productivity Press. Originally published as a Japanese book entitled *Sochi Kogyo no TPM in 1992.* Tokyo: Japan Institute of Plant Maintenance.

Umeda, M. (2001). *Seven Key Factors for Success on TQM.* Tokyo: Japanese Standards Association.

Open Access This chapter is licensed under the terms of the Creative Commons Attribution 4.0 International License (http://creativecommons.org/licenses/by/4.0/), which permits use, sharing, adaptation, distribution and reproduction in any medium or format, as long as you give appropriate credit to the original author(s) and the source, provide a link to the Creative Commons license and indicate if changes were made.

The images or other third party material in this chapter are included in the chapter's Creative Commons license, unless indicated otherwise in a credit line to the material. If material is not included in the chapter's Creative Commons license and your intended use is not permitted by statutory regulation or exceeds the permitted use, you will need to obtain permission directly from the copyright holder.

6

Kaizen as a Key Ingredient of Industrial Development Policy

Keijiro Otsuka

Eradication of poverty in the world is one of the main goals of international society. Indeed, included among the United Nation's the Millennium Development Goals (MDGs) was the goal to cut the poverty ratio in half from 1995 to 2015. Some of the eight development goals, including halving poverty, were achieved, but some other goals were not. Hence, the Sustainable Development Goals (SDGs) were announced in 2016, with 17 goals and 169 targets, with an unchanged or even increasing emphasis on reducing the incidence of poverty. Although we fully support the idea of setting up such goals, they are not very useful unless we find strategies to achieve them. Yet, to the best of our knowledge, there has been little discussion about effective development strategies to

---

This chapter heavily draws on "Training-Infrastructure-Finance (TIF) Strategy for Industrial Development in Sub-Saharan Africa," prepared by Research Group on Strategic Support for Industrial Development in SSA and published by JICA Research Institute, October 2017.

K. Otsuka (✉)
Graduate School of Economics, Kobe University, Kobe, Japan
e-mail: otsuka@econ.kobe-u.ac.jp

© The Author(s) 2018
K. Otsuka et al. (eds.), *Applying the Kaizen in Africa*,
https://doi.org/10.1007/978-3-319-91400-8_6

achieve the MDGs and SDGs. Thus, there is no universally accepted effective strategy to develop industries.[1]

In order to reduce poverty, build peace in conflict-affected countries, and rehabilitate the devastated economy in disaster areas, it is imperative to create decent employment opportunities for the poor and the vulnerable by developing labor-intensive manufacturing industries. Furthermore, the creation of factory jobs for women tends to improve women's economic and social status (Heath and Mobarak 2015). Thus, the development of industries ought to be a central theme of development issues.[2]

So far in this book, we have stressed the importance of *Kaizen* in stimulating industrial development in SSA, by proving the theoretical background and empirical evidence of its impact in Chap. 1, reviewing important roles played by *Kaizen* in Japan's Official Development Assistance (ODA) in Chap. 2, showing the general impacts of *Kaizen* in Chap. 3 and in Ethiopia in particular in Chap. 5, and proposing standardized and practical *Kaizen* useful for SSA in Chap. 4. We do not mean to imply, however, that a thorough implementation of *Kaizen* is sufficient for successful industrial development. Actually, it is not. The point we want to emphasize is that *Kaizen* is a central and indispensable ingredient of industrial development policies. There is no question that beyond competent entrepreneurs, basic infrastructure and credit are needed for successful industrial development. We simply argue that *Kaizen* is an excellent entry point, the most effective first step toward industrial development that is badly needed for sustainable development, particularly when foreign direct investment (FDI) is made. The sole purpose of this final chapter is to specify an effective strategy to develop industries for poverty reduction and inclusive income growth in SSA, while recognizing the decisively important role played by *Kaizen* in the process of industrial development in SSA.

---

[1] For example, World Bank (2012) discusses the importance of creating productive jobs, but not a strategy to do so.

[2] Needless to say, the development of agriculture is also a critical development issue in SSA (Otsuka and Larson 2013, 2016; Otsuka et al. 2016). Agriculture, however, does not offer ample employment opportunities for the poor (David and Otsuka 1994; Otsuka et al. 2009; Estudillo and Otsuka 2016), so the development of the nonfarm sector is indispensable for inclusive economic development.

The rest of this chapter is organized as follows. In Sect. 6.1 we explain why our approach, which emphasizes *Kaizen* as an entry point to industrial development, is recommended. In this section, we also compare our approach with those recommended by the emerging literature on industrial policies in SSA. We discuss why the sequence of policy measures from *Kaizen* to industrial parks and financial support is expected to be effective for industrial development in Sect. 6.2. We clarify the role of *Kaizen* in attracting FDI and facilitating learning from FDI in Sect. 6.3. We conclude this chapter by making a proposal to realize the industrial development in SSA in Sect. 6.4.

6.1 *Kaizen* as an Entry Point to Industrial Development

We propose a logical sequence of support measures beginning with *Kaizen* training of entrepreneurs followed by investment in infrastructure and financial support, with the aim of attracting foreign direct investment (FDI) and facilitating learning from FDI. We call our strategy—consisting of training, infrastructure investment, and financial supports—TIF, which is portrayed in Fig. 6.1. We recommend the TIF strategy, because the rates of return on investment in infrastructure including industrial parks as well as physical capital will be low, if there are few promising entrepreneurs. Thus, investment in human capital of entrepreneurs should precede investment in infrastructure. While we do not argue that training workers is unimportant, we believe that the training of entrepreneurs, who are major decision makers, has often been neglected in the past, even though it is likely to be more important than worker training. We also do not argue that the proposed sequences must always be followed strictly in a step-by-step way over time. In practice, training, investment in infrastructure, and financial support may be carried out simultaneously. In other words, the proposed sequence is logical, but not intended to be strictly followed as discrete steps. We simply would like to emphasize that the rates of return on investment in infrastructure and physical capital tend to be high when the ability of potentially promising entrepreneurs has been enhanced.

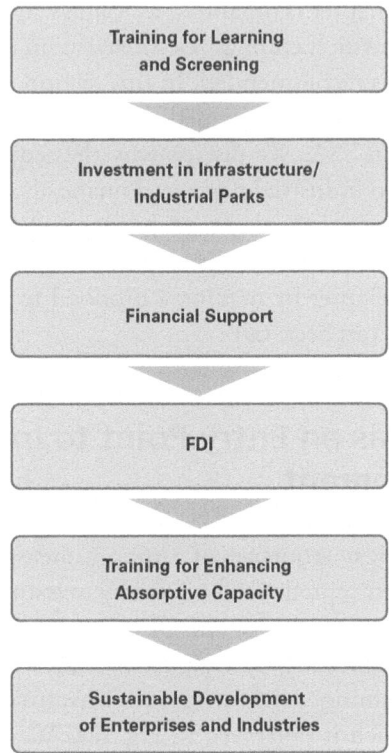

Fig. 6.1 A recommended logical sequence of industrial development policies. (Source: Prepared by the author)

We would also like to emphasize that training of entrepreneurs is useful not only for improving the ability of entrepreneurs but also for identifying promising and non-promising entrepreneurs. Thus, targeted support for admitting promising enterprises to industrial parks and providing financial support to them becomes feasible after the training of entrepreneurs. This is another reason to conduct *Kaizen* training at the outset of the industrial development process.

More fundamentally, we advocate this approach because (1) adequate training of entrepreneurs and investments in infrastructure are not amenable to market mechanisms, (2) there is a room for the government and aid agencies to provide financial support considering the underdevelopment of financial sectors in developing economies, and (3) the TIF approach is likely to play the role of vanguard in attracting FDI by establishing a favorable production climate for FDI. The spectacular impact of training of 130 newly recruited employees for garment production in Bangladesh by the Daewoo Corporation of Korea is well-known (Mottaleb and Sonobe 2011). Within two years, after eight months of training in Korea, almost all of them left to start their own garment businesses, which has resulted in unprecedented jump-start of a gigantic new industry. This incidence clearly indicates that private entrepreneurs do not have adequate incentives to invest in human capital of their employees because of the possibility of labor turnover.

We must also note that FDI does not immediately lead to the development of industries in developing countries because foreign enterprises have incentives to protect production and management know-how from competing enterprises. In order to facilitate learning from FDI, further investments in human capital of entrepreneurs as well as workers are required, so as to enhance the absorptive capacity of the local enterprises.

We recommend developing labor-intensive industries in SSA, where unskilled workers are abundantly available. Lin (2014) argues that to be successful, industrial development must follow the comparative advantage of the economy, whereas Chang (Lin and Chang 2009) argues that developing countries should adopt proactive industrial policy, which takes into account a dynamically changing comparative advantage. We fully agree with their arguments that industrial policy should support the development of industries that have and will continue to have comparative advantages. However, it is not clear how to identify such industries in practice or whether the government can find them without major failures (Kruger 2011). Yet, in principle, we advocate the development of labor-intensive industries in SSA.

Lin appears to assume implicitly that there are no spontaneously developed industries in SSA, suggesting that promising industries are missing in SSA. According to our own as well as others' research in SSA (Sonobe and Otsuka 2011; Higuchi et al. 2016; Mano et al. 2012; Oyeyinka and McCormick 2007), however, there are a large number of informal industrial clusters in SSA. They have spontaneously formed and, hence, are obviously market-led. Many of them are slowly developing, but the fact that such industrial clusters have emerged without any support from the government implies that these clustered industries have clear comparative advantages. We argue that we should support the development of such clustered industries, which we believe have the potential to grow and become formal sectors. Our argument is in line with the finding of Hidalgo et al. (2007) that industrial development entails continuous processes of upgrading the quality of products and production processes and developing slightly new products, rather than the sudden emergence of new industries.

Without any doubt, a major source of industrial development, particularly in developing countries, is technological progress, which in turn depends on learning useful knowledge from abroad. Since acquired useful knowledge spills over, the private benefit of knowledge acquisition is exceeded by the social benefit. Since the private benefit is lower than social benefit, the incentives to acquire useful knowledge are lower than social optimum, resulting in socially inadequate learning with "missing knowledge." Thus, Noman and Stiglitz (2015, 2016) recommend that governments in developing countries should play the role of catalyst in facilitating learning useful knowledge from abroad. We agree with this and further argue that the efficient management of enterprises is critically "missing" knowledge, based on our own empirical research in SSA (Sonobe and Otsuka 2011, 2014). The acquisition of such missing knowledge will promote a structural change in Africa from a lower productivity sector to a higher productivity sector (Page 2015).

It is true that not only management knowledge but also a trained workforce, infrastructure, and efficient credit markets are missing in most developing countries. There is no question that such missing factors are constraints on growth. Thus, it appears useful to remove major constraints, as is argued by Hausmann, Rodrick, and Velasco (2008). We must recognize, however, that if we remove one constraint, other constraints appear, so we have to anticipate changes in major constraints when we formulate an effective industrial policy. For example, the lack of infrastructure may not be a major constraint when there are no growing firms. It becomes a major constraint, however, when a number of trained entrepreneurs plan to expand their operations, resulting in congestion. According to our research, training of entrepreneurs has high payoffs even without investing in infrastructure and providing cheap credit, because trained entrepreneurs use the existing resources more efficiently, as was argued in Chaps. 1 and 3 (also see Sonobe and Otsuka 2011, 2014; Higuchi et al. 2016; Mano et al. 2012). Subsequently, those entrepreneurs who wish to expand their businesses face such constraints as congestion, the lack of spacious industrial parks, and the lack of credit for constructing new factories. That is why we argue for the logical sequence of investing in entrepreneurial talents particularly by *Kaizen* training, infrastructure or industrial parks, and a credit system, which are key to successful industrial development.

6.2 From *Kaizen* to Industrial Parks and Financial Support

Although we advocate logically sequential support for industrial development from *Kaizen* training of entrepreneurs to infrastructure investments and financial support, we do not argue that investment in infrastructure or financial support should be delayed until the *Kaizen* training of entrepreneurs is completed. Our proposed sequence is logically sequential but may overlap or may even be reversed over time. Thus, training, infrastructure investment, and financial support may be made in parallel, or additional training may be required after investments in infrastructure are made because an inadequate supply of entrepreneurial talent is later found to be a major bottleneck on further development. The important point is that the *Kaizen* training of entrepreneurs confers substantial benefits even without improving infrastructure and providing financial support (Mano et al. 2012; Sonobe and Otsuka 2014; Suzuki et al. 2014; Higuchi et al. 2015, 2016). Furthermore, we expect that such training will enhance payoffs to investments in infrastructure and the provision of financial support by enhancing the ability of entrepreneurs and making it possible to identify promising and non-promising entrepreneurs. Thus, the training of entrepreneurs ought to be an effective entry point to industrial development.

Competent entrepreneurs who take the *Kaizen* training program will likely want to apply newly learned management policies and adopt progressive management plans, for example, employing more workers, installing more machines, and moving to industrial parks to construct new larger factories. It then becomes possible to offer targeted support for them by providing space in industrial parks and financial support for the construction of new factories. Thus, the TIF approach relies on complementarity between *Kaizen* training and investment in infrastructure as well as financial support.

6.2.1 Investment in *Kaizen* Training

A variety of human resources with different skills, knowledge, and talents are required for economic development. For example, distribution systems must develop alongside the economy to transport goods from one place to another, and hence there must be competent staff capable of managing ports, airports, transportation and communication systems, and storage and distribution centers. This illustrates how important it is to invest in human resources for economic development. We believe that particularly scarce but critically important human resources in developing countries are competent managers and owners of enterprises, whom we refer to as entrepreneurs (Bruhn et al. 2010). They are major decision makers and must play the role of innovators.

To be innovative, entrepreneurs must invest in their human capital. A lot of time, effort, and resources are needed for such investments. However, they cannot know in advance the quality of trainers, instructors, and teachers from whom they will learn and, hence, returns on human capital investments are uncertain. Moreover, employers may not be interested in investing in hired managers who have the potential to become capable entrepreneurs, because they may quit their current jobs in the future. Therefore, we cannot assume that market forces lead to adequate investment in entrepreneurial human capital. Governments in developing countries should guarantee the quality of trainers, nurture a number of *Kaizen* experts, and support the training of entrepreneurs in a sustainable fashion, as we argued in Chaps. 1 and 5. If the government is not prepared to play such a role, donor agencies and international organizations should assist the investment in entrepreneurial human capital.

A useful lesson may be learned from the successful experience of Thailand's Eastern Seaboard Development Plan (1982–95). This was a regional development plan based on the construction of harbors, highways, and industrial parks with aims of reducing congestion in Bangkok due to successful industrialization and utilizing natural gas deposit discovered in Gulf of Thailand. The government of Japan supported the design of a development plan, provided loans, and assisted with FDI of Japanese companies in industrial parks. Furthermore, Japan invested in managers of infrastructure and employees of Japanese companies, particularly engineers and middle-level managers. As a result, huge industrial clusters of automobile production have been built with a large number of local enterprises and ample employment opportunities. According to ex-post assessment of the plan (Ariga and Ejima 2000), 30,000 new jobs were created in Laem Chabang City, which is located in the middle of the Eastern Seaboard, and more than 10,000 new jobs were created in Map Ta Phut Industrial Estate in the 1990s when the plan was completed. The success was attributed to the coordination of investments in human capital, infrastructure, and factory buildings and other physical capital. Also noteworthy is the dissemination of *Kaizen*, which emphasizes a participatory approach of workers to production management and quality control.

The quality of management has increasingly received the attention of development economists as a major factor affecting the performance of enterprises in developing countries, because it is found that firms in low-income countries are significantly more likely to suffer from poor management than their counterparts in high-income countries (Bloom et al. 2016). Thus, it is recommended that aid agencies and international organizations assist governments in developing countries in institutional building toward the goal of spreading good management practices. Indeed, there have been a number of such projects and programs. The Ethiopian *Kaizen* Institute is an excellent example of institutional innovation (Chap. 5). The World Bank and International Labor Organization nurtured a number of trainers who can provide business development services and master trainers who can train trainers in a large number of developing countries. There has also been assistance given directly to local firms, not through the government, such as the provision of training programs for entrepreneurs under the names of women entrepreneur programs and micro and small enterprise (MSE) training programs. Microfinance institutions have also provided business development services for their potential clients.

In recent years, there has been a considerable increase in interest among development economists in assessing the impacts of these kinds of management training programs on the trained enterprises by using randomized controlled trials (RCTs). Almost all such studies find that training has favorable effects on management practices, and several studies also find that training improved business performance measured in sales revenue, profits, productivity, and so on. Nonetheless, to our knowledge such assistance programs and projects have not led to the kind of notable industrial development in which a number of training participants grow into large firms, thereby creating a large number of jobs, nor has there been industrial development comparable to that on the Eastern Seaboard in Thailand. Presumably, the reason is that the assistance is intended to help those who start small or self-employed business and those who want to sustain their businesses. Little assistance is intended to help those who have been successful and are interested in substantially expanding their businesses by employing a large number of workers. Instead, they focused on financial literacy, how to make a business plan, elementary marketing, and entrepreneurship. Knowledge of these items is useful for any size of businesses, but it does not help entrepreneurs solve problems they would face when increasing the number of their employees. It is especially difficult to nurture an efficient workforce with workers who are not educated, not accustomed to working as part of a team, or who do not aspire to acquire new skills. In industrial clusters or cities in developed countries in which a number of medium and large enterprises are located, small business owners can easily invite a former manager of a larger firm to teach them how to cope with the problems that arise from the expansion of operation and employment size. For the majority of entrepreneurs in low-income countries, however, such experienced advisors are unavailable and, hence, it is difficult for them to learn how to manage larger enterprises.

Low-income countries in SSA potentially have a comparative advantage in labor-intensive industries due to the abundance of those who cannot earn high incomes and would accept the offer of low-wage jobs. Actually, however, such a potential advantage has not been realized because it is difficult to turn these people into efficient workers who supply effective labor at a low wage. For a low-income country to achieve industrial development on a large scale, the potential comparative advantage in labor-intensive industries must be actualized. It is true that the development of labor-intensive industries is not indispensable for high growth. It may be easy to raise the economic growth rate by making the country a focal point of outsourcing of call center services, data entry services, and other back office services from developed countries. As experienced already by India and the Philippines, however, this type of economic growth may end up with jobless growth that offers jobs to college graduates, but not to the less educated population.

To achieve economic growth with equity, low-income countries ought to seek the development of labor-intensive industries, which in turn necessitate the dissemination of management practices and skills that allow firms to employ a large number of employees and turn them into an effective labor force. Fortunately, there is an inexpensive, human-friendly approach to such management, as has been discussed intensively in this volume (see particularly Chap. 3). It is called *Kaizen*. According to the Oxford Dictionary of English, this is "a Japanese business philosophy of continuous improvement of working practices, personal efficiency, etc." It is not just philosophical but also scientific,[3] in the sense that it has been developed through observations and experiments by a number of firms.

Kaizen is designed to facilitate coordination of the division of labor between managers and workers, between production divisions, and between workers. The total quality control achieved through joint participation of managers and workers is just one of many successful examples of *Kaizen* activities. Indeed, an RCT (randomized controlled trial) of *Kaizen* for medium-size enterprises in the textile industry in India found a significant impact of *Kaizen* training on management practices and enterprise performance (Bloom et al. 2013). Similarly an RCT in the

---

[3] See Chap. 1 on the definition of *Kaizen*.

garment industry in Vietnam also found a significant impact of *Kaizen* training on management practices and performance (Suzuki et al. 2014).

SSA has in general a comparative advantage in labor-intensive industries such as the textile, garment, leather shoe, and simple metal-processing industries, where *Kaizen* training is found to have profound impacts on management practices and enterprise performance (Mano et al. 2012; Higuchi et al. 2015). Yet, the fact that many of these industries failed to develop strongly indicates the severe lack of managerial human capital in the area, capable of managing a number of workers in a participatory fashion (Sonobe and Otsuka 2014).

As is demonstrated in Fig. 1.4, the results of an RCT in the garment industry in Tanzania by Higuchi et al. (2016), where not only classroom lectures but also on-site training by instructors was offered, are instructive. It is clear that improved management practices, measured by a management score,[4] were increasingly adopted more or less equally for a while after the training by the groups receiving both classroom and on-site training, only classroom training, and only on-site training. The control group receiving no training also adopted some improved management practices due to imitation. The management score, however, began declining 1.5 years after the training, presumably because the trainees sorted out irrelevant practices. A major finding is that only the group receiving both classroom and on-site training continued to increase value added, which indicates that the combination of conceptual training in the classroom and practical training on-site leads to the sustainable growth of enterprises.

The finding of RCTs that *Kaizen* training improves enterprise performance by improving management practices, even without improving infrastructure and providing subsidized credit, strongly indicates that the *Kaizen* training is an effective first step for industrial development. Thus, it seems clear that it is desirable to train a number of specialists in *Kaizen* and offer a number of *Kaizen* training courses, thereby increasing the number of competent entrepreneurs. This is what has been happening in Ethiopia, where the government established the Ethiopian *Kaizen* Institute, where Japanese *Kaizen* experts have been sent to train selected Ethiopians who will later be dispatched to factories and training centers (see Chap. 5).

---

[4] This is measured by the number of improved management practices out of 27 recommended ones.

If competent entrepreneurs are nurtured by the management training, many enterprises will develop, which will lead to congestion in the existing industrial clusters as well as in other original locations. Then the demand for industrial parks in the suburbs of cities will increase. Investment in industrial parks will have high returns if the government allocates space to promising entrepreneurs. If the government also provides financial support only to those promising entrepreneurs, the risk of failure in the allocation of investment funds will be reduced. In this way, the TIF approach is likely to significantly enhance the likelihood of success of industrial development.[5]

Finally, it should be stressed that the policy of increasing the number of competent entrepreneurs by means of *Kaizen* training will contribute to the establishment of competitive markets, which, in turn, is expected to reduce corruption and preferential treatment of specific industries and enterprises (Otsuka and Sonobe 2011).

6.2.2 Investment in Industrial Parks

Industries tend to be concentrated geographically. This is because of the benefits of agglomeration economies, including savings on transaction costs between enterprises due to the locational proximity, development of labor markets of skilled workers, and spillovers of useful information, such as innovative new ideas (Sonobe and Otsuka 2006). Indeed, there are many promising informal industrial clusters in SSA, such as a car repair-cum-metal processing cluster in Kumasi in Ghana, a leather shoe cluster in Addis Ababa in Ethiopia, and garment clusters in Dar es Salaam in Tanzania (Sonobe and Otsuka 2011). In addition to the agglomeration economies, clustering contributes to saving investment costs in infrastructure, because the construction of industrial parks equipped with transportation and communication infrastructures and water and sewage facilities is less costly than investments in such infrastructures over wide areas. Thus, the establishment of industrial parks which house enterprises

---

[5] Although we did not discuss it explicitly, general education of the labor force particularly through schooling is extremely important. We did not take up this issue, as it is a part of overall economic and social policies, rather than specifically industrial development policy.

producing similar and related products, for example, part suppliers and assemblers, ought to be a part of effective strategy to develop manufacturing industries.[6]

The establishment of industrial parks, however, may fail to invite domestic enterprises to the parks unless there are growing enterprises looking for larger spaces to expand the operation of their businesses. This is why we advocate the training of entrepreneurs as a first step for industrialization. It is also worth emphasizing that the success of Thailand's Eastern Seaboard Development Plan (ESDP), which was alluded to before, rested on the fact that the construction of industrial parks and other infrastructure coincided with the congestion of industrialized areas in Bangkok and the transformation process of the entire economy from light- to heavy-industry-centered structures, which created huge demand for production space with a sufficient supply of infrastructure (Ariga and Ejima 2000).[7] According to our own observations, industrial parks were constructed outside of the old urban industrial centers, when the original locations became congested due to the expansion and development of clustered enterprises in China and Taiwan. The relocation of the production bases to industrial parks led to the transformation from informal to formal clusters in these countries.

The establishment of industrial parks will help attract FDI, which is widely recognized as a conduit to transfer improved production technologies and management practices from developed to developing countries. FDI, however, will not be attracted without the availability of disciplined workers, experienced middle-level managers, suppliers of simple parts and components, and the more than minimum development of supporting industries, such as machine repair sectors. FDI policies also need to be

---

[6] According to Hashino and Otsuka (2016), producer associations play an important role in introducing new technologies and assuring the product quality in dynamically growing clusters. If such producer associations exist, support for and cooperation with them can be an effective way to develop industrial clusters.

[7] According to Mieno (2013), ESDP was initially designed with two major aims in accordance with the fourth and fifth Five Year Plan in the 1970s: to reduce the excessive concentration of industries in the Bangkok metropolitan area by shifting growing light industries to the Laem Chabang port area and to construct a government-led petrochemical industry utilizing natural gas in the Gulf of Thailand, based in Map Ta Phut port. Industrialization since the mid-1980s has oriented to FDI-led machinery industry, which is different from the envisaged initial plans to develop light industries and government-led petrochemical industries.

liberalized and further supports for FDI implemented. The quality of industrial parks also matters. Since construction companies and general trading companies in Japan have accumulated experience in the construction of industrial parks, public–private partnerships can be deployed for the construction of industrial parks in SSA. Such partnerships will stimulate FDI of private manufacturing companies.

ODA is expected to help attract FDI. This is particularly the case in Japanese ODA (Kimura and Todo 2010). In order to do so, ODA must be allocated to human capital development and the establishment of infrastructure, which are not amenable to market mechanisms. In particular, we advocate the *Kaizen* training of entrepreneurs and the construction of industrial parks, because these are expected to be cost effective and conducive to industrial development.

6.2.3 Financial Support

Since the main function of financial intermediation is to allocate an appropriate amount of investment funds, the development of a financial system is indispensable for the development of the entire economy. In order to achieve this function, the financial sector needs the capacity to assess the potential performance of enterprises and the profitability of their projects. While information asymmetry generally impedes efficient transactions in the credit market, financial institutions must reduce inefficiency by means of information processing.

The development of the financial sector is slow in many developing countries, which means that the problem of asymmetric information is not overcome in a number of countries. Consequently, the financial sector fails to allocate enough funds to promising investments. In order to improve management of the financial sector, human resources must be trained and, at the same time, continuous and long-term lending experience needs to be accumulated. Furthermore, legal and institutional governance systems must be in place to facilitate efficient financial transactions. In addition, monopolistic elements of the financial sector by large conglomerates, if any, must be removed to reduce distortions in financial markets.

Therefore, on the one hand, the general support for the development of the financial sector can be efficiency-improving. On the other hand, it may be desirable to introduce selective financial support by aid agencies and international organizations, which supplement the insufficient function of the underdeveloped financial sector. In particular, selective support for promising entrepreneurs within a context of the TIF approach can be highly desirable.

Japan has developed a two-step loan program for the purpose of targeted financial support.[8] Under this program, Japan provides loans to development-oriented public or semi-public financial organizations in developing countries, which, in turn, provide loans to end-users who would not otherwise have access to formal loans. Prior to the 1990s, the main end-users used to be small-scale farmers in Southeast Asia. Since then, loans to small and medium-sized enterprises (SMEs) through public-sector organizations increased, as increases in FDI raised the demand for such loans. It is critically important to recognize that the two-step loan is one way to support SMEs, whose production and management efficiency can be improved by the training of managers.

Although there are many successful two-step loan programs, the reasons for their success are not necessarily clear (Hayashi 1995). One possible though unlikely explanation is that local financial institutions possess sufficient capacity to identify promising enterprises and projects, and the two-step loan programs simply utilize their latent capacity. Another possibility, which we believe is more plausible, is that the two-step loan provides opportunities for local financial institutions to accumulate lending experience to new loan users and thereby develop their abilities to find promising projects that otherwise would not have been supported.

---

[8] As another attempt to apply Japan's experience of SME financial support to developing countries, credit guarantee schemes also seem promising. Recently, the schemes are being applied to a few Southeast Asian countries (e.g., Yoshino and Taghizadeh-Hesary 2016). Apart from Japan's experience, the International Finance Corporation (IFC) launched the SME Ventures Program in 2007 in order to create jobs and promote robust economic growth by providing the risk capital and strategic advice to SMEs in developing counties. For example, one of the IFC's projects, Central Africa SME Fund (CASF) targeting the Central African Republic (CAR) and the Democratic Republic of the Congo (DRC), provided the risk capital of debt and equity to over 30 companies during the period from 2011 to 2015, which resulted in the creation of some 500 jobs at the targeted companies. This IFC program is worth analyzing further. http://xsmlcapital.com/funds/central-africa-sme-fund/

Recently, variants in two-step loans have arisen. For example, offering a package of loans and management training to SMEs run by the Small Business Finance Corporation is now being widely applied in Asian countries. This attests the complementarity between loans and management training which is consistent with the TIF approach. In other words, we recommend providing two-step loans to those competent entrepreneurs who have participated in *Kaizen* training programs. Since Japanese SMEs also launch production in developing countries, the two-step loans are used to support them. Recently, not only public-sector financial institutions but also private institutions have become involved in two-step loan programs. In any case, we recommend the use of two-step loans as a part of a package of industrial development policies. At the same time, we must recognize that the economic rationale for the success of two-step loans as an aid scheme is not yet completely understood. Therefore, further academic research in this field is called for.[9]

In the literature on finance in developing countries, there is a debate as to whether market-based or bank-based financial systems work better to facilitate economic development (La Porta et al. 1998; Levine 2002). The history of development of financial sectors in developing countries in Asia, however, strongly suggests that the first priority should be the development of a financial intermediary rather than a capital market. This is because commercial banks do not function well in providing loans to SMEs and, as a result, informal inter-business trade credit plays a major role in promoting their development (McMillan and Woodruff 1999; Allen et al. 2005). To build a better functioning financial system particularly for SMEs, shifting from informal trade credit to formal bank credit by enhancing the capacity of the commercial banking sector is key, and a relevant policy scheme is vital (i.e., Hellman, Murdock and Stiglitz 1997). On the other hand, it may not be unrealistic that in the long-term process of developing a financial system, well-targeted two-step loan programs can assist both the development of banking sectors and the TIF approach to industrial development.

---

[9] The loan program discussed here must be distinguished from microfinance, which is designed to reduce poverty at the household level without regard to the industrial development.

6.3 *Kaizen* for Attracting and Taking Advantage of FDI

Globally the amount of FDI has been increasing dramatically since the mid-1980s, as has FDI from Japan (Ito and Kruger 2000; Lall and Urata 2003). Both deregulation of financial transactions in developed countries and the liberalization of FDI policies in developing countries have contributed to this expansion. Japanese FDI also increased because of the appreciation of the Japanese yen, which led to the relocation of production bases to other Asian countries. Interestingly, Japanese FDI is highly concentrated in the manufacturing sector, which reflects the comparative advantage of Japanese multi-national enterprises (MNEs) in manufacturing sectors in developing countries.

One reason for the rapid increase in FDI is the shift from exports to local production for sale in developing countries. Another is the fragmentation of production processes in which the best production locations across country borders are selected, in order to create global value chains. In this globalization process, the role of domestic enterprises as partners of MNEs has become increasingly important.

The TIF approach is useful to lay foundations for attracting FDI. In fact, FDI is attracted to developing countries that have competent entrepreneurs, disciplined workers, and well-equipped industrial parks. Considering that the amount of FDI is nine times as large as ODA as of 2014,[10] and that foreign firms bring about improved technologies and management practices, it is of utmost importance for developing countries to attract FDI (Crespo and Fontoura 2007). Anticipating FDI in the future, it is highly desirable to let MNEs participate from the beginning in the design and implementation of the *Kaizen* training programs for entrepreneurs.

It is a mistake to assume that once FDI is made, domestic enterprises automatically learn advanced technologies and management methods, as horizontal knowledge spillovers from MNEs to domestic enterprises in the same industry are limited. The major beneficiaries from MNEs are domestic enterprises in upstream industries, which provide parts and

---

[10] FDI amounted to US$136 billion, whereas ODA amounted to US$16 billion in 2014 (https://www.jetro.go.jp/world/japan/stats/fdi.html; http://www.mofa.go.jp/mofaj/gaiko/oda/files/000137908.pdf).

components to foreign affiliates (Javorcik 2014). This means that while foreign firms effectively protect know-how from their rival firms, they order the production of specific parts and components by local enterprises with instructions detailing the production methods. In other words, the initial effect of FDI is to stimulate the development of industrial sectors producing parts and components. The other side of the same coin is that in order to attract FDI, the development of part-supplying industries is very important.

Typically such part suppliers are subcontractors who receive orders from foreign affiliates as well as materials and production instructions. In order to secure cheap, high-quality parts, foreign affiliates have incentives to provide production training for entrepreneurs and workers in such domestic enterprises. But if these domestic enterprises passively receive orders and produce parts and components without undertaking market research, technology choice, procurement of materials, production designs, and marketing, they are unlikely to make sizable profits or grow. Such passive entrepreneurs are termed as captive suppliers by Gereffi et al. (2005). Pre- and post-production activities are known to be core competencies of leading MNEs and a major source of profits (Humphrey and Schmitz 2002). In other words, the management abilities of local entrepreneurs do matter. Managerially competent entrepreneurs will try to absorb not only the knowledge of production methods but also knowledge of management, encompassing pre- and post-production activities. Only if local entrepreneurs learn advanced management methods can their enterprises become independent and earn a large share of profits. This view on the importance of management ability for the absorption of advanced knowledge is consistent with the recent literature referenced earlier, which argues that what is really missing in developing countries is managerial human capital (Bloom et al. 2013, 2016; Bruhn et al. 2010; Sonobe and Otsuka 2014).

We must clearly recognize that foreign companies are willing to provide training in production, but not in management. This means that the attraction of FDI is not the end of industrial policy but the beginning of a new phase of industrial development in which management ability must play a key role. Therefore, the TIF approach aims not only to attract FDI but also to strengthen the absorptive capacity and management abilities of domestic enterprises. Indeed, we recommend the provision of advanced *Kaizen* training programs by the government and aid agencies to enhance the absorptive capacity of local enterprises (see Fig. 6.1). Such training may lead to "imitative innovation," which can have ground-breaking impacts on productivity growth of local enterprises and industrial development in developing countries (Sonobe and Otsuka 2006, 2011). In order to realize such industrial development, it is of utmost importance to generate a new cohort of highly competent management consultants knowledgeable about *Kaizen* in SSA.

6.4 Conclusions and Implications

Unlike modern service sectors, such as those related to information and communication technology (ICT) and the financial sectors that employ highly educated workers, light manufacturing industries are capable of providing ample employment opportunities for the uneducated, women, and youth, thereby making it possible to achieve inclusive growth. The starting point of our proposal is the recognition that there are many spontaneously developed industrial clusters in SSA, producing garments, textile, shoes, processed foods, furniture, metal products, and simple machineries. Their development is market-led and obviously in line with their comparative advantage. In our view, these industries fail to develop because of the market failures, ranging from socially inadequate investment in managerial human capital and infrastructure to the absence of efficient financial markets. Thus, our proposal aims to correct these market failures by supporting management training, investments in infrastructure, and the provision of credit.

Our second premise is that the transfer of useful technology and management knowledge from advanced countries is the prerequisite for industrial development in SSA. Based on Japan's experience of supporting the miraculous development of East Asian economies and empirical evidence accumulated in SSA, we propose to disseminate *Kaizen* in this area.

Our proposal is unique in its recognition of the complementarities among policy measures. It seems obvious to us that rates of return on investment in industrial parks will be very low unless there are many promising and growing local enterprises. Similarly, the provision of cheap credit does not make sense if there are only a small number of promising enterprises, or if promising entrepreneurs cannot be identified. In contrast, empirical evidence clearly shows that *Kaizen* training of entrepreneurs is effective even without any other policy supports. Thus, we recommend the TIF approach, beginning with the *Kaizen* training of entrepreneurs, which is useful not only for enhancing entrepreneurial abilities but also for identifying promising entrepreneurs, followed by targeted supports for promising enterprises by means of investments in industrial parks and the provision of credit (see Fig. 6.1).

Considering the increasing importance of FDI as a conduit to transfer advanced technologies and improved management practices from developed to developing countries, we propose that the TIF approach should be designed to attract FDI from the beginning. For this purpose, we recommend private enterprises interested in FDI, practitioners of foreign aid, and development economists participate in designing the TIF approach in practice.

It is a mistake to assume that once FDI is made, local enterprises will learn useful knowledge and grow accordingly. While the presence of FDI provides an opportunity to learn, whether the host country enterprises learn useful knowledge and grow depends on their absorptive capacity. At this stage, advanced management and technological training becomes crucial. In all likelihood, if such investments are made, local enterprises will continue to grow, which will lead to the development of local industries and stimulate the development of the entire economy.

It must be stressed that practitioners, MNEs, and economists must make concerted efforts to design an effective TIF approach. Due considerations must be given to the unique features of countries in SSA, which can be significantly different from those of Asian countries. Furthermore, success or failure in each step of the TIF approach, including investment in infrastructure and financial support for competent entrepreneurs, hinges on the development of human resources capable of effective operation and maintenance. If concerted efforts are made successfully, we are wholly confident that the TIF strategy, which is deeply based on the diffusion of *Kaizen*, will lead to sustainable and inclusive industrial development in SSA.

Because of the confidence of all the contributors to this volume that *Kaizen* ought to play a central role in promoting the development of industries in SSA, we explained why *Kaizen* is so important in Chap. 1, its role in Japan's ODA policy in Chap. 2, the impacts of *Kaizen* in Chap. 3, how the standardization of *Kaizen* is related to *Kaizen* training programs offered by Japan International Cooperation Agency (JICA) in SSA in Chap. 4, and the importance of institutionalizing *Kaizen* dissemination activities and customizing them to suit particular environments of developing countries in Chap. 5. In order to implement the TIF strategy successfully, it is critically important at the outset to boost entrepreneurs' awareness of *Kaizen*, multiply the number of competent *Kaizen* experts, maintain the quality of *Kaizen* training, and customize the contents of *Kaizen*. These points were discussed in previous chapters, and it is hoped that those countries interested in getting started on *Kaizen* dissemination can learn enormously from this book.

References

Allen, F., Qian, J., & Qian, M. (2005). Law, Finance, and Economic Growth in China. *Journal of Financial Economics, 77*(1), 57–116.

Ariga, K., & Ejima, S. (2000). *Tai Okoku Tobu Rinkai Kaihatsu Keikaku Sogo Inpakuto Hyoka* (Comprehensive Assessment of Thailand's Eastern Seaboard Development Plan). *Kaihatsu Kenkyusho Ho, Report of Development Research Center, 2*, 41–69.

Bloom, N., Eifert, B., Mahajan, A., McKenzie, D., & Roberts, J. (2013). Does Management Matter? Evidence from India. *Quarterly Journal of Economics, 128*(1), 1–51.

Bloom, N., Sadun, R., & Reenen, J. V. (2016). *Management as a Technology*, National Bureau of Economic Research, NBER Working Paper No. 22327.

Bruhn, M., Karlan, D., & Schoar, A. (2010). What Capital Is Missing in Developing Countries? *American Economic Review, 100*(2), 155–169.

Crespo, N., & Fontoura, M. P. (2007). Determinant Factors of FDI Spillovers: What Do We Really Know? *World Development, 35*(3), 410–425.

David, C. C., & Otsuka, K. (Eds.). (1994). *Modern Rice Technology and Income Distribution in Asia*. Boulder: Lynne Rienner.

Estudillo, J. P., & Otsuka, K. (2016). *Moving out of Poverty: An Inquiry into Inclusive Growth in Asia*. London: Routledge.

Gereffi, G., Humphrey, J., & Sturgeon, T. (2005). Governance of Global Value Chain. *Review of International Political Economy, 12*(1), 78–104.

Hashino, T., & Otsuka, K. (2016). *Industrial Districts in History and the Developing World*. Dordrecht: Springer.

Hausmann, R., Rodrik, D., & Velasco, A. (2008). Growth Diagnostics. In N. Serra & J. E. Stiglitz (Eds.), *The Washington Consensus Reconsidered: Towards a New Global Governance*. Oxford: Oxford University Press.

Hayashi, K. (1995). Seicho wo Kyoyusuru Kiban to Shokibo Kinyu (Foundation for Shared Growth and Small-Scale Finance). *Kaihatsu Kinyu Kenkyu (Review of Development Finance), 2*(4), 91–99.

Heath, R., & Mobarak, A. M. (2015). Manufacturing Growth and the Lives of Bangladeshi Women. *Journal of Development Economics, 155*(1), 1–15.

Hellman, T., Murdock, K., & Stiglitz, J. (1997). Financial Restraint: Toward a New Paradigm. In M. Aoki, H. K. Kim, & M. O. Fujiwara (Eds.), *The Role of Government in East Asian Economic Development: Comparative International Analysis*. Oxford: Oxford University Press.

Hidalgo, C. A., Clinger, B., Barabási, A. L., & Haussman, R. (2007). The Product Space Conditions the Development of Nations. *Science, 317*(5837), 482–487.

Higuchi, Y., Nam, V. H., & Sonobe, T. (2015). Sustained Impacts of *Kaizen* Training. *Journal of Economic Behavior and Organization, 120*, 189–206.

Higuchi, Y., Mhede, E. P., & Sonobe, T. (2016). Short- and Medium-Run Impact of Management Training: An Experiment in Tanzania. Mimeo, National Graduate Institute for Policy Studies.

Humphrey, J., & Schmitz, H. (2002). How Does Insertion in Global Value Chains Affect Upgrading in Industrial Clusters? *Regional Studies, 36*(9), 1017–1027.

Ito, T., & Kruger, A. O. (Eds.). (2000). *The Role of Foreign Direct Investment in East Asian Economic Development*. Chicago: University of Chicago Press.

Javorcik, B. S. (2014). Does FDI Bring Good Jobs to Host Countries? *World Bank Research Observer, 30*(1), 74–94.

Kimura, H., & Todo, Y. (2010). Is Foreign Aid a Vanguard of Foreign Direct Investment? A Gravity-Equation Approach. *World Development, 38*, 482–497.

Krueger, A. (2011). Comments on 'New Structural Economics' by Justin Yifu Lin. *World Bank Research Observer, 26*(2), 222–226.

La Porta, R., Lopez-de-Silanes, F., Shleifer, A., & Vishny, R. W. (1998). Law and Finance. *Journal of Political Economy, 106*, 1113–1155.

Lall, S., & Urata, S. (2003). *Competitiveness, FDI, and Technological Activity in East Asia*. Cheltenham: Edward Elgar.

Levine, R. (2002). Bank-Based or Market-Based Financial Systems: Which Is Better? *Journal of Financial Intermediation, 11*(4), 398–428.

Lin, J. Y. (2014). *The Quest for Prosperity: How Developing Economies Can Take Off*. Princeton: Princeton University Press.

Lin, J. Y., & Chang, H. J. (2009). Should Industrial Policy in Developing Countries Conform to Comparative Advantage or Defy It? A Debate Between Justin Lin and Ha-Joon Chang. *Development Policy Review, 27*(5), 483–502.

Mano, Y., Yishino, A. Y., & Sonobe, T. (2012). How Can Micro and Small Enterprises in Sub-Saharan Africa Become More Productive? The Impacts of Experimental Basic Managerial Training. *World Development, 40*(3), 458–468.

McMillan, J., & Woodruff, C. (1999). Interfirm Relationships and Informal Credit in Vietnam. *Quarterly Journal of Economics, 114*(4), 1285–1320.

Mieno, F. (2013). The Eastern Seaboard Development Plan and Industrial Cluster: A Quantitative Overview. In M. Nissanke & Y. Shimomura (Eds.), *Aid as Handmaiden for the Development of Institutions: A New Comparative Perspective*. London: Palgrave Macmillan.

Mottaleb, K. A., & Sonobe, T. (2011). An Inquiry into Rapid Growth of the Garment Industry in Bangladesh. *Economic Development and Cultural Change, 60*(1), 67–89.

Noman, A., & Stiglitz, J. (Eds.). (2015). *Industrial Policy and Economic Transformation in Africa*. New York: Columbia University Press.

Noman, A., & Stiglitz, J. (2016). *Efficiency, Finance and Varieties of Industrial Policy*. New York: Columbia University Press.

Otsuka, K., & Larson, D. (Eds.). (2013). *An African Green Revolution: Finding Ways to Boost Productivity on Small Farms*. Dordrecht: Springer.

Otsuka, K., & Larson, D. (Eds.). (2016). *In Pursuit of an African Green Revolution: Views from Rice and Maize Farmers' Fields*. Dordrecht: Springer.

Otsuka, K., & Sonobe, T. (2011). A Cluster-Based Industrial Development: Policy for Low-Income Countries. Policy Research Working Paper, 5703, Washington, DC: World Bank.

Otsuka, K., Estudillo, J. P., & Sawada, Y. (Eds.). (2009). *Rural Poverty and Income Dynamics in Asia and Africa*. London: Routledge.

Otsuka, K., Nakano, Y., & Takahashi, K. (2016). Contract Farming in Developed and Developing Countries. *Annual Review of Resource Economics, 8*, 353–376.

Oyeyinka, B., & McCormick, D. (Eds.). (2007). *Industrial Clusters and Innovation Systems in Africa: Institutions, Markets, and Policy.* Tokyo: United Nations University Press.

Page, J. (2015). Structural Change and Africa's Poverty Puzzle. In L. Chandy et al. (Eds.), *Last Mile in Ending Extreme Poverty.* Washington, DC: Brookings Institution Press.

Sonobe, T., & Otsuka, K. (2006). *Cluster-Based Industrial Development: An East Asian Model.* Basingstoke: Palgrave Macmillan.

Sonobe, T., & Otsuka, K. (2011). *Cluster-Based Industrial Development: A Comparative Study of Asia and Africa.* Basingstoke: Palgrave Macmillan.

Sonobe, T., & Otsuka, K. (2014). *Cluster-Based Industrial Development: Kaizen Management for MSE Growth in Developing Countries.* Basingstoke: Palgrave Macmillan.

Suzuki, A., Vu, H. N., & Sonobe, T. (2014). Willingness to Pay for Managerial Training: A Case from the Knitwear Industry in Northern Vietnam. *Journal of Comparative Economics, 42*(3), 693–707.

World Bank. (2012). *World Bank Development Report 2013: Jobs.* Washington, DC: World Bank.

Yoshino, N., & Taghizadeh-Hesary, F. (2016). *Optimal Credit Guarantee Ratio for Asia.* Asian Development Band Institute Working Paper Series, No. 586.

Open Access This chapter is licensed under the terms of the Creative Commons Attribution 4.0 International License (http://creativecommons.org/licenses/by/4.0/), which permits use, sharing, adaptation, distribution and reproduction in any medium or format, as long as you give appropriate credit to the original author(s) and the source, provide a link to the Creative Commons license and indicate if changes were made.

The images or other third party material in this chapter are included in the chapter's Creative Commons license, unless indicated otherwise in a credit line to the material. If material is not included in the chapter's Creative Commons license and your intended use is not permitted by statutory regulation or exceeds the permitted use, you will need to obtain permission directly from the copyright holder.

Appendix: Teaching Material for Classroom Training and the Manual for In-Company Training

Kimiaki Jin, Tsuyoshi Kikuchi and Seiji Sugimoto

Introduction

This appendix is prepared based on extracts from the manuals created for the *Kaizen* consultants trained by the JICA project in Ethiopia and other countries in Africa. JICA has produced manuals for each technical cooperation project in several countries, and their contents were initially designed to assist consultants who work for a *Kaizen* promoting institute (KPI) as a government agency. Therefore, *Kaizen* is characterized as public support to private sector development.

Since *Kaizen* technologies cover very broad tools, methodologies, and systems, the original manuals are voluminous and comprehensive.

K. Jin
Japan International Cooperation Agency (JICA), Tokyo, Japan
e-mail: Jin.Kimiaki@jica.go.jp

T. Kikuchi • S. Sugimoto
Consulting Division, Japan Development Service Co., Ltd., Tokyo, Japan
e-mail: go-kikuchi@jds21.com; sugimoto@cba.att.ne.jp

© The Author(s) 2018
K. Otsuka et al. (eds.), *Applying the Kaizen in Africa*,
https://Doi.org/10.1007/978-3-319-91400-8

However, this appendix covers only a brief outline of two of the possible tools (5S and *Muda* elimination) and a mean quality benchmark (Quality Control Circle; QCC), which are the basics of the *Kaizen* technologies to be applied in the early stages of its introduction.

Training activities for consultants as well as members of a company who want to introduce *Kaizen* can be divided into classroom training (CRT) and in-company training (ICT). For CRT, this appendix highlights those training materials that explain the contents of lectures. For ICT, the appendix includes a manual for *Kaizen* consultants who provide consultation services to a company. The contents are as follows:

Part 1: 5S and *Muda* Elimination (CRT)

- 5S;
- Finding problems;
- *Muda* (waste) elimination.

Part 2: 5S and *Muda* Elimination (ICT)

- Organizing *SEIRI*, Sort activity;
- 3S activities for eliminating *Muda*.

Part 3: Quality Control Circle (CRT)

- Overview of a Quality Control Circle (QCC).

Part 4: Quality Control Circle (ICT)

- Conducting a QCC meeting.

The expected participants of the CRT and ICT are (1) consultants who want to be *Kaizen* consultants and (2) *Kaizen* core team members of the company consisting of top managerial staff and section or department managerial staff who are directly responsible for the production line or process.

When *Kaizen* activities are implemented in a company, *Kaizen* committee and 5S committee (the decision-making body for sorting unnecessary items) are formed. The *Kaizen* committee directs the activities of 5S, *Muda* elimination, and the QC Circle, which is an implementation unit for the small group activities of frontline workers.

Part 1: 5S and *Muda* Elimination (Classroom Training)

A. Five S (5S)

  I. Introduction of 5S

   1. What is 5S?
      5S is an entry point for *Kaizen*. Quality and productivity improvement cannot be realized without the implementation of 5S, especially the first stage of 2S (Sort and Set-in-order). 5S is highly cost-effective and easy to understand and is a prerequisite for other *Kaizen* activities. The 5S title stands for: *Seiri* (Sort), *Seiton* (Set-in-order), *Seiso* (Shine), *Seiketsu* (Standardize), and *Shitsuke* (Sustain).

   2. What is Sort?
      Sort out unnecessary items in the workplace, dispose of them, and keep only those items necessary for current production.

   3. What is Set-in-order?
      Decide where to put necessary items in the workplace, arrange them to maintain easy access, and display signs that can be found immediately and returned or replenished properly.

   4. What is Shine?
      Clean workplace floors, equipment, and facilities, provide an inspection at the same time, and ensure that they are in good operating condition.

   5. What is Standardize?
      Keep the workplace clean by integrating Sort, Set-in-order, and Shine activities into everyone's regular work.

   6. What is Sustain?
      Develop the self-disciplined habit of maintaining and following the procedures, rules, and arrangements of the organization.

   7. What is the role of the supervisors of the workplace?
      Demonstrate leadership in implementing 5S, organize training activities, and patrol to ensure the proper implementation of 5S.

8. The commitment of managers
   Although 5S is a participatory activity in each workplace, its success depends strongly on the commitment of managers. A lack of commitment will undermine the sustainability of 5S.

II. Let's Start Planning 5S activities

1. Let's start:
   Planning processes are (i) work organization, (ii) recognition of the current condition, (iii) target areas, (iv) goal setting, (v) planning, (vi) budgeting, and proceeding to implementation.

2. Work organization:
   - 5S promotion teams are formed in each workplace to promote 5S activities;
   - The 5S committee is a decision-making body for sorting unnecessary items based on proposals made by workers in a participatory manner; and
   - The *Kaizen* committee is a management body that provides guidance and supervision not only over company-wide 5S activities but is also responsible for directing 5S, QC Circle activity, and other *Kaizen*-related activities.

3. Recognition of current conditions:
   Recognition of the current condition in the workplace is achieved by collecting the information required to identify problems, sharing them among the participants in 5S activity, and setting target areas and expected goals. 5S promotion team members take initiatives and give instructions.

4. Planning and budgeting:
   Using the 5S total evaluation sheet (see Table A1) as a checklist for planning of 5S activities. The necessary materials such as red-tags (see Table A2), boards, cleaning tools, and paint are prepared with appropriate budgeting.

Table A1 5S total evaluation sheet

	A	B	Evaluation Items	Evaluation points	Remarks about problems
Sort		O	1) Necessary things and unnecessary things can be identified easily.		
		O	2) Unnecessary things are discarded, or clarified in time limit for handling.		
		O	3) Quantity of each thing is kept as specified.		
		O	4) Bulletins and control sheets are replaced with updates.		
			Sub-total		
Set in order		O	5) Things are located at each given place.		
		O	6) Fixed positions of things are clarified by signboard, delineating, etc.		
		O	7) Things are positioned so as to facilitate first-in first-out system.		
		O	8) Small improvement realizes easy transfer of things into and from each given place.		
			Sub-total		
Shine		O	9) There are no stain, trash, dust, etc. (facilities, floor, building, lights, etc.)		
		O	10) Upstream solutions are provided against stain, trash, dust, etc.		
		O	11) Voluntary inspection of facilities is conducted.		
		O	12) Processes, aisles, etc. are delineated with paint colors, etc. so that cleaning area can be easily identified		
		O	13) There are no stain/separation/unevenness/cracks in painted /delineated part on the floor		
		O	14) There are no obstacles on aisles. (cart, pallets, parts, etc.)		
		O	15) Cleaning is facilitated with creative efforts.		
			Sub-total		
Standardize	O		16) Judgement criteria for necessary/unnecessary things are specified.		
	O		17) Judgement criteria for disposing unnecessary things are specified.		
	O		18) Quantities of necessary things are specified.		
	O		19) Fixed positions of necessary things are specified by signboard, layout chart, etc.		Items to evaluate the system of 3S (Red Tag Operation, Signboard Operation, and Tidy-it-up Operation)
	O		20) Heights of racks, etc. are specified.		
	O		21) Method/procedure/responsible person/time frame of cleaning are specified.		
	O		22) Contents/procedure/responsible person/time frame of voluntary facility inspection are specified.		
	O		23) Workers keep neat appearance and have no stain on their clothes, etc.		
	O		24) Progress/normality/abnormality in 3S (Sort, Set-in-order, Shine) can be easily identified.		
	O		25) Comfortable worksite is maintained through repeated 3S activity.		
			Sub-total		
Sustain	O		26) Annual policy for 5S activity is set.		
	O		27) Annual basic plan for 5S activity is set.		
	O		28) 5S activity plan is set for each worksite.		
	O		29) Awareness campaign, education, events, and patrols are included in activity plan.		
	O		30) 5S evaluation sheet is specially prepared for each worksite.		
	O		31) Supervisor prepares "Sustain Evaluation Sheet "for workers.		
	O		32) Supervisor repeatedly instructs workers on their weak points to Sustain.		
	O		33) Patrols by the person in each duty position are provided.		
	O		34) Responsible persons for patrols properly give advices and take actions.		
	O		35) Activity bulletin board is efficiently utilized for timely notice and understandability.		
	O		36) Bottom-up activities such as small improvements are invigorated.		
			Sub-total		

A: Evaluation of appearance	Total points	/108
B: Evaluation of system completion	Achievement rate	%

<Evaluation criteria>

3 points	85% or more
2 points	60% or more but less than 85 %
1 points	30% or more but less than 60 %
0 points	Less than 30 %

Source: *Kaizen* manual for JICA project in Ethiopia

Table A2 Red-tag

	Red Tag		
Classification	1. Raw material	5. Machine	
	2. Material in process	6. Mold, Jig	
	3. Fabricated materials	7. Tools	
	4. Product	8. Others	
Name of applicant:			
Quantity		Amount (Bs.)	
Reason	1. Unnecessary	5. Unexplained	
	2. Defective	6. Others	
	3. Not urgent		
	4. Mill ends		
Department			
Action	1. Put off		Done
	2. Return		
	3. Transfer to storage of Red Tag		
	4. Special keeping		
	5. Others		
Date	Paste on	Action on	
No.			

Source: *Kaizen* manual for JICA project in Ethiopia

III. Let's implement 5S

1. Sort activity:
    - The process of this activity is preparation ⇒ putting a red-tag (see Table A2) on the item to be potentially discarded ⇒ evaluation of unnecessary items ⇒ disposal of unnecessary items ⇒ cleaning with everyone together;

- Use red-tags for proposing classifications and the reasons for doing so. Each person contributes at least four red-tags, one tag for one item;
- The evaluation of unnecessary items needs decision-makers ('sorters') who are given authority by the 5S committee;
- Red-tag items are moved to the holding area (by type, by member) before the evaluation. Evaluate the 'red-tag items' in a holding area by two levels of sorters.
- *Example*: (a) materials, evaluation by the group leader; (b) parts, first evaluation by the group leader and second by the head of the section; (c) facilities, first evaluation by the head of the section and second by the head of the division:
- Dispose of unnecessary items;
- Decide on the location and method for keeping necessary tools and materials; and
- Never put red-tag on people even as a joke!!!

2. Set-in-order activity:

- The sequence of this activity is clarification of targets for the Set-in-order activity ⇒ decision on the location and method ⇒ decision on the display method ⇒ preparation of tools for the Set-in-order activity ⇒ decision on the schedule and allocation ⇒ indication of zones and positions and relocation of items under Set-in-order ⇒ application;
- Preparation of tools for labelling, signing, zoning, and setting of tool boards;
- Indicating zones of work area, aisle, storage site, and other designated zones by painting on the floor. Installing tool boards and placing location plates, shelf plates, item plates, and number plates; and
- Placing machines, tools, items, and materials in allocated space.

3. Shine activity:
   - This process is the preparation of cleaning tools ⇒ determining the time and the allocation of clean area ⇒ determining and display of cleaning rules, and giving an explanation to all the members ⇒ determining the person in charge of the tools ⇒ preparing the cleaning manual to explain usage to all the members ⇒ cleaning workplace according to rules and procedures;
   - Decide on the distribution and allocation of the cleaning area (time, person in charge) by making a table; and
   - Implementation of cleaning.
4. Standardize activity:
   - Standardization and thoroughness of Sort activity/Set-in-order activity/Shine activity by making rules and guidelines and setting routine activities; and
   - Standardization of activities in a QC circle when it is established.
5. Sustain activity:
   - Approach the activity repeatedly and patiently to sustain 5S activity; and
   - The success of 5S depends on the supervisor's ability to sustain the gains acquired through the 5S activity.
6. Patrol:
   - Top management patrol (making a tour of the workplace); and
   - The 5S committee members and the 5S promotion team members use the 5S checklist to ensure implementation.

B. Finding Problems

I. How to find problems in operations.
   1. The focal points to check to find out existing problems are:
      - The six major production elements: quality, cost, production volume, delivery, safety, and motivation;

- The four Ms: man, machine, material, and method; and
- The three Ms: *muda* (waste), *mura* (unevenness), and *muri* (overburden).

2. Check the following six major production elements:

   - Quality: reduce DPU (defect per unit), improve quality, eliminate claims, reduce irregularities, reduce quality dispersion, prevent errors, improve reliability;
   - Cost: reduce control costs, reduce processing, manage time, reduce materials, reduce unit requirements;
   - Production volume: increase production volume, increase productivity, prevent accidents, reduce the amount of materials required, change design;
   - Delivery: shorten the work period, simplify procedures, decrease inventory;
   - Safety: decrease errors from negligence, reduce fatigue duty, maintain a comfortable environment, maintain proper sections and arrangements, clean workshop, maintain hygiene; and
   - Motivation: increase motivation, maintain active work for *Kaizen* activities, increase operators' attendance ratios, clean environment, maintain good relationships.

3. Check the four Ms:

   - Man: experience and knowledge, exact job assignment, health condition, quality assurance, job training, observance of the standards, service record;
   - Machine: machine performance, processing productivity, inspection, troubleshooting, oil consumption control, material quality damages, abandonment, replacement, maintenance, grinding, storage conditions;
   - Material: quality grade, brand names, quality of materials, volume, mixture of materials, treatment, production in-process; and
   - Method: operation standard, procedure, irregularities, layout, location, room temperature, humidity, lights, air-condition, noise, transportation, preparation for work, adjustments.

4. Finding existing problems by checking the three Ms of quality control:

- *Muda*: production factors that increase cost, in other words all non-value-adding things;
- *Mura*: variation in work distribution, production capacity of machinery, and material specifications; and
- *Muri*: mental and physical overburden on operators, and overburden on production machinery.

II. Seven keys to solve problems

1. The seven keys:
   The keys are (1) think 'why?', (2) grasp of current status, (3) data sorting, (4) confirmation of plans, (5) support, (6) flexibility, and (7) follow-up.

2. Think 'why?'
   Pick up any *Kaizen* point anywhere, make it a rule to think 'why?' or 'is it OK?'

3. Grasp of current status:
   If you found any problems, collect as much data as possible to determine its cause.

4. Data sorting:
   The collection and classification of data must be included in routine work. Make check sheets to be filled with answers to such questions as what material, what machine, who, when, and how. These records must be classified by lot number so that the causes of problems may be easily found.

5. Confirmation of plans:
   Pick up the items that are clearly described as targets so that the focus of subsequent activities is well defined.

6. Support:
   Support by other members is appreciated. Lots of opinions from various angles can be expected.

7. Flexibility:
   Utilization of brainstorming should result in more ideas and better solutions.

8. Follow-up:
   After confirmation of the effects, recurrence must be prevented through a standardization of check systems.

III. Seven steps of the *Kaizen* procedure

1. Seven steps:

   The first step: find problems;
   The second step: set the *Kaizen* targets;
   The third step: make schedules;
   The fourth step: survey the issues found in problems;
   The fifth step: create *Kaizen* plans;
   The sixth step: act according to these plans; and
   The seventh step: confirm the results of *Kaizen*.

2. First step: find problems
   Identify present and future problems. Investigate the size of those problems. Assess the targets concerned and select appropriate issues to focus on.

3. Second step: set the *Kaizen* targets
   Set a *Kaizen* target (for each problem) with expected results. Get approval from managers.

4. Third step: make schedules
   While solving these problems, make clear systems for support and sharing. Draw up plans that include any specific procedures.

5. Fourth step: survey the issues found in problems
   To place focus on the *Kaizen*, collect data and analyse these. Methods of thinking, the use of specific approaches, and the sorting out of results are important.

6. Fifth step: create *Kaizen* plans
   Develop good ideas into improvement plans (*Kaizen* plans) based on the results of the analysis of the current status. Brainstorming is the most effective method to get all members' opinions.

7. Sixth step: act according to the *Kaizen* plan
   Proceed with the *Kaizen* activities on schedule under the designated terms, no matter what may happen.
8. Seventh step: confirm the results of *Kaizen*
   Confirm the achievements made. Evaluate all steps from the plan to action to make a record for the next step.

IV. Alliances developed by *Kaizen*

1. This covers the use of alliances, devices, or arrangements in production lines, which can be one of the alternatives used to solve problems identified through the *Kaizen* process.
2. Andon:
   An 'Andon' is an indicator informing team leaders and supervisors of the current workshop situation using colour boards, flashing lights, and/or automated announcements. They quickly recognize any problems when each machine or process is in operation, and what the causes of the troubles might be. The types of Andon are:
   1. Calling Andon: used to request parts;
   2. Warning Andon: used to identify the occurrence of irregularities on the lines; and
   3. Progress Andon: used to identify the progress of operation on the lines with a short cycle time.
3. U-line:
   A U-line is a layout in which the inlet and outlet are positioned in the same direction to avoid working back for a single operator when he/she performs all machining or assembly operations in production. For multiple operators, the layout should be arranged by considering the distribution of operations.
4. In-lining:
   In-lining is a way to make the production lines simple and effective by integrating parts processing into the main line for unit production. Part processing includes sub-machined parts

or other parts separated from the main line and found in lot production but not in one-piece flow. This makes it easier to watch the status of the flow.

5. Unification:
   Even if a flowing line cannot be formed, odd operations can be combined in one place in an operator's work sequence. Combining odd or inefficient operations together in a place is called unification.

6. Multi-process handling and multi-skilled operators:
   Multi-process handling means that a single operator manages multiple machines and processes in product processing and assembling. This is the primary factor for constructing lines requiring a small number of operators. A multi-skilled worker can deal with several machines or processes as described above. The supervisor of the workplace can make a flexible placement of operators when someone within the same team or section is absent.

7. A.B. control/two-point control:
   A.B. control is a devised automatic control function. For example, it controls machine movements when they start or stop working depending upon the number of workplaces piled up between the preceding process and the following process. A.B. control is used as an arrangement for time control to realize just-in-time procedures.

8. Cell production line:
   This is a production line in which a single operator manages all the machining or assembly operations in unit production. This is contrasted with a conveyer-driven line. Advantages: quality assurance can be ensured. The production output or efficiency of each operator can be clarified. Changes in the production volume can be dealt with flexibly. Operators can obtain a feeling of work achievement. Conditions for a cell production line: an operator must be able to perform multiple operations. Each operator must therefore be multi-skilled.

C. The Seven *Mudas*

1. '*Muda*' means waste in Japanese. The seven *Mudas* in a standard production system are:
   (1) *Muda* of overproduction, (2) *Muda* of inventory, (3) *Muda* of waiting, (4) *Muda* in transporting, (5) *Muda* of defect-making, (6) *Muda* in motion, and (7) *Muda* in processing.
   The following are the typical causes and outcomes to be checked in connection with the above seven *Mudas*.

2. Overproduction:
   Cause: workforce and facilities above production needs, big lot production, big and fast production machine, and products are produced continuously;
   Possible Outcomes: disturbance of flow, increase in inventory (products, stock in-progress), increased defects, deterioration of the turnover ratio of funds, too much in advance preparation of materials and parts, and disturbance of flexibility in planning.

3. Inventory:
   Cause: weak inventory control awareness, bad facility layout, big lot production, bottleneck processes, anticipated production, speculative production;
   Possible Outcomes: lengthened delivery time, nipping an improvement in the bud, waste of space, need for inspection of transportation, expansion of working capital needs.

4. Waiting:
   Cause: bottleneck processes, bad facility layout, trouble in previous process, capacity imbalance, big lot production;
   Possible Outcomes: waste of manpower, time, and machines. Increase in the in-process inventory.

5. Transporting:
   Cause: bad facility layout, big lot production, single-skilled worker (over-specialization), sedentary operation;
   Possible Outcomes: waste of space, deterioration of production, increase in transportation processing, expansion of transportation facilities, occurrence of scratches and dents.

6. Defect-making:
   Cause: emphasizing inspection in downstream processes, poor methods and standards for inspection, excessive quality requirements, lack of standard operation;
   Possible Outcomes: increase in material cost, productivity deterioration, increase in personnel and processes for inspection, increase in defects and claims.

7. Motion:
   Cause: isolated operation, craftsmanship traits prevail, bad layout, no education or training;
   Outcome: increase in manpower and processing, minimization of skills, unstable operation, unnecessary movement.

8. Processing:
   Cause: lack of analysis of the proper order of processing, lack of analysis of contents of operation, improper jigs and their use, insufficient standardization, lack of analysis of materials;
   Possible Outcomes: unnecessary processing/operations, increases in manpower and in processing, lower work efficiency, increases in defects.

Part 2: 5S and *Muda* Elimination (In-Company Training)

A. Organizing '*SEIRI*': Sort Activity

I. Activities in the session

1. *Kaizen* core team of the company is organized:
   The members consist of top managerial staff and section or department managerial staff who are directly responsible for the production line or process.

2. Explanation of overview of *Kaizen* and selection of two (2) model workplaces:
   Kaizen consultants explain the overall concept of *Kaizen*, the implementation process, and the basic stages of company diagnosis and guidance activities, to make sure that they are understood.

Kaizen core team selects two model workplaces where model *Kaizen* activities are to be carried out.

3. Instruction to put relevant mini-posters on appropriate places: *Kaizen* consultants explain the relevant mini-posters to be put in appropriate places.

- Basic mini-posters
  At least the following mini-posters should be put in appropriate places:
  – Promises (points of *Kaizen*);
  – Definitions of 5S;
  – Why are *Kaizen* activities necessary?
  – *Kaizen* house (see Fig. A1);
  – *Muda*—anything unnecessary; and
  – Seven *Mudas*

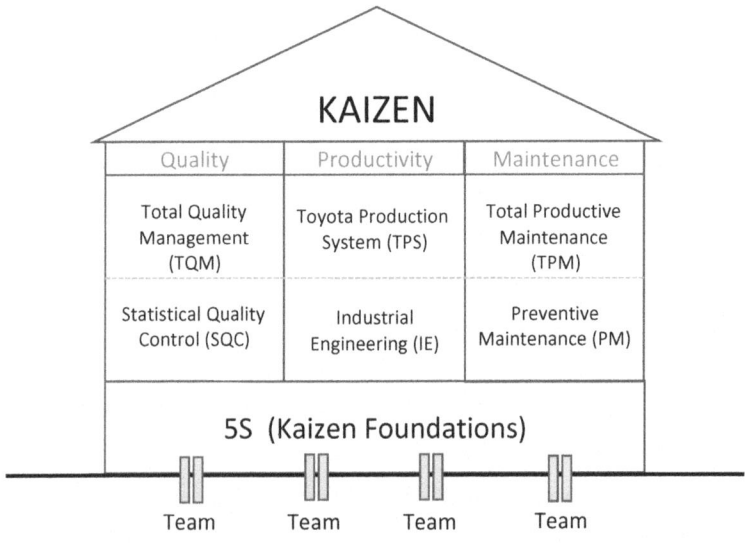

Fig. A1 *Kaizen* house. (Total Quality Management (TQM), Toyota Production System (TPS), and Total Productive Maintenance (TPM) are three major pillars of *Kaizen* and 5S gives foundations for these three pillars. Teamwork of the staff sustains all of them.) (Source: Created by the authors)

KAIZEN consultants can show other mini-posters and assist *Kaizen* core team members in selecting any additional mini-posters for specific purposes to be identified.

- *Kaizen* board
  Kaizen consultants may suggest that a *Kaizen* board should be prepared by the company so that information sheets including mini-posters can be put onto it and made available for dissemination. Preferably, there should be a total of three *Kaizen* boards, namely, one general *Kaizen* board and one for each model workplace. The number, size, materials, and other related issues of the *Kaizen* board(s) should be decided by the company.

4. Rapid assessment of a model workplace by '3S' concepts:
   '3S' means Sort, Set-in-order, and Shine—the first three S of the 5S. *Kaizen* consultants will use the Form-1 '*MUDA* checklist' (see Table A3) and explain the result.

5. Understanding workflow in the layout chart:
   A company is expected to provide *Kaizen* consultants with standard operation sheets (see Table A4) or existing descriptions of workflow and layout. *Kaizen* consultants will request that the company provide them for the next visit if they are not yet ready.

6. Identification of lists and the formulation of criteria for 3S:
   Kaizen consultants will explain about each form in order to assist *Kaizen* core team members in (i) listing all the items at the selected workplace; (ii) sorting all the items into necessary and unnecessary items by setting up operation standards; and (iii) setting in order all the necessary items for stock at the workplace by determining required quantities.

7. Instructions to conduct homework:
   The Sort activity is suggested to be repeatedly exercised at two (2) model workplaces until the participants in *Kaizen* activities can become accustomed to repeatedly conducting the Sort activity. Participants are also encouraged to teach other company staff what and how to do so.

Table A3 *Muda* checklist

Plant Assessment Sheet

Shop:　　　　　　Process:　　　　　　Date:　　　　　　Person in charge:

Type of Muda		Wasteful of Bad Condition	Check (bad)	Cause and corrective actions
1. Muda of overproduction		1. Production without concrete plan/production not dependent on actual demand		
		2. Production dependent on demand forecast		
		Sub Total		
2. Muda of inventory		1. Overstock of raw materials for more than two months of consumption		
		2. Large amount of work-in-process (WIP) between each process		
		Subtotal		
3. Muda of waiting		1. Machine downtime due to no work, imbalance in production process or operational problems		
		2. Worker downtime due to no work, imbalance in production process or machine operation problems		
		Subtotal		
4. Muda in transportation		1. Long-distance transportation of work-in-process between production sites		
		2. Transportation of work-in-process to/from storage other than the regular stockyard		
		Subtotal		
5. Muda of defect-making		1. High rate of defects in work in-process		
		2. High rate of defects in final products		
		Subtotal		
6. Muda in motion		1. Movement without value addition such as searching and transporting tools/materials		
		2. Motion with long time for set up and adjustment of tools/materials in the process		
		Subtotal		
7. Muda in processing		1. Unnecessary processing/assembling by using time/resource consuming methods or too many parts		
		2. Reworking in production process due to poor preparation/operation		
		Subtotal		

Evaluation point

3 points	Always observed
2 points	Often observed
1 points	Slightly observed
0 points	Not observed

Source: Created by the authors

Table A4 Standard operation sheet

Source: Kaizen manual for JICA project in Ethiopia

Accordingly, *Kaizen* core team members are asked to conduct homework jointly with other workers of the company, that is, in-company *Kaizen* activities, with a focus on the following specific activities related to the Sort activity:

- Identify items to be stocked in the workplace through classifying items into necessary and unnecessary items;
- Note down 'standards' or 'rules' to classify items through the Sort activity (write all the standards or rules down on blank paper even using handwriting);
- Be ready to present results including the presentation of standards or rules for sorting items;
- Through familiarization with the Sort activity, explain about the '5S Evaluation Sheet' as a sample format that helps them to effectively analyse the current conditions of workplace environments. At the same time, advise *Kaizen* core team members to carefully look at the sheet for possible modification and adaptation in that workplace.

II. Expected outputs

1. The capability of *Kaizen* core team members to formulate, revise, and manage operation standards for sorting and Set-in-order at the workplace is enhanced;
2. The capability of *Kaizen* core team members to implement Sort and Set-in-order activities is enhanced;
3. The capability of *Kaizen* core team members to assess the current workflow of the model workplace and suggest ideas to improve it is enhanced;
4. The capability to understand purposes, contents, and methods of the homework is developed;
5. Plant assessment results are created; and
6. Session reports are prepared by *Kaizen* core team members.

B. '3S' Activities in *Muda* Elimination

  I. Activities in the session

  1. *Kaizen* consultants review performance of the homework given in the last session on the previous day and give advice on any issues to be identified or raised. This means that *Kaizen* consultants must make a rapid assessment on the company's performance on the Sort activity. In the situation where the Sort performance is not at a satisfactory stage, *Kaizen* consultants will ask the company to continue their exercises on the Sort activity.

  2. Exercise 3S activity within the scope of *Muda* elimination:
     - *Kaizen* consultants refer to the list of the stock at the workplace which was prepared during the last session(s);
     - Based on the above list, the consultants assist *Kaizen* core team members in exercising 3S activities; and
     - The consultants remind *Kaizen* core team members that 3S activities are an integral part of activities for the elimination of *Muda*.

  3. Confirm and review present standard operation sheets:
     - The consultants ask about the availability of the standard operation sheet at the selected workplace;
     - If it is available, the consultants assist *Kaizen* core team members in assessing their standard operation sheets to determine whether their current operations have any unnecessary processes or not. Then, the team moves into revising and improving standard operation sheets, if issues were identified; and
     - In cases where the company has not prepared and used the standard operation sheet, the consultants show *Kaizen* core team members a sample sheet and advise them to prepare this with their assistance.

  4. The consultants explain about '*Muda* in motion' and '*Muda* in processing' and assign the analysis of the layout and 5S result as homework for the *Kaizen* core team. The consultants also give explanations on the outcome and cause by *Muda* type. This session

aims to explain the contents of homework to be performed by the company at two (2) model workplaces in-between sessions:

- The consultants assess how much awareness or consciousness on the importance of *Muda* elimination has been raised;
- The consultants ensure the understanding of participants about the basic idea and method for preparing a standard operation sheet. The consultants may further support the *Kaizen* core team and selected workers at two (2) model workplaces to improve the present standard operation sheet; and
- The consultants also make sure that *Kaizen* core team members are ready or motivated to prepare an action plan for 5S by using the sample form.

    – Encourage *Kaizen* core team members to deepen their understanding that 'no assessment or evaluation can be possible without the preparation of an action plan for 5S'. In other words, these exercises or the preparation of an action plan implies the actual application of the PDCA cycle.

5. The consultants will send the report of the visit to the KPI within three days.

II. Expected outputs

1. Clearer understanding of *Kaizen* activities will be increased through involvement in 3S activities. These activities should result in the creation of a safer and more workable environment in the workplace. In parallel with this, it is often observed that those who realize changes in the workplace environment are motivated to more actively participate in 3S activities;
2. Additional open workspaces will be created by the Sort activity. Effective use of these spaces will make it possible to further undertake the Set-in-order activity to develop a more efficient work performance system. Through this process, frontline employees at a workplace will realize that they can change their workplace environment through better work conditions by their participation in idea creation and planning;
3. Those who carry out Sort and Set-in-order activities based on an action plan should realize that they can manage the process of

improvement. In other words, they may now understand the full significance of the PDCA cycle.

Part 3: The Quality Control (QC) Circle (Classroom Training)

A. How to organize a QC Circle

  I. Concept of the QC Circle

   1. What is a QC Circle?
      - The QC Circle is a small group with five to seven members formed in the workplace to improve workflow on the production floor.

  II. The Role of the QC Circle

   1. The QC Circle in the promotion of quality control:
      - Identifying daily problems in the frontline workplace;
      - Devising unique work processes and expanding process control;
      - Acquiring and improving techniques and skills required to carry out work; and
      - Gaining experience as a QC Circle leader contributing to the development of knowledge and skills.

   2. Basic principles of QC Circle activities:
      - Fully reveal human capabilities and eventually draw out possibilities;
      - Respect humanity and build a pleasant, vital, and satisfying workplace; and
      - Contribute to the improvement and development of the company.

   3. Benefits of QC Circle activities:
      - Closer relationships between workers and management;
      - Cultivation of cooperation among workers;
      - Job satisfaction;
      - Increased motivation at work;
      - Building self-confidence;

- Development of leadership among workers;
- Encouragement of creativity among workers; and
- Improvement of systems and work procedures.

III. Stages in QC Circle development

1. Preparation:
   - Management prepares for installation of a QC Circle;
   - Potential leaders of the Circle observe other QC Circle activities/study QC Circle in other workplaces.

2. Installation of the Circle:
   - Management declares commitment to QC Circle activities;
   - Establishment of (a) QC Circle organization, (b) steering committee, (c) QC Circle office, and (d) facilitator and appointment of their members is carried out; and
   - Preparation of QC Circle installation plan that includes (a) in-house training and (b) volunteers for a pilot circle.

3. Implementation of activities:
   - Launch of the pilot circle;
   - Tackling of the first problems by following the QC story;
   - Case presentation for management; and
   - Evaluation of the pilot circle.

4. Sustaining the QC Circle:
   - Company-wide implementation of the QC Circle concept;
   - Conduct QC Circle meetings; and
   - Evaluation by the steering committee and the QC Circle office.

B. What is the QC Story?

I. The Concept of the QC Story

1. What is the QC Story?
   The QC Story is a series of problem-solving steps as well as a *Kaizen* reporting procedure. It is based on scientific and evidence-based problem-solving techniques. It includes easy steps to enable understanding of the *Kaizen* scenario.

2. Features of the QC Story:
   The QC Story is applicable not only for quality problems but also for other issues such as productivity and cost problems. The QC story includes the utilization of scientific problem analysis tools such as 7 QC tools.

II. Steps of the QC Story

1. Ten steps of the QC story:
   (1) Preparation ⇒ (2) selection of *Kaizen* subject ⇒ (3) comprehend current situation ⇒ (4) activity planning ⇒ (5) cause analysis ⇒ (6) countermeasures ⇒ (7) comprehend results ⇒ (8) standardization and training ⇒ (9) identification of remaining problems ⇒ (10) planning for the next QC plan.

2. Preparation:
   Review of the background of the *Kaizen* subject; company name, number of employees, annual sales, organization form, year of foundation, main products, production type, production process, and so on.

3. Selection of the *Kaizen* issues:
   - Problems are equal to the goal of the ideal situation, minus the current situation;
   - Problems are found through interviews with management and workers and observation in the workplace;
   - *Kaizen* issues are selected from problems based on priorities such as importance, urgency, and magnitude of impact; and
   - Selection of the *Kaizen* subject with the consent of the owner of the company.

4. Comprehend current situation:
   - Understand the current situation through brainstorming and cause and effect diagrams;
   - Comprehend the current situation in a quantitative manner through observation;
   - Gather stratified data and graph them;
   - Comprehend the variability of data; and
   - Set objectives for change (what, how many/how much, by when).

5. Activity planning:
   Make a *Kaizen* activity plan and set up role sharing through identifying activity items, people in charge, and the time frame.

6. Cause analysis:
   - Investigate the root causes of problems;
   - Identify the causes of problems through brainstorming;
   - Focus on those causes that seem to be important though cause and effect diagrams and why-why analyses; and
   - Confirm important causes with data (facts).

7. Countermeasures:
   - Seek countermeasures that could remove the root causes, and implement them;
   - Generate countermeasures by confirming root causes;
   - Focus on the countermeasures to be implemented;
   - Create an action plan for the preferred countermeasures; and
   - Implement that action plan.

8. Comprehend results:
   - Comprehend results and compare them with objectives;
   - Compare the qualitative performance with the target value;
   - Comprehend the spread effect; and
   - Compare the qualitative effect.

9. Standardization and training:
   - Standardize effective countermeasures;
   - Register the standardized process;
   - Train workers to sustain the standardized process; and
   - Confirm results.

10. Identification of remaining problems:
    - Review the good and bad points of the above processes and reflect on the next application of the QC Story; and
    - Collect data on remaining problems.

11. Planning for the next step:
    - Use the reflection task to identify the next *Kaizen* activity;
    - Come up with remaining problems for the next *Kaizen*; and
    - Prepare the next *Kaizen* plan.

C. 7 QC tools

1. 7 QC tools are Pareto diagrams, histograms, cause and effect diagrams, stratification, scatter diagrams, check sheets, and control charts. However, some of the manuals and guidebooks of the 7 QC tools include graph as one of the seven instead of stratification.
2. Each of these 7 QC tools is explained in the following section by analysing the process of problem-solving in a food processing factory. These steps are in accordance with seven out of the ten steps in the QC Story, namely, from the second step (selection of *Kaizen* issues) to the eighth step (standardization and training).
3. A Pareto diagram (see Fig. A2) is used to select *Kaizen* issues. Pareto analysis is a method for identifying the few vital causes that contribute to most of the problems. This tool is particularly useful for option selection, prioritization, and implementation. In the system shown in Fig. A2, the non-standard weight of the products can be selected as a target for *Kaizen*;
4. A histogram (see Fig. A3) is used to comprehend the current situation and set the target.

    A histogram is a graph showing the distribution of occurrences and is constructed by dividing the range of a group of measurement data into a certain number of segments and indicating these in the graph. Figure A3 shows the distribution of the weight of products, that is, the essential data to set the target weight to be achieved by *Kaizen*. Then, the schedule of *Kaizen* activities can be prepared as the seven steps indicate;
5. Using a cause and effect diagram (see Fig. A4) to analyse the causes of the problem. Such a diagram is like a fish bone which provides well-arranged information on the relationship between quality characteristics and influence factors. Figure A4 gives the potential causes of the non-standard weight of products based on the four Ms (man, machine, material, and method);

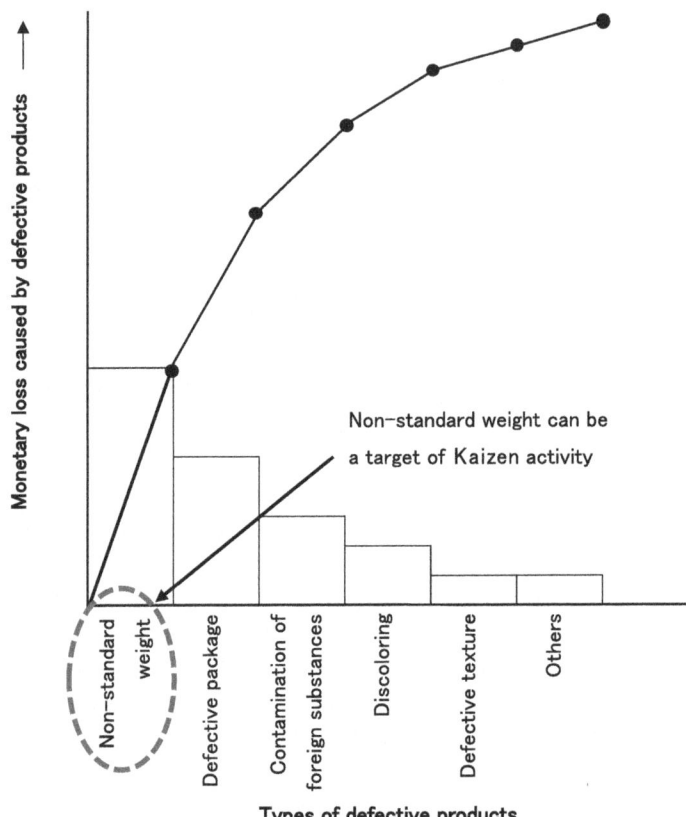

Fig. A2 Pareto diagram. (Source: Created by the authors)

6. Using stratification (see Fig. A5) to disaggregate the cause of a problem. Stratification is used to arrange the different parts of something into separate layers or groups. It is a technique used in combination with other data analysis tools. Figure A5 stratifies the distribution of weight based on packaging machines;
7. Using a scatter diagram (see Fig. A6). Scatter diagrams are graphs that show the relationship between variables. Variables represent possible causes and effects. Figure A6 shows the relation between temperature and the weight of products;

Appendix: Teaching Material for Classroom Training... 253

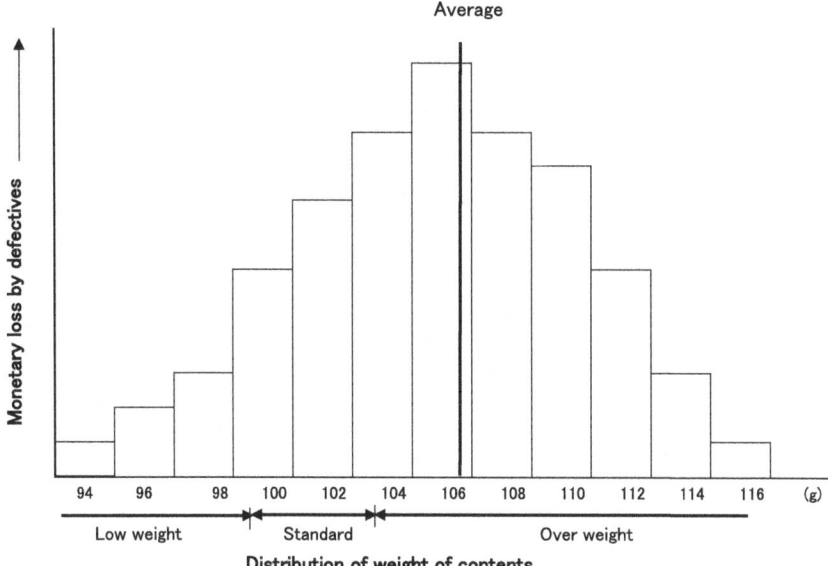

Fig. A3 Histogram. (Source: Created by the authors)

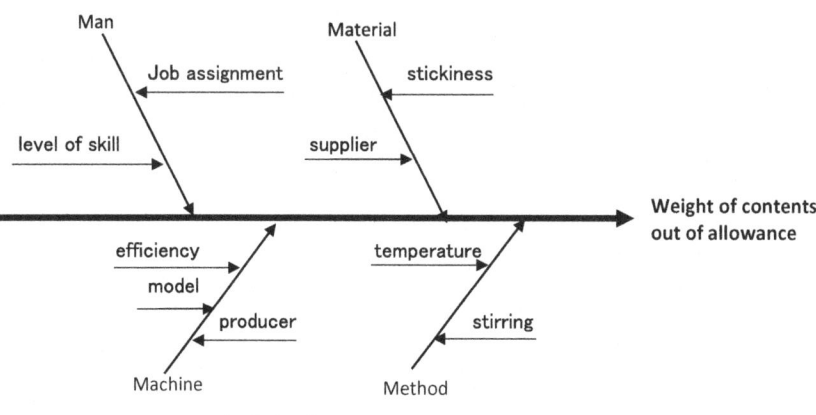

Fig. A4 Cause and effect diagram. (Source: Created by the authors)

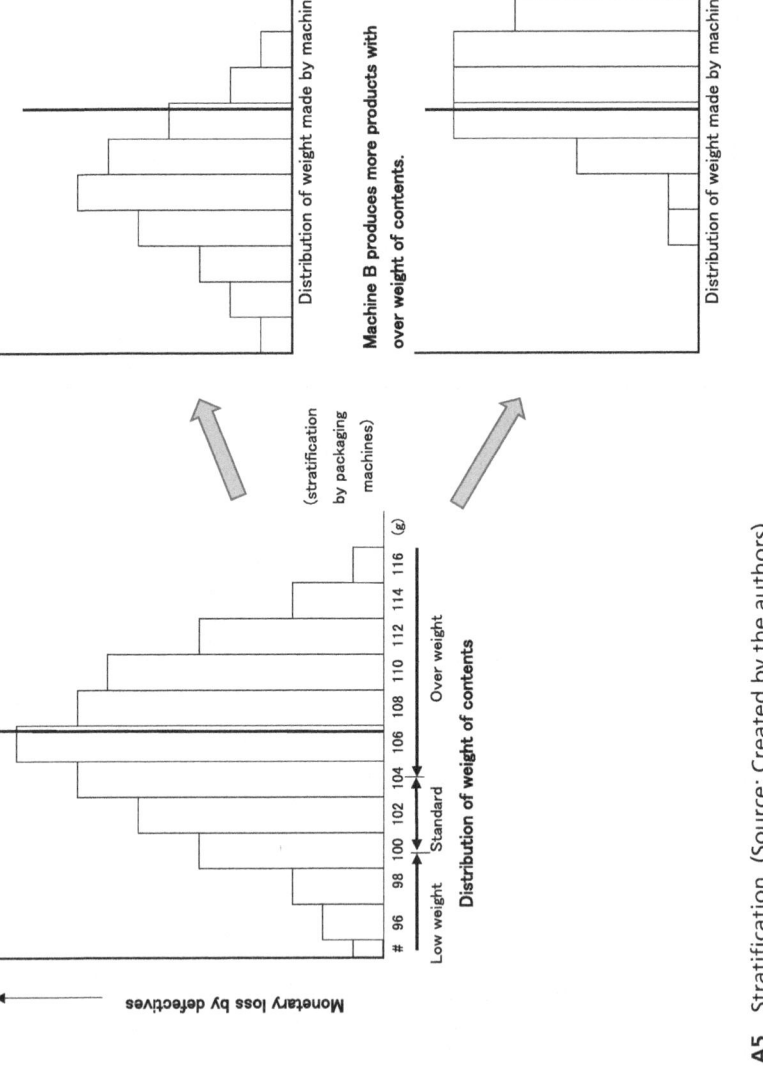

Fig. A5 Stratification. (Source: Created by the authors)

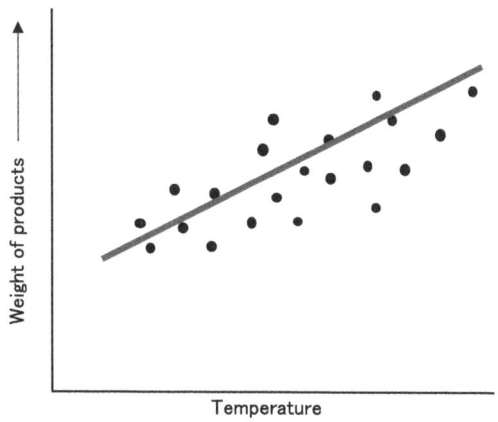

Relation between temperature and weight of products

Fig. A6 Scatter diagram. (Source: Created by the authors)

Temperature check sheet

	8:00	8:30	9:00	9:30	10:00	10:30	11:00	11:30	12:00	13:00
Temperature of production room										
Setting temperature of packaging machine										

Fig. A7 Temperature check sheet. (Source: Created by the authors)

8. Using a check sheet (see Figure A7) to create countermeasures. A check sheet is a tool for collecting the required data, such as defective items, causes of defects, location of defects, and their frequency, and is summarized in the form of a table, diagram, chart, or drawing. In this case, the check sheet in Fig. A7 was prepared to indicate temperatures in the production room and packaging machine for necessary action;
9. A graph (see Fig. A8) can be used to comprehend the results of *Kaizen* as the change of percentage of defective products is indicated;
10. Using a control chart (see Fig. A9) to monitor and standardize the countermeasures. A control chart is a statistical tool used to distinguish between the variations in a process that result from common

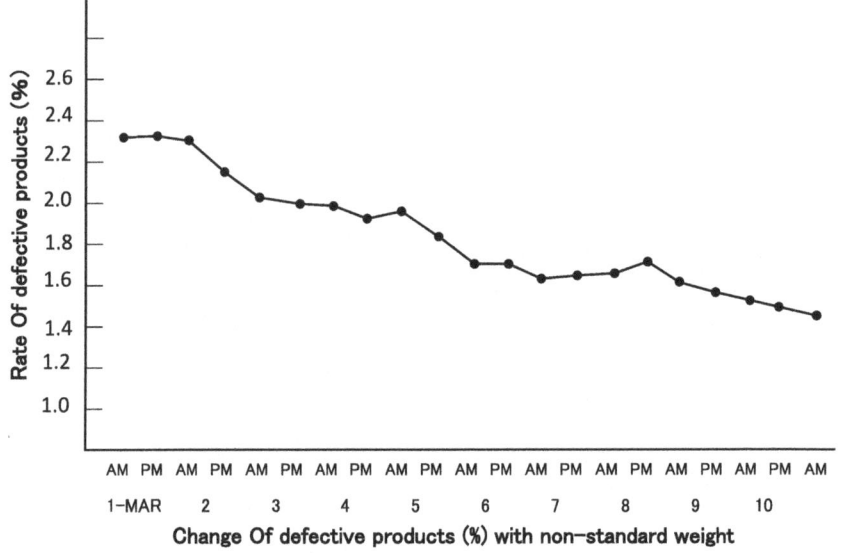

Fig. A8 Graph. (Source: Created by the authors)

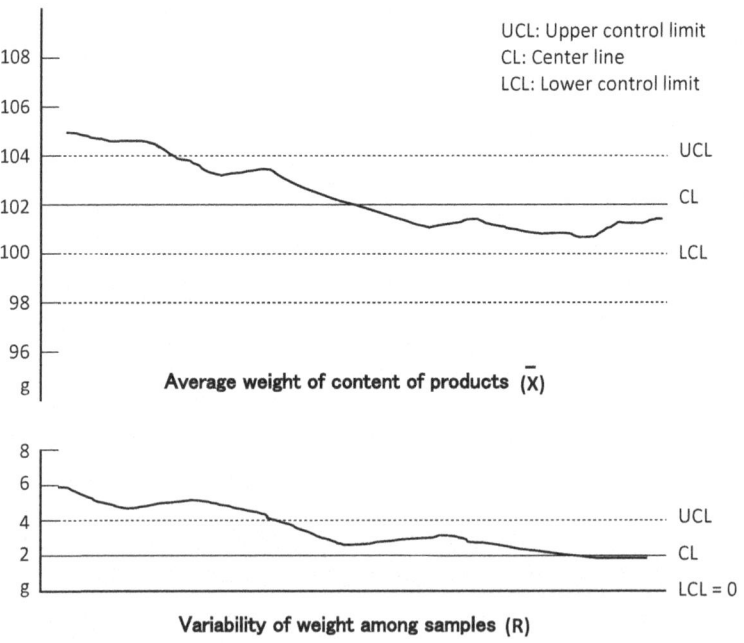

Fig. A9 Control chart. (Source: Created by the authors)

causes, and the variations resulting from special causes. In Fig. A9, the upper graph indicates a change of average weight of contents of product to be adjusted within the standard weight range (100–104 g). The lower graph indicates the variability of the sample weight (the difference between the heaviest sample and lightest sample) of products, which is essential to reduce the defective rates of products.

Part 4: Quality Control (QC) Circle (In-Company Training)

A. Conducting the QCC Meeting

I. Activities in the session

1. The *Kaizen* consultants review and grasp the present condition of the QCC condition in the company and give necessary guidance to QCC activities:

    - *Kaizen* consultants may remind participants that inappropriate identification of problems due to insufficient analysis may lead to ineffective results from *Kaizen* activities;
    - It often happens that in such cases QCC members will replace the past theme with a new one by concluding that QCC activities would not bring about any changes without an examination on the selection of the theme; and
    - This kind of trend may further lead to declining motivation, resulting in the cessation of QCC activities. Thus, exercises in identifying and analysing problems should be repeatedly continued.

2. The consultants request a model QCC to perform meeting and monitor it in accordance with the QCC guidelines;
3. The consultants let participants understand the QC Story method for QCC activities and tackling knowledge deficiencies;
4. The consultants will send the visit report to the KPI within three days.

II. Expected outputs

1. Sufficient knowledge to handle a QC Circle in the company;
2. Sufficient knowledge to make better improvements at the company.

Index[1]

A

Affinity diagram, 80
Africa Kaizen Initiative, 140
African-style of *Kaizen*, 27, 61
African Union Commission (AUC), 53
Argentina, 52, 81, 89, 94, 134n33, 160
Arrow diagram, 80
Asian Productivity Organization (APO), 50
Association diagram, 80
Association for Overseas Technical Scholarship (AOTS), 50, 51
Association of Southeast Asian Nations (ASEAN), 33, 46

B

Black Belt (BB), 115, 127, 131, 132, 132n29
Botswana, 5, 26, 54, 55
Bottleneck, 96–97, 108, 205
Bottom-up approach, 72, 97, 98, 117, 122–125
Brazil, 52
Burkina Faso, 54, 55
Business Process Re-engineering (BPR), 38, 39, 112–114, 121–123, 122n14, 154, 188
Business process outsourcing, 7

C

Cameroon, 5, 52, 134n32, 140n38, 141n39, 143
Cause and effect diagram, xvii, 80, 93, 102, 249–251
Chamy, Jam, 121

---

[1]Note: Page numbers followed by 'n' refer to notes.

Check sheet, xvii, 80, 102, 234, 251, 255
China, 2, 54, 71, 212
Cirera, X., 48, 140, 146
Classroom Training (CRT), 25, 39, 61, 155, 156, 166, 168, 181, 193, 210, 226
Colombo Plan, 32
Component entrepreneurs, 21, 111, 155, 172, 174, 175, 212, 217
Control chart, xvii, 80, 102, 251, 255
Core capacities, 40, 41, 55, 58–61, 63
Costa Rica, 51, 51n11, 140n38
Council of Ministers, 164, 193
Cross-Functional Team (CFT), 19, 20, 83, 98, 125, 136
Current state, 70–72, 98, 107
Customization, 11, 27, 36–39, 41, 53, 55, 60–64, 143, 144, 162, 173, 190, 191, 194–195

D

Department for International Development (DFID), 34
Development strategies, 73, 159, 199
Dissemination, vii, viii, xv, 5, 6, 20–21, 27, 28, 37, 43–56, 74, 104, 108, 128, 128n23, 132, 132n30, 139, 141, 146, 151, 159, 162, 164, 166, 172, 173, 176, 181, 192, 207, 209, 220, 241

Division of labor, 3, 3n1, 209
DMAIC (define, measure, analyze, improve and control), 112, 115, 117, 126–127, 129, 132n29

E

Eastern Seaboard, 207, 208, 212
Egypt, 5, 52, 134n32, 140n38
Entrepreneurial human capital, 201, 203, 206, 207
Ethiopia *Kaizen* Institute (EKI), vii, 54, 56, 74, 143, 152, 153, 157, 160, 163–175, 177, 179–183, 185–190, 192–196
Ethiopia *Kaizen* Model, 159, 175
Extrinsic motivation, 101

F

Financial market, 213, 218
Financial sector, 203, 213–215, 218
Financial support, 25, 201, 202, 205–215, 214n8, 219
Fishbone diagram, 80, 94
Five S (5S), xx, 17, 19, 38, 40, 47–51, 54, 56, 58, 60, 79–80, 89, 98, 102, 105, 106, 108, 136, 156, 172, 174n4, 190, 194, 226–247
Fordism, 10, 11, 21
Foreign direct investment (FDI), 42, 43, 50, 54, 140, 141, 147n41, 200, 201, 203, 207, 212–214, 212n7, 216–219

Index

G

Gap, 10, 62, 70–72, 101n10, 107, 121, 184
Gazette, 164, 193
Gemba, 35, 39, 53, 188, 188n5, 195
General Electric Company (GE), 115, 116, 122, 131
Ghana, 1, 5, 52, 134n32, 140n38, 141n39, 211
Green Belt (GB), 115, 117, 127, 132, 132n29
Growth and Transformation Plan (GTP), 152, 159, 168, 177–180, 186

H

Hammer, M., 121
Histogram, xvi, 80, 102, 251
Human capital of entrepreneurs, 201, 203
Human Resource Development (HRD), 33, 35, 41, 44, 57, 165, 166, 180, 186
Human-oriented management, 163

I

Ideal state, 70–72, 107
Inclusive income growth, 200
In-company Training (ICT), 61, 155, 156, 166, 168, 193, 225–258
Industrial clusters, 25, 203, 204, 207, 208, 211, 212n6, 218
Industrial Engineering (IE), 12, 13, 16, 47, 48, 74, 75, 78, 105, 106, 172

Industrial parks, 25, 201, 202, 205–216, 218, 219
Industrial policy, viii, 201, 203, 204, 217
Inherent technologies, 74–76, 108
Innovation, 3n1, 18, 38, 42, 49, 53, 54, 73, 103, 108, 118n12, 124n16, 160, 179, 207, 218
Interchangeable parts, 10
International Labor Organization (ILO), 25n7, 49, 207
International Standards Organization (ISO), 20, 28, 39, 87, 89, 112, 113, 125–133, 137, 138, 146, 147
Internet of Things (IoT), 62, 92
Intra-lot waiting (lot processing delay), 85, 85n6
Intra-process waiting, 85
Intrinsic motivation, 100n10, 101
Investment in infrastructure, 2, 201, 205, 206, 219
Ishikawa diagram, 80

J

Japan Emigration Service (JEMIS), 32
Japanese Standards Association (JSA), 127n22, 130
Japanese-style of *Kaizen*, 28, 103, 113, 113n2, 114, 122–126, 136n34, 137, 142
Japan External Trade Organization (JETRO), 50
Japan Industrial Management Association (JIMA), 112n1, 114n6, 115n7, 116

Japan Management Association
(JMA), 11, 82, 86, 113n4,
163, 173
Japan Productivity Center (JPC), 11,
33, 113n4, 142n39
Jidoka, 15, 78, 118–120, 118n12
Joint Coordination Committee, 165
Jones, D.T., 116, 119
Just-in-Time (JIT), 15, 78, 116,
116n10, 118, 118n12, 119,
121, 237

K

Kaizen award, 185, 196
Kaizen consultants, vii, viii, 74n2,
75, 94, 100n10, 130n25, 152,
157, 160, 166, 180, 225, 226,
239–241, 245, 257
Kaizen movement, viii, 26, 27, 44,
152, 159, 171, 173, 180, 181,
195, 196
Kaizen Promotion Team (KPT), 61,
174, 174n4, 175, 179–183,
185, 191, 195, 196
Kaizen training, 23, 42, 51, 164,
165, 167, 201, 202, 205–211,
213, 215, 216, 218–220
Kanban, 15, 21, 86, 116
Kenya, 1, 5, 52, 72n1, 101n10,
131n28, 134n32, 140,
140n38, 141n39
Knowledge spillovers, 216

L

Labor-intensive industries, 5, 203,
209, 210
Labor productivity, 58, 182

Labor union, 11, 83
Labor-intensive manufacturing
industries, 200
Labour-Management Relations
(LMR), 47
Lead time, 85, 85n5, 90, 157
Lean Production System (or Lean),
78, 84, 87, 112–114,
116–120, 127, 133
Learning by doing, 36, 39–42,
47, 62
Lee Kuan Yew, 33, 44,
46, 162–163

M

MAIC (measure, analyze, improve
and control), 115
Malaysia, 44, 50, 140n38, 143,
160, 167
Malcolm Baldrige National Quality
Award (MBNQA), 115
Maloney, W., 48
Management
ability, 75, 214, 217, 219
knowledge, 11, 41, 74, 104, 108,
115, 144, 204, 217, 218
technologies, 49, 58, 74–76,
74n2, 78, 83, 107, 108, 113,
113n4, 147n41, 212, 216,
218, 219
Managerial human capital, 210,
217, 218
Market failures, 218
Master Black Belt (MBB), 115, 117,
127, 132n29
Matrix data-analysis diagram, 80
Matrix diagram, 80
Meta-*Kaizen* technology, 76

Millennium Development Goals (MDGs), 199, 200
Mind-set, 37, 41, 55, 58–60, 63, 72, 98
Minh, N.D., 143, 144
Motorola Inc., 114, 114n5, 115, 122, 131
Mottainai, 72, 72n1, 73, 107
Muda, xx, 13, 15, 16, 18, 53, 78, 82–85, 87–91, 91n9, 98, 102, 105, 107, 108, 114n7, 116, 118–121, 123, 136, 156, 172, 194, 226–247
Muda elimination, 16, 82–84, 87–89, 98, 105, 108, 114n7, 118–121, 123, 136, 156, 226–247
"*Muda, muri, mura*," 15, 16, 118–120, 233

N

Nakano, M., 116, 116n11, 118–120, 120n13, 124n18
New 7 QC tools, 80
New Partnership for Africa's Development (NEPAD), 26, 53, 140
Nonaka, I., 38
Non-value adding activities, 6, 154

O

Official Development Assistance (ODA), 32–35, 43–55, 62, 108, 200, 213, 216, 216n10, 220

On-site training, 23, 25, 210
On-the-job training (OJT), 40, 47, 49, 52, 61, 81, 103
Organisation for Economic Co-operation and Development (OECD), 32
Osada, H., 167, 175
Overseas Technical Cooperation Agency (OTCA), 32

P

Pan Africa Productivity Association (PAPA), 142n39, 145
Paraguay, 52, 57
Pareto chart, xvi, 80, 94, 251
Partial optimization, 96, 97, 122, 123
Participatory approach, 37, 38, 41, 207
Plan-Do-Check-Act (PDCA), 18, 19, 136, 159, 246, 247
Possible cause, 93, 94, 252
Poverty reduction, 200
Pre- and post-production activities, 217
Preventive maintenance, 13, 78, 105, 106, 108
Problem, 3, 7, 8, 16, 23, 35, 48, 60, 62, 70–72, 80, 82, 83, 86, 93, 94, 97–99, 102, 104, 115–117, 119–121, 122n14, 124–126, 131n26, 132, 133n31, 136, 136n35, 142, 155, 159, 167, 172, 190, 208, 213, 226, 228, 232–237, 247–252, 257

Problem-solving, 72, 83, 102, 112, 114, 115, 117, 136, 155, 167, 172, 190, 248
Process Decision Program Chart (PDPC), 80
Promising entrepreneurs, 25, 201, 211, 214, 219

Q

Quality Control Circle (QCC), 16, 18–20, 47, 48, 50, 54, 55, 83, 98, 155, 159, 165, 167, 172, 174, 174n4, 175, 190, 190n6, 191, 226, 257–258
Quality Control Story (QC Story), 83, 102, 108, 117, 136, 156, 248–251, 257
Quality Management System (QMS), 20, 115, 127, 127n22, 130, 189
Quality, productivity, cost, delivery, safety, morale, and environment (QPCDSME), 4, 8, 15, 17

R

Randomized controlled trials (RCTs), 23–25, 208–210
Rate of return to investment, 201, 218
Relations diagram, 80
Republic of the Congo, 5, 214n8
Roos, D., 116
Root causes, 72, 80–82, 93, 94, 250
Royal Statistical Society (RSS), 130

S

Scatter diagram, xvii, 80, 102, 251, 252
Seiketsu, 17, 227
Seiri, 17, 226, 227, 239–244
Seiso, 17
Seiton, 17, 227
Senegal, 5
Sequence of support measures, 49, 201
Sequential support, 205
Set-up changes, 82, 85, 85n4
Seven Quality Control Tools (7 QC Tools), 80, 102, 108, 155, 251–257
Shindanshi (Small and Medium Enterprise Management Consultant), 21
Shitsuke, 17, 227
Singapore, 33, 43, 44, 46–48, 55–57, 60, 61, 63, 143, 160–162, 164, 193, 194
Single Minute Exchange of Die (SMED), 21, 85
Six Sigma (SS), 20, 28, 38, 39, 89, 97, 112–117, 120, 125–128, 131–134, 131n27, 132n29, 137, 138, 143, 147
Skill matrix, 157
Small- and medium-sized enterprises (SMEs), 20–21, 42, 47, 50, 52, 73, 89, 102, 130–138, 143, 144, 147, 153, 214, 214n8, 215
Smallholder Horticulture Empowerment and Promotion (SHEP), 58
Start/Improve Your Business, 25n7

Statistical Quality Control (SQC), 12, 13, 15n4
Stern, T.V., 113, 123, 127, 137
Stratification, xvii, 80, 102, 251, 252
Sub-Sahara Africa, vii, xv, 1, 33, 34, 41, 53
Sudan, 5
Suggestion system, 60, 83, 98, 136
Sustainable Development Goals (SDGs), 199, 200

T

Tacit knowledge, 34, 38, 39, 87, 143–145
TAM THE, 143–144
Tanzania, 1, 5, 18, 23, 24, 52, 134n32, 140n38, 141n39, 210, 211
Task-achieving, 70–72, 83, 117
Task set, 71
Taylorism, 10, 11
Technical and Vocational Education and Training Institutes (TVET), 152, 164, 166, 167
Technical assistance (TA), 33, 34, 147n41
Technical cooperation (TC), 31–44, 48–50, 55, 57, 62, 225
Thailand, 33, 43, 49, 50, 140n38, 160, 207, 208, 212, 212n7
TIF approach, 26, 203, 206, 211, 215–217, 219
TIF strategy, 201, 219, 220
TIISO model, 176, 186
Tokyo International Conference for African Development (TICAD) VI, 26, 140

Top-down approach, 72, 98, 117, 123–125
Total optimization, 96, 97, 122, 123
Total Productive Maintenance (TPM), xvi, 13, 16, 19, 48, 51, 74, 76, 78, 83, 103, 105, 106, 108, 112, 142, 172, 174, 174n4
Total Quality Control (TQC), 12, 13, 15, 15n4, 19, 20, 47, 48, 76, 112, 112n1, 114, 189, 209
Total Quality Management (TQM), xvi, 12, 13, 15n4, 19, 20, 43, 60, 74, 76, 83, 105, 106, 108, 112–114, 112n1, 114n6, 116, 117, 120–122, 125n19, 133, 134, 137, 138, 142, 147, 172, 174, 174n4, 189, 190, 190n6
Toyota Production System (TPS), xvi, 10, 15, 50, 75, 78, 82, 84–87, 87n8, 92, 105–108, 112–114, 114n7, 116, 118–120, 118n12, 125n20, 133, 134, 137, 137n36, 138, 142, 144, 147, 172, 174
Training-Infrastructure-Finance (TIF), 26, 201, 203, 206, 211, 214–217, 219, 220
Training of entrepreneurs, 201, 202, 204–206, 213, 219
Training Within Industry (TWI), 12, 13, 82, 136
Tree diagram, 80
Tunisia, viii, 5, 52, 126n21, 132n30, 134n32, 134n33, 137, 140n38, 141n39
TVET trainers' trainers (TTTs), 166, 167
Two-step loan, 214, 215

U

Union of Japanese Scientists and Engineers (JUSE), 11, 12, 19, 20, 50, 51, 83, 99, 112n1, 113n4, 167, 174

United Kingdom Accreditation Service (UKAS), 130

United Nations Industrial Development Organization (UNIDO), 54

V

Visualization, 82, 119, 120, 136

W

Wakon Yosai, 36, 37

Welch, J.F.J., 115

Western-style of *Kaizen*, 20, 28, 113, 114, 122–126, 137, 142

Why-Why Analysis, 80, 94, 136, 250

Womack, J.P., 116, 119

World Bank, 2, 33–35, 54, 56, 147n41, 200n1, 207

Z

Zambia, 5, 52, 134n32, 140n38, 141n39

Zenawi, M., vii, viii, 42, 53, 54, 153, 186

The manufacturer's authorised representative in the EU is Springer Nature Customer Service Centre GmbH, Europaplatz 3, 69115 Heidelberg, Germany. If you have any concerns regarding our products, please contact ProductSafety@springernature.com

Printed and bound by CPI Group (UK) Ltd, Croydon, CR0 4YY

23/03/2026

02076666-0011